THE TECHNIQUE OF VARIATION

THE TECHNIQUE OF VARIATION

A STUDY OF THE
INSTRUMENTAL VARIATION FROM
ANTONIO DE CABEZÓN TO MAX REGER

BY

ROBERT U. NELSON

UNIVERSITY OF CALIFORNIA PRESS
BERKELEY AND LOS ANGELES
1962

UNIVERSITY OF CALIFORNIA PRESS
BERKELEY AND LOS ANGELES
CALIFORNIA

CAMBRIDGE UNIVERSITY PRESS
LONDON, ENGLAND

Third Printing, 1962

MANUFACTURED IN THE UNITED STATES OF AMERICA

Acknowledgments

To the many persons who have helped forward this study I am most grateful. Generous counsel was given at the outset by Dr. Willi Apel, Professor Walter Piston, and Dr. Otto Kinkeldey, and later by Professor G. Wallace Woodworth, Professor Edward Ballantine, and Dr. Donald J. Grout. Among my colleagues at the University of California, Los Angeles, I am indebted to Dr. Walter H. Rubsamen for suggestions concerning the early chapters, to Dr. Hugh Gilchrist Dick for helpful advice in matters of English style, and to Dr. Wayland D. Hand and Dr. L. Gardner Miller for assisting with the translations. Thanks are due to the local editors of the University of California Publications in Music and to Mr. David R. Brower of the University of California Press editorial staff, Berkeley, for their careful reading of the manuscript and for many suggestions in the interest of greater clarification. I also wish to thank Dr. Edwin J. Stringham for information regarding copyrights and printing techniques, and Dr. Gerhard Albersheim for checking portions of the manuscript. The university library staff has been unfailingly coöperative; in particular, Mrs. Jean C. Anderson and Mr. Neal R. Harlow have assisted by obtaining materials from other libraries. My typist, Miss Marjorie Macdonald, has likewise aided greatly through her expert copyings of the manuscript. A final word of appreciation is reserved for my wife, whose help and encouragement have been constant.

Acknowledgment is made to the following firms for permission to use copyrighted material:

Novello and Company, Ltd., London, and The H. W. Gray Company, Inc., New York (examples 102, *a*, and 103–106; van den Borren quotations, pp. 11, 17, 22; Spitta quotations, pp. 62, 64).

Drei Masken Verlag, Berlin (Viecenz quotations, pp. 13, 20 f.).

Associated Music Publishers, Inc., New York (Leichtentritt quotations, pp. 14, 17 f., 25, 96 f.; Mies quotation, p. 86; Luithlen quotation, p. 124; examples 43, 46–49, 54, 56, *b*, 56, *c*, 57, 59, 61, 62, 66, 67, 70, 71, 85, *b*, 93, 132–144).

Durand et Cie, Paris, and Elkan-Vogel Company, Inc., Philadelphia (d'Indy quotations, pp. 14, 18, 26, 125; examples 107, 109).

Kistner und Siegel, Leipzig (Stöhr quotation, p. 25).

G. Schirmer, Inc., New York (Goetschius quotations, pp. 25, 27; examples 145–163).

Augener, Ltd., London (Prout quotations, pp. 85 f.; 161, note 12).

American Music Center, Inc., New York (Copland excerpts, p. 159, note 54).

Charles Scribner's Sons, New York (Santayana quotation, p. 121).

The Macmillan Company, New York (Stanford quotation, p. 1; Colles quotation, p. 112).

Joseph Williams, Ltd., London (Tovey quotation, p. 161, note 12).

Clayton F. Summy Company, Chicago (examples 1, 3–11, 13–20, 25, *a*, 27–29, 40–42, 44, 45, 55, *b*, 63, 64, 98, 102, *d*, 110–131).

J. and W. Chester, Ltd., London (example 50).

G. Ricordi and Co., Inc., New York (examples 2, 12, 21–24, 25, *b*, 26, 30–39, 53, 55, *a*, 56, *a*, 58, 65, 68, 69).

                                                                R. U. N.

January, 1948.

Contents

Introduction

THE PRINCIPLE of variation underlies all music. Its effect can be found not only in the variation form proper but also in such diverse manifestations as the early cantus firmus mass, the variation suite, the variation ricercar, the *double* of the dance suite, the modified recurrence of the principal theme in the rondo, the varied reprise of the classical sonata and symphony, the nineteenth-century cyclical treatment, the *idée fixe* of Berlioz, and the Wagnerian leitmotif.[1]

Because the principle of variation is epitomized by the variation form itself, teachers have long advocated learning the techniques of composition through the writing of variations. As early as 1868, Adolf Bernhard Marx, after stating that there is hardly a form which does not make incidental yet decided use of variation, declares that the student who wishes a comprehensive training in composition will make himself at home in the variation.[2] Charles Villiers Stanford, writing more than forty years later, expresses this idea still more emphatically, asserting that

Variations are to free composition what counterpoint is to technique—the master-key of the whole building. Interesting in themselves to elaborate, they are of still greater service in training the mind to deal easily with the most difficult problems in works of larger proportions. Sections of sonata form, such as the episodes between the statements of themes, the development (or free fantasia), and the coda, all depend upon the knowledge of writing variations; and the repetitions of the main themes themselves become far more intrinsically interesting in the hands of a composer who is well practiced in variation writing. It should be clearly understood that we do not use the term variation from the point of view of mere ornamentation or passage writing on the basis of a theme. It is easy even among the old masters to distinguish those who knew every nook and corner of this branch of their craft from those who did not, by comparing their powers in this form.[3]

Many writers have made the variation form the object of their studies, but none of their works includes an extended treatment of the variation as a whole.[4] The special studies are concerned, of necessity, with individual composers, periods, schools, or types; while the books on composition and form, although often surveying the entire field, treat the subject incompletely. Hugo Leichtentritt recognized this situation when he wrote that "eine umfassende Behandlung der Variationskunst wäre Gegenstand genug für ein ausgedehntes Spezialwerk."[5]

It is the purpose of the present study to undertake such a "comprehensive special work" covering the field of the instrumental variation. No attempt will be made to deal with the general problem of variation

---

[1] For footnotes to text, see p. 155.

in music, except so far as the variation form provides a partial solution, nor to deal with the still broader problem, philosophical in its essence, of the relation between unity and variety (or variation) in art as a whole. Instead, the method used here will be (1) to make a critical examination of existing explanations of the variation in order to reconcile them into a more consistent series of basic constructive principles; and (2) to show the successive historical manifestations of these constructive principles under the influence of changing styles.

The music investigated is the literature of the instrumental variation from its earliest significant appearance in the sixteenth century to its more mature form at the opening of the twentieth. The history of the variation in the period antedating the Spanish lutenists is alluded to only cursorily; similarly, the field of the contemporary variation (embracing works by Schönberg, Hindemith, Stravinsky, and the like) is left for later investigation. The study is not concerned, except in an incidental way, with hybrid forms like the variation suite and variation ricercar; nor does it undertake to treat works built upon the plan of a theme with a single variation (the dance pair, for example) or those consisting of a single variation of a theme not stated, as in the chorale prelude. The chorale variation, however, is discussed at length. Variation cycles which compose parts of larger works are considered equally with those which constitute independent pieces, but all concert arrangements, paraphrases, and transcriptions are excluded.

Because secondary sources adequately provide the information needed in a study of this kind, concerned as it is with broad trends over several centuries, reprints rather than original manuscripts have been consulted throughout. The aim has been to inspect as many variations as possible, not merely the most significant ones; hence all readily available scores have been analyzed.

CHAPTER I

The Categories of Variation Technique

BECAUSE the variation has had a longer history than any other instrumental form, its use having been uninterrupted for more than four centuries, and since, during this long span, it has undergone many changes in type, style, and technical treatment, a study of its development presents diverse and stimulating problems. Certain of these problems are general in character. What kinds of variations have existed at different periods? How did each originate, and what influence did each exert upon succeeding types? What effect have changing styles had upon variation development? There are also questions which are more specifically technical. What is the nature of the variation theme? What modifications are applied to the theme? Is there a relationship or balance between those elements of the theme which are modified and those which remain unchanged? Are there basic technical plans which underlie the variations of different periods?

From the first systematic beginning of the variation, in the second quarter of the sixteenth century, to the emergence of the contemporary style in the first quarter of the twentieth, variation types have succeeded one another with methodical regularity. In this period of approximately four hundred years seven distinct kinds may be distinguished:

1. Renaissance and baroque variations on secular songs, dances, and arias.

2. Renaissance and baroque variations on plain songs and chorales.

3. The baroque basso ostinato variation.

4. The ornamental variation of the eighteenth and nineteenth centuries.

5. The nineteenth-century character variation.

6. The nineteenth-century basso ostinato variation.

7. The free variation of the late nineteenth and early twentieth centuries.

Renaissance and baroque variations on secular songs, dances, and arias were the first type to appear. Characteristic pieces are William Byrd's *Walsingham*, based upon the melody of an English secular song of the sixteenth century; the *Pavana italiana* of Antonio de Cabezón, built, as the title suggests, upon a pavane (the ceremonious court dance of the early sixteenth century); and the numerous aria variations (*Aria prima, Aria secunda,* etc.) of Johann Pachelbel, the themes of which were apparently original with the composer. In pieces of this kind, the primary aim was the decoration and embellishment of the theme by means of new figurations and counterpoints. A similar decorative purpose, it is true, governed the creation of the later ornamental variation (as seen, for example, in Haydn's *Variations in F Minor*), yet there are important stylistic differences between the two groups. Whereas the figuration of the ornamental variation is strikingly regular and symmetrical, that of the earlier type is less set; its texture, furthermore, is often more contrapuntal than that of the ornamental species. Then, too, the variations on secular songs, dances, and arias came at a time when music was less definite harmonically, owing to modal influences, than it was during the period of the ornamental variation. Because of their flexibility of harmony and figuration, together with their simple and often folklike themes, these variations show an agreeable freshness and ingenuousness. In common with most pre-nineteenth-century types, they maintain the essential structure of the theme throughout a series.

Renaissance and baroque variations on plain songs and chorales are distinguished from those on secular themes not alone through their use of liturgical subjects but also by their more serious and complicated style. Unlike the preceding type, which was sometimes intended for performance on the lute, and more often for the various kinds of keyboard instruments (clavichord, harpsichord, organ, etc.—in short, all those embraced by the generic term *clavier*), the variations on plain songs and chorales were conceived in greater part for the organ. Often, too, they adhere less closely to the theme than do the secular pieces. John Bull's *Salvator Mundi* is a typical plain-song variation; a well-known example of the chorale variation is *Vom Himmel hoch da komm' ich her* by J. S. Bach.

Ostinato variations, as a class, differ from the preceding variations by virtue of their continuous construction; the component variations, instead of being separated by cadential breaks into a succession of isolated units, are joined to produce an uninterrupted flow of movement. Equally important as a distinguishing characteristic, the ostinato variation is generally built upon a short melodic phrase, normally four or eight measures long, which, ideally, recurs without change from the beginning of a piece to the end. Actually, such a completely literal recurrence of the ostinato is comparatively rare, for, as will be shown more fully in chapter iii, the ostinato theme is frequently figured or otherwise altered; sometimes, too, more than one theme appears in the same composition. There are also occasional pieces so free in their construction as to lack any consistent use of an ostinato melody, the ostinato element in such variations being reduced to a recurring series of chords, or even, when the freedom is extreme, to a recurring cadence pattern.

Almost without exception, those ostinato variations which are built upon a recurring melodic phrase utilize the theme as a bass, hence are *basso ostinato* variations, although a few ostinato pieces, such as *A Grounde* by the English virginalist Thomas Tomkins, maintain the ostinato theme chiefly outside of the bass. Basso ostinato variations have been important in two different epochs, the baroque period and the nineteenth century. The *baroque basso ostinato* variation shares with the chorale variation the traits of seriousness and contrapuntal complexity, yet it is often more massive and brilliant than the ecclesiastical pieces. In contrast to the borrowed themes in vogue in other baroque variation types, most of its underlying basses are either original themes or consist of stock thematic patterns used jointly by different composers (see pp. 66–68). Prominent examples of the baroque basso ostinato variation are the passacaglias and chaconnes of Buxtehude, and J. S. Bach's famous *Passacaglia in C Minor*.

The ornamental variation of the eighteenth and nineteenth centuries is the successor to renaissance and baroque variations on secular songs, dances, and arias. Both types aim at the figural decoration of the theme, as indicated above, and the distinction between them is therefore primarily stylistic. Because of the undisputable relationship existing between the two, some writers on the variation make no attempt at a differentiation; Leichtentritt, for example, uses the term *ornamenting variation* to denote all simple variations impartially whose basis is the decoration or embellishment of the chief theme outlines.[1] But the stylistic divergence between the two classes is too wide to be ignored, and in this study *ornamental variation* will be used in the restrictive sense of a specific eighteenth- and nineteenth-century decorative type, to which belong Haydn's *Variations in F Minor*, the variations movement from Schubert's *Death and the Maiden Quartet*, and similar embellishing variations. In conformity with the straightforward style of the classic period, this type exhibits greater simplicity than its prototype in the renaissance and baroque periods, and because of its avoidance of contrapuntal complexities, the connection between theme and variations is singularly transparent. Secular songs and dances continue, occasionally, to serve as themes but the main reliance is upon operatic excerpts and original subjects. Many of the finest variations are set, not for clavier, but for chamber music ensembles.

The nineteenth-century character variation contrasts strongly with earlier types in general. Whereas previous variations tend to preserve the expression of the theme throughout a series, the separate members of the character variation frequently alter the expression, or "character," of the theme profoundly. Thus in Beethoven's *Diabelli Variations*, one of the most celebrated of all character variations, the theme is a rapid waltz, variation 1 is a slow and majestic march, variation 2 uses a quietly animated style, and so on. Another important difference from earlier types is that in place of a purely figural and ornamental treatment we find here, for the first time, an emphasis upon the development of motives from the theme. The character variation is thus not only more dramatic than its predecessors, through its sharp contrasts of mood, but also more organically constructed as well. Of greater length than its immediate forerunner, the ornamental variation, it is likewise more elaborate in every way.

The technique of character change is actually very old, being traceable to an early prototype of the variation, the dance pair; but its use in the early period of variation history was slight compared to its use in the nineteenth century. Hence, although one may justifiably apply the name *character variation* to separate members of certain early variation series (the scherzo-like fifth variation of Frescobaldi's *Partite sopra l'aria della Romanesca*, for example), and even to pre-nineteenth-century sets in their entirety (notably to Bach's *Goldberg Variations*), it is not possible to speak of the character variation as a *type* before the nineteenth century.

The nineteenth-century basso ostinato variation springs, as does its baroque ancestor, from a bass theme, and shows the same continuity of design, but it differs from the early type in two important respects. Under the influence of the character variation and the general nineteenth-century impulse toward subjective expression, its component members often depart widely from the expression of the theme; they also present the theme more frequently in upper voices. For these reasons the nineteenth-century type is less homogeneous in style than the baroque variations and less true to the strict basso ostinato principle. In contrast with the earlier species, which was intended in large part for keyboard instruments, two of the most celebrated examples from the nineteenth century are for orchestra—the *Allegro energico* from Brahms' *Fourth Symphony*, and the *Finale* from the same composer's *Haydn Variations*.

The free variation of the late nineteenth and early twentieth centuries is the last important type prior to the contemporary period. It marks a significant departure from all earlier species in that the bond between variations and theme is now frequently a theme motive rather than the theme in its entirety. This means that the structural and harmonic pattern of the theme is often discarded in favor of a free development, and that the free variation approaches, in plan and treatment, forms like the rhapsody and fantasia. As in the character variation, so in the free variation the expression of the theme is altered materially. Many of the most typical examples, such as Franck's *Variations symphoniques* and Strauss's *Don Quixote*, are for orchestra.[2]

The basis of the foregoing differentiation into broad variation types is partly the kind of theme employed. Such is the distinction which sets off the basso ostinato variation, with its characteristic bass theme and attendant harmony, from variations built upon a melodic subject and the attendant harmony—ornamental variations, certain chorale variations, and the like. Again, the classification has to do in part with the treatment accorded the theme; this criterion distinguishes all pre-nineteenth-century types from the free variation. Finally, the setting up of categories is carried out partly in accordance with differences in general style; as brought out above, the technical procedures employed in the eighteenth- and nineteenth-century ornamental variation are often the same as those of the earlier variations on secular songs, dances, and arias, yet there exist significant stylistic differences between the two types.

We come now to the examination of the specific technical procedures which underlie these many types. This, the chief task of the present chapter, demands initially a more precise understanding of the variation theme and of the modifications which the theme may undergo.

The variation theme may be regarded as a complex of separate, though interdependent elements. Conspicuous among these elements are melody, bass, harmony, structure (meaning the plan of parts and phrases), tempo, dynamics, rhythm, and instrumental tone color. Some themes lack certain of these elements altogether—the basso ostinato theme lacks a *superius* melody, the cantus firmus theme has no supporting harmony—but even these exceptional examples contain most of the elements mentioned.

Every element contained in the theme may, potentially, be changed. Each change may vary from a slight modification, whose effect is a simple embellishment or decoration, to radical alterations which threaten the recognizability of the original element or may even destroy it completely; hence infinite possibilities are open to the composer. Alterations of the melodic subject, for example, comprise coloration; sundry kinds of figuration, ranging in effect from a close, almost literal adherence to the melody to a freely arched elaboration which coincides with the melody only at occasional intervals; embellishment by means of conventional ornaments; and far-reaching transformation of the melody through the auxiliary action of changed meter, dynamics, tempo, and the like. The creation of theme motives to be developed in the course of the variations also involves, as a rule, modifications of the melodic subject. Changes in the subordinate voices, or harmony, are similarly varied. They include not only figuration but the application of various contrapuntal devices, such as imitation and invertible counterpoint; the addition of lyric countermelodies; even the employment of fugue and strict canon. They comprise, furthermore, many specifically harmonic alterations: change of mode; change of cadence; the addition of new chords in an attendant, embellishing capacity; the omission of chords, with a view to simplifying the harmony; the use of pedal point; and various degrees of reharmonization, from the use of isolated substitute chords to the virtually complete recasting of the harmony. Changes in the structure of the theme embrace expansions or contractions in the lengths of single phrases; the suppression or addition of phrases; the use, within a single variation, of varied restatements to take the place of literal repetitions in the theme ("double variation"); and the insertion of preludes, postludes, interludes, and transitions. Finally, a wide array of changes is possible in those elements most directly concerned with the expression or character of the theme. The rhythm may be altered, either moderately by the introduction of new figural patterns or more drastically through the use of new meters; tempo and dynamics may experience a similar wide range of modifications; and a variation may be transferred in pitch to a new register or, especially if written for the orchestra, may exploit diverse tone colors.

The technique of variation is conventionally thought of as embracing primarily the foregoing *alterations* or *changes* which may affect a theme. Change of harmony is conceived to be a variation technique; similarly, changes in structure, melody, figuration, expression, and the like are regarded as variation techniques. But it is obvious that in any true variation certain elements of the theme must remain constant as others change. Thus in the cantus firmus variation the melodic subject remains constant while the adjoining voices undergo changes of figuration, counterpoint, and harmony. Were all the elements of the theme to undergo strong change simultaneously we should have, not variation, but complete antithesis and contrast. In order to attain, therefore, a more accurate conception of the term variation technique it becomes necessary to enlarge the customary meaning to include, not merely single changes, or groups of changes, but *combinations of changes with constants.* Everything which happens to a theme, under this new meaning, whether of change or inaction, is a part of the technical treatment the theme receives; the cantus firmus plan is just as completely a variation technique as change of expression. If, in this study, a distinction continues to be drawn at times between "variation plans" (meaning the broad categories into which variations may be divided) and "variation techniques" (meaning the specific changes which a theme undergoes), it is only in deference to customary practice and to secure the greater clearness which accompanies the use of accepted meanings.

The history of the variation has shown a pronounced tendency for particular groups of changes to ally themselves with particular groups of constants. Thus have evolved, in a purely empirical way, the broad techniques or plans of variation writing referred to above through the example of the cantus firmus variation. Up to the latter part of the nineteenth century practically all variations were constructed on a plan which, while changing now the melody of the theme, now its harmony, now its figuration, now two or more of the elements in concert, nevertheless remained true to its essential structural outlines; the variations of Beethoven and Brahms, no less than those of Cabezón, Frescobaldi, and Bach, exemplify this principle of structure retention. Toward the close of the nineteenth century, as has been shown, a radically new conception was introduced, wherein the separate variations, instead of following the structural pattern of the theme, customarily broke away from it altogether, establishing their connection with the theme mainly through the use of theme motives or of transformations of the melodic subject; this is the plan which was followed in such works as Franck's *Variations symphoniques.* By the beginning of the contemporary period, therefore, in the early twentieth century, there were in existence two diametrically opposed ways of constructing variations: the age-old *structural* plan, wherein the basic relationships of parts, sections, and phrases present in the theme were preserved in the variations, and the comparatively recent *free* plan, in which these theme relationships were generally disregarded.

The distinction between the structural and free plans of variation writing is fundamental to an understanding of the form as a whole, and many writers on the variation have recognized its importance. Thus d'Indy draws a line between variations in which the structure of the theme is preserved intact (*la variation ornementale, la variation décorative*) and those in which the theme structure is extended or modified (*la variation amplificatrice*).[3] In the same way Leichtentritt discusses separately the relatively simple *ornamenting variation, contrapuntal variation,* and *character variation,* on the one hand, and the more complicated "*Variationen der Variationenform,*" such as Richard Strauss's *Don Quixote* and Reger's *Hiller Variations,* on the other.[4] Again, Goetschius distinguishes between the *small* (or *simple*) *variation form,* in which "no *essential* alterations of the design of the Theme are permissible"[5] and the *large* (or *higher*) *variation form,* in which "the variations are more properly *Elaborations* than mere modified duplications of the Theme."[6] These men confirm what was stated above, that the crux of a really basic distinction is the degree of structural correspondence existing between variations and theme. So long as the structural design of the theme is maintained, the resulting series is essentially conservative; this means that variations as stylistically and chronologically divergent as Buxtehude's *D-Minor Passacaglia,* Haydn's *Variations in F Minor,* and Reger's *Variations on a Theme by Mozart* exhibit a fundamental affinity. When, contrariwise, the structural design of the theme is abandoned, the resulting series shows so little connection with traditional variations as to become virtually a new form. It is from this point of view that one must consider d'Indy's *Istar*, Elgar's *Variations on an Original Theme*, and Strauss's *Don Quixote*, works which in their breadth of dimensions and freedom of development often approach the symphonic poem.

Within the basic twofold division may be distinguished still further differences of plan. These relate without exception to the structural family of variations, since the design of the free variation is too heterogeneous to make further classification practicable. Three contrasting kinds of structural variations present themselves: the *cantus firmus*, the *melodico-harmonic*, and the *harmonic*.

In the *cantus firmus* plan the successive variations adhere closely to the melodic subject while creating for it new figural and harmonic settings. As a rule the subject is presented literally; occasionally it receives an incidental embellishment. The underlying principle of this treatment originated in polyphonic vocal music hundreds of years before the advent of the variation form proper; the various kinds of late medieval organa and clausulae, the motet of the thirteenth and fourteenth centuries, and the fifteenth-century mass (*Missa L'homme armé*, etc.) are all manifestations of the cantus firmus idea.[7] In the fifteenth and sixteenth centuries the principle was transferred to organ music,[8] and during the middle sixteenth century Cabezón used it as the basis for writing variations, choosing as his cantus fermi the melodies of contemporary songs and dances.[9] Cabezón's lead was followed by the English virginalists, especially Byrd, and by Sweelinck and Scheidt on the continent, all of whom used the cantus firmus principle conspicuously in varying secular themes. Beginning with Bull, Sweelinck, and Scheidt, and continuing as late as J. S. Bach, the treatment found an even more important place in the variation of liturgical melodies, at first of plain songs and later of chorales. Throughout this early period the cantus firmus variation exhibited, because of its contrapuntal manner and its freedom from the harmony of the theme, considerable complexity of effect; hence it is not surprising that with the passing of the baroque style, around 1750, the cantus firms plan virtually disappeared. In comparison, therefore, with the other structural designs, both of which continued to be actively used throughout the nineteenth century, it was relatively short-lived.

Various terms are now current to designate variations built on the cantus firmus principle. Viecenz uses the name *cantus firmus treatment* (*Cantus-firmus Praxis*); van den Borren employs the term *polyphonic variation*.[10] Leichtentritt regards variations of this kind as belonging to a larger class which he calls the *contrapuntal variation*, and d'Indy similarly considers them as an early stage of a larger group which he calls the *decorative variation*.[11] If, unlike d'Indy and Leichtentritt, one considers these variations as forming a distinct species, a point of view which will be supported during the following discussion, the choice among existing terms lies with *cantus firmus treatment* and *polyphonic variation*. Of these, *cantus firmus treatment* (or *cantus firmus plan* or *cantus firmus technique*) has the advantage of naming definitely the constructive principle involved, the retention of the literal melodic subject and its embellishment through contrapuntal figuration; hence this term is adopted here.

Discussion of the characteristics and possibilities of the cantus firmus plan must necessarily consider the definitions and descriptions of the men referred to above. Van den Borren, whose account of the different variation plans is unusually specific, possibly because he confines his analysis to the English virginal variations, emphasizes that in the typical variation of this kind the melodic subject changes its location among the voices as the series progresses:

The melodic subject submitted to variation maintains its simplicity from one end to the other of the piece; from variation to variation it passes from one voice to another, and each time it is surrounded with fresh figural counterpoints.[12]

Van den Borren takes pains to point out that this transfer of the cantus firmus from part to part follows no prescribed order (soprano, alto, tenor, bass, for example); on the contrary the transfer is generally carried out quite unsystematically. Thus, *The Woods so Wild*, by William Byrd,

comprises fourteen variations, very irregular in structure, and presenting a mixed aspect at several points. In the first two the subject is in the *superius*, the bass being different in each of them. It passes to the alto in the third, in which we meet again with the bass of the first variation, a sort of countrified drone. In the fourth it undergoes a strong figuration, and is distributed between the upper parts; there is the same drone bass. This reappears in the fifth variation, in which the subject passes to the *superius*, and also in the sixth, in which it occupies the tenor. The seventh variation treats it in the *superius* with a new bass. In the eighth it disappears altogether, but we find the drone bass again. The ninth variation brings it back, almost completely disguised, and with a free bass. The variations 10, 11, 12 have a common bass on which are erected counterpoints having no relation with the subject. The latter reappears in the alto in the thirteenth variation, and in the *superius* in the fourteenth. These last two variations have a completely free bass. As we see, the polyphonic element is at several points crowded out by a harmonic element, which appears under the archaic form of the popular drone.[13]

It is apparent from the foregoing analysis that van den Borren classifies a variation set as belonging to the cantus firmus category even when certain of the component variations fail to exemplify cantus firmus treatment. His statement that *The Woods so Wild* belongs here means essentially that most of the component variations, but not necessarily all of them, exhibit the earmark of this type, *i.e.*, contrapuntal figuration centering around a cantus firmus. Such elasticity in the application of terms is a necessity in any system of classification which attempts to give names to variation series in their entirety rather than to the component members only. For, as we shall see, it is not merely variations of the cantus firmus variety which fail to maintain consistently a single technique; variations built upon quite different plans show the same characteristic departures from the hypothetical norms.

Because of this fact it may well be asked at this point if an alternative method of classification might not be desirable, one which, instead of attempting to name the over-all plan of an entire series, would concentrate on naming the plans of the component variations. The question is perhaps this: Did the composers of the past, as they prepared to write variations, resolve to build a set entirely upon a single plan or did they rather decide to construct variation 1 according to one plan, variation 2 according to another, and variation 3 according to a third? From the evidence of hundreds of variation sets we learn that although in most of them composers refused to bind themselves completely to either of these decisions, they generally had a reasonably consistent over-all plan in view. Thus the baroque passacaglia writers worked from the given bass theme, or from the harmony suggested by the theme, throughout an entire piece, as Bach did also in his *Goldberg Variations*. Likewise Haydn and Mozart followed a single plan in most, even if not all, the variations of a given series, that of ornamenting the melody, as well as the harmony, of the theme. One concludes that theorists are on firm ground when they attempt to assign names to entire series of variations, and that these larger classifications, with their attendant qualifications and exceptions, give an essentially true reflection of the attitude of variation composers. It will be noted, furthermore, that the use of these terms to denote the plans of entire sets does not preclude their being applied, in addition, to the component members; to say that Byrd's *The Woods so Wild is* a cantus firmus variation (in the sense of a cantus firmus series) does not prevent our saying that variations 1 to 3 of this work are single cantus firmus variations, in distinction to variation 4, which is built upon quite another plan.

To van den Borren's concept of an immutable melodic subject surrounded by ever-new counterpoints, Viecenz adds the important idea that a considerable degree of harmonic change is possible in the cantus firmus variation. Following a discussion of the chaconne and passa-caglia, whose technique he says consists in the addition of new material rather than in the change of the old, he states:

Eine analoge Diagnose ergibt eine Untersuchung der Formen, in denen eine Stimme einen Cantus firmus vorträgt, der durch andere, sich selbst und einander imitierende Stimmen umspielt wird. (Vergl. die Choralvariationen.) Die Veränderung trifft auch hier nicht die als cantus firmus repräsentierte *res facta*, die höchstens figurativ bereichert wird. Die harmonische Ausbeute wird eine mannigfaltigere, sobald der cantus firmus nicht im Basse liegt, da in diesem Falle nicht die Notwendigkeit einer gleichzeitig Basscharakter tragenden Stimme Einschränkungen auferlegt.[14]

Trans.: An analogous diagnosis [to that obtained from the chaconne and passa-caglia] is yielded by an examination of forms in which a voice carries a cantus firmus which is embellished by other voices imitating the cantus firmus and each other. (Compare chorale variations.) Here, again, the change does not affect the *res facta*, represented as the cantus firmus, which at most is enriched figurally. The harmonic result becomes a more manifold one as soon as the cantus firmus does not lie in the bass, since in this case [*i.e.*, when the cantus lies outside the bass] those limitations are removed which stem from the fact that a melodic voice must serve, at the same time, as a bass.

Viecenz says, it will be noted, that the cantus firmus is occasionally figured; nevertheless he clearly regards such figurations as exceptional, for he proceeds to stress the idea that the principal changes take place in the accompanying voices rather than in the given melody:

Das Prinzip des Variierens trifft hier wie auch bei den Chaconnebildungen nicht in der Hauptsache das musikalisch Gegebene einer *res facta*, sondern befasst sich vielmehr mit der Darstellung ein und desselben unveränderten Grundgedankens in Verbindung mit anderen Gedanken, die einem neuen Schöpferakt entspringen. Die Neubildungen können sich derart in den Vordergrund drängen, dass der eigentliche Ursprungskern zum blossen Schatten verblasst. (Vgl. die Cantus-firmus-Praxis des 15. Jahrhunderts.)[15]

Trans.: Here, as in chaconne formations, the principle of variation does not affect, in the main, the given musical condition of the *res facta*, but is concerned, rather, with the presentation of one and the same unchanged basic idea in connection with other thoughts which spring from a new creative act. The new formations may push themselves into the foreground to such a degree that the actual basic idea dwindles to a mere shadow. (Compare the cantus firmus treatment of the fifteenth century.)

Viecenz's contention that the principal change takes place outside the cantus firmus is incontestable; likewise true is his statement that the accompanying voices may intrude themselves to such an extent as to reduce the original melody to a mere shadow. But in emphasizing in this way the importance of the supporting voices he seems to imply that the function of the cantus firmus is no more than that of an architectural brace or prop. This implication is unfortunate. For even though a cantus firmus in a middle voice may be completely covered and subordinated by the surrounding voices, it immediately takes on melodic significance when transferred to the *superius*. Then, too, it easily attains prominence when, as is so often the case in variations for the organ, it is played upon a contrasting manual, no matter what its location. It would seem, in short, that composers have tried fully as often to enhance the given melody and bring it into prominence as they have to subordinate it; that they have regarded it fully as much in the light of a picture to be successively reframed as of a mere column supporting an edifice.

Leichtentritt and d'Indy add little to the descriptions already given. Leichtentritt mentions the cantus firmus plan in connection with the baroque chorale variation, some of which utilize a successive resetting of the unaltered chorale melody:

Eine zweite Art der Variation, die kontrapunktische, ist zumal in den Orgelwerken schon vom 17. Jahrhundert an gepflegt worden. In den Choralvorspielen z. B. wird der cantus firmus, die Choralmelodie, entsprechend den verschiedenen Textstrophen des Chorals oft mehreremal nacheinander in verschiedener Weise behandelt, so dass der Charakter der Musik sich ändert, entsprechend dem Stimmungsgehalt der einzelnen Strophen.[16]

Trans.: A second kind of variation, the contrapuntal, has been cultivated especially in works for the organ from the seventeenth century on. In chorale preludes, for example, the cantus firmus (the chorale melody) is often treated differently several times in succession, in accordance with the different stanzas of the chorale text, so that the character of the music is altered according to the mood content of the single stanzas.

D'Indy likewise describes the cantus firmus variation by means of the chorale variation. Writing of Bach's three *Chorale partitas* he says:

Plusieurs de ces Variations appartiennent à l'ordre purement *contrapontique* et *décoratif:* le Thème reste à peu près immuable et s'expose en *même temps* que les contrepoints que l'entourent.[17]

Trans.: Many of these variations belong to the purely contrapuntal and decorative category: the theme remains virtually unchanged and is revealed at the same time as the counterpoints which surround it.

He says further that the *variation décoratif* (his name for the general group which embraces the cantus firmus variation) has its basis in polyphonic ornamentation, and thus underscores once more the dependence of the plan upon the contrapuntal style:

Dans cet état *polyphonique* de la Variation, le Thème subsiste *intrinsèquement:* il ne *varie* pas; la Variation circule *autour de lui,* s'en inspire, le commente et l'imite, sans l'atteindre ni le pénétrer: elle devient purement *extrinsèque.*[18]

Trans.: In this polyphonic state of the variation the theme subsists intrinsically; it does not change; the variation revolves around it, draws inspiration from it, comments on it, and imitates it, without affecting or penetrating it: the variation becomes purely extrinsic.

It is significant that Leichtentritt, d'Indy, and Viecenz see a close connection between the cantus firmus plan and that of the basso ostinato variation. Leichtentritt connects the two through their common use of the contrapuntal style; similarly d'Indy and Viecenz find a correspondence in their common employment of what d'Indy calls *l'ornement polyphonique*. But in spite of their stylistic and technical resemblances it may well be questioned if the two plans are essentially one, as these writers would have us believe. In the first place, *l'ornement polyphonique* implies the presence of an immutable melodic line, or subject, and the basso ostinato variation meets this condition much less fully than those built on the cantus firmus plan; as we shall see later, decoration and change of the given subject are frequent and characteristic in the basso ostinato variation, whereas in the cantus firmus variation they are exceptional. A more compelling reason for considering the two plans as distinct is that the theme of the cantus firmus variation is heard melodically whereas the bass subject of the basso ostinato variation is heard as a harmonic support. A melodically functioning cantus firmus (such as one finds in examples 3–15) generally has intrinsic interest; hence a composer tends not only to preserve the subject intact but to bring it occasionally into prominence. Then too, such a cantus firmus imposes relatively few harmonic restrictions upon the variations which it inspires. On the other hand, the type of cantus firmus which functions as a bass, and which becomes thereby what we call a basso ostinato, serves primarily as the representative of a harmonic succession; because it rarely possesses intrinsic interest, ordinarily consisting, instead, of stereotyped formulas of tones (see examples 53–55), composers do not hesitate to leave it in the background nor to obscure its identity by figuration or by more essential changes. In distinction to the true cantus firmus theme, which tends to encourage harmonic change, the basso ostinato, through its implication of fixed chord roots and progressions, tends to restrict and limit the harmony. This tendency, it must be admitted, is not always respected, for certain baroque basso ostinato variations, especially those written under French influence, show harmonic departures as great as those of the average cantus firmus variation; nevertheless, many of the most typical basso ostinato pieces, including the justly admired *Passacaglia in C Minor* of J. S. Bach and the organ passacaglias and chaconnes of Buxtehude, display a harmonic constancy altogether foreign to the cantus firmus type. For these reasons, and chiefly because the essence of the cantus firmus variation is adherence to a recurring melody whereas that of the basso ostinato variation is adherence to a recurring bass subject, with its attendant harmonic implications, the two will be considered in this study as representing distinct treatments.

We turn next to another of the structural plans, the *melodico-harmonic*. As its name indicates, this treatment is marked by the simultaneous retention of the melodic subject and the theme harmony. The melodic subject remains in the soprano, where it undergoes incidental alteration, generally by means of figuration; to a lesser degree the supporting voices are similarly altered or figured. Occasionally the bass receives the chief figuration; at such times the melodic subject tends to resume its original form. The theme harmony is subjected to frequent modifications of detail, even though its main outlines are preserved. The underlying principle, like that of the cantus firmus plan, originated earlier than the variation proper; clearly seen in the colored organ piece as early as Paumann, it can be traced back to a still more significant prototype in the dance pair.[19] This simple form, dating from at least the fourteenth century, is at times virtually a variation set in miniature, in which a slow duple-meter dance is followed by a faster triple-meter dance built on the melodic and harmonic outlines of the first. Melodico-harmonic elaboration of this kind was introduced into the variation form proper by the Spanish lute and keyboard composers, Navaréz, Mudarra, and Cabezón, who used it to vary secular songs and dances.[20] The English virginalists, strongly attracted to the melodico-harmonic treatment, made it their ruling procedure,[21] and during the entire baroque period it formed the basis of many variations in Germany, where it appeared not only in variations on secular themes but in chorale variations as well. The Viennese classic composers, together with their immediate successors, found the melodico-harmonic plan the ideal vehicle for their elegant and at times showy clavier variations; Mozart, Beethoven, Weber, and Chopin all used it in this manner. In addition it served a more serious purpose, throughout the late eighteenth century and the entire nineteenth, as the basis for separate movements of chamber-music works by Haydn, Mozart, Beethoven, Schubert, and Brahms.

Variations built, in this way, by means of elaborations of the given melody and harmony are variously designated. Leichtentritt calls them *ornamenting variations* (*auszierende Variationen*); d'Indy mentions them as a later stage of the *decorative variation;* van den Borren employs the name adopted here, *melodico-harmonic variation.*[22] Blessinger and Viecenz refer to them less explicitly, but on the basis of the examples cited Blessinger appears to have this class in mind when he speaks of the *figural variation*, as does Viecenz when he discusses the *figural varia-*

tion and the *melodic variation.*[23] Of these terms, *ornamenting, decorative,* and *figural* are too general in meaning to serve adequately as names of a technical plan, and *melodic variation,* although technical, overlooks what is plainly the distinguishing characteristic of this procedure: the simultaneous retention of both the melody and the harmony, a twofold binding which explains much of the peculiar nature and limitation of the plan. The only name which takes account of the underlying constructive principle is van den Borren's *melodico-harmonic,*which although coined with reference to the variations of the English virginalists, is applicable to an entire category from Cabezón through the nineteenth century.

Describing the melodico-harmonic plan, van den Borren says that

its principle is simple enough, but its applications are at times complex . . . from variation to variation, the bass and *superius* alternately undergo figurations which alter their outlines, without, however, doing violence to the principle according to which the two extreme parts form the frame of each variation. It is hardly necessary to say that . . . the subject is placed in the *superius;* the bass is nothing but a permanent harmonic foundation.[24]

Leichtentritt stresses the predominantly decorative aspect of the plan. Speaking of examples among the early Spanish *diferencias* and the English virginal variations, Leichtentritt says:

Die ältere Variation ist fast ausnahmlos ausschmückender Art. Sie löst die Melodie des Themas gern in kleinere Notenwerte auf, umspielt sie mit Läufen, Trillern, Arpeggien, verwendet die Versetzung in verschiedene Oktaven. Die Harmonie des Themas wird gewöhnlich in den Variationen im wesentlichen beibehalten.[25]

Trans.: The older variation is almost without exception of decorative character. It likes to break up the melody of the theme into shorter note values, to adorn it with runs, trills, and arpeggios, and to apply transposition into different octaves. The harmony of the theme is usually retained, in essence, in the variations.

He goes beyond van den Borren when he states that the plan underlies variations subsequent to the virginalists, mentioning among its later manifestations the *doubles* of the French suite composers and certain of the variations of Haydn, Mozart, and Beethoven.

D'Indy, along with Leichtentritt, recognizes the melodico-harmonic treatment in the *doubles* of the eighteenth-century dance suite and, more especially, in *le Thème varié,* his name for the variation of the eighteenth and nineteenth centuries. Of *le Thème varié* he says, "Cette forme . . . procédait à la fois du genre *ornemental* employé dans les *doubles* et du genre *décoratif* en usage dans la *Chaconne* et la *Passacaille.*"[26] Since the "genre *ornementale*" relies upon melodic embellishment and the "genre *décoratif*" exhibits a constant bass line, d'Indy's reference to the melodico-harmonic plan is unmistakable. Beyond this brief mention, however, he contributes little to the technical under-standing of the treatment, for his further discussion of *le Thème varié* is vague and confusing. Along with such undeniable examples of the melodico-harmonic plan as Handel's *Harmonious Blacksmith* and the variation movement from Mozart's A-major *Piano Sonata* (K. 331) he cites Bach's *Goldberg Variations*, Beethoven's *Diabelli Variations*, and Brahms' *Haydn Variations*, all of which employ, not the melodico-harmonic, but the harmonic plan.

Both Leichtentritt and d'Indy warn that the melodico-harmonic plan may easily be abused, and point to the brilliant but shallow varia-tions of the bravura pianists in the early nineteenth century to confirm their view. Thus Leichtentritt says:

Die Gefahr liegt nahe, dass diese Variationsweise, wenn sie nicht mit hervor-ragendem Geschmack und Geschick verwendet ist, in ein seichtes Tonge-klingel, ein virtuoses Brillantfeuerwerk ohne Gehalt ausartet. In der Tat hat diese Richtung schliesslich zu modischen Salonvariationen des 19. Jahrhun-derts (Herz, Hünten, Kalkbrenner usw.) geführt, zu einem Tiefstand, der mit echter Kunst kaum noch Beziehung hat.[27]

Trans.: There is danger that this variation method, if not employed with out-standing taste and skill, will degenerate into a superficial tinkling, a virtuoso display of brillant fireworks, without content. Actually, this tendency finally led to the fashionable salon variation of the nineteenth century (Herz, Hünten, Kalkbrenner, and others), to a low watermark, which scarcely bears relation to true art.

D'Indy's scorn of these tawdry variations, and of their composers, whom he calls *célèbres inconnus*, is particularly sharp:

Depuis le début du xixᵉ siècle jusque vers 1830, l'engouement pour le genre *Thème varié* ne connut plus de bornes ... Tous les compositeurs se livrèrent à la "confection en gros" de *Thèmes variés*; quelques-uns ... consacrèrent leur vie entière à ce genre de production ... la palme, dans ce tournoi, revient certainement à l'abbé Gélinek, qui fournissait ses éditeurs de cahiers (*Hefte*) comprenant chacun *six Thèmes variés* ... , et l'on connaît de ce Gélinek *cent huit* cahiers de Variations! Le second prix doit être décerné à Czerny, qui n'écri-vit pas moins de *mille* œuvres, parmi lesquelles on compte près de *la moitié* en *Thèmes variés!*[28]

Trans.: From the beginning of the nineteenth century until about 1830, the craze for the *Thème varié* type knew no bounds ... All composers gave them-selves over to the wholesale manufacture of *Thèmes variés*; some of them ... dedicated their entire life to this kind of production ... the victory in this contest went definitely to Abbé Gélinek, who supplied his publishers with manuscript books containing six *Thèmes variés* each ... , and there are eight hundred known manuscript books by this Gélinek! The second prize must be awarded to Czerny, who wrote no fewer than a thousand works, about half of which are *Thèmes variés!*

The reason that composers such as Gélinek and Czerny were able to write variations in such enormous quantities is directly traceable to the nature of the melodico-harmonic plan: instead of demanding essential changes in the theme this treatment requires only a simple, ornamental elaboration of the given melody and harmony, and in a non-contrapuntal style such elaborations can be achieved with almost mechanical facility.

In defense of the plan it must be emphasized that the elaborations which it calls forth need not be superficial nor obvious. Indeed, one of the peculiar glories and mysteries of the variation form lies in the way composers of first rank—Byrd, Bach, and Mozart, to name but a few,—working from simple melodico-harmonic premises, have attained results so subtle and ingenious, and so far removed, seemingly, from the theme.[29]

The remaining plan to maintain the structural integrity of the theme is the *harmonic*. Like the melodico-harmonic, it preserves the general structural and harmonic outlines of the theme, but unlike that treatment, it abandons the melody of the theme entirely or, at most, maintains but an incidental contact with it. By escaping the melodic control of the theme the plan becomes the vehicle for variations of unusual flexibility.

The harmonic treatment has as its constructive principle a recurring series of chords which, appearing first in the theme, underlies each of the variations in turn. Frequently, though not always, such a recurring harmonic succession is associated with an uninterruptedly recurring bass line, or basso ostinato, a device which appeared first in early vocal music. Propper traces the idea of the basso ostinato back to the organ point of the Middle Ages, as exemplified in *organum purum*, and shows its later and more developed manifestations in the recurring basses of the Montpellier Codex, *Sumer is icumen in*, and the masses of the fifteenth century.[30] According to this authority, the basso ostinato found its way into instrumental music in the sixteenth and seventeenth centuries by means of gamba, guitar, and lute music, especially in connection with the practice of improvising upon a ground. The earliest instance of such instrumental usage is the *Tratado de glosas* of Diego Ortiz (Rome, 1553), whose numerous basso ostinato pieces, called *recercadas*, and intended by Ortiz to serve as models for gamba improvisation, may be regarded as incipient passacaglias.[31] Toward the close of the sixteenth century and the beginning of the seventeenth the harmonic plan appeared in variations on secular songs and dances and in basso ostinato compositions written by the English virginalists and

Italian organists, notably Byrd and Frescobaldi. During the seventeenth and eighteenth centuries it continued to form the basis for basso ostinato variations, especially the popular passacaglia and chaconne; and in the nineteenth century, it underlay most of the character variations of Beethoven, Schumann, and Brahms, as well as of basso ostinato variations by Brahms and Reger. Numerous significant works, among them J. S. Bach's *Goldberg Variations* and the *Diabelli Variations* of Beethoven, attest to the importance of this plan, while its almost uninterrupted continuance for over three centuries is evidence of its vitality. In the baroque period it was often the servant of contrapuntal development; in the nineteenth century it served equally well the exigencies of a more homophonic style, as well as of the development of motives from the theme.

Variations constructed in this way on the plan of a constantly recurring bass and harmony, like those already discussed, have received different names. Blessinger terms the species *ostinato variation;* van den Borren, *harmonic variation;* Goetschius, *basso ostinato;* Viecenz, *chaconne treatment (Chaconne-Praxis);* Luithlen, *bass variation.* Stöhr describes it but gives it no name, while Goetschius and Luithlen draw a distinction between variations in which the bass is constant and those in which the harmony remains fixed.[32] Such a distinction is of doubtful value. One reason is that the bass and harmony work together reciprocally in these variations, as Viecenz points out in the following paragraph. Another reason is that only very rarely is a bass retained literally throughout a series of variations (see pp. 72 ff.). Because all the terms used to denote this plan recognize the fundamental constructive principle involved, that of a recurring bass line with its attendant harmonic implications and restrictions, any one of the terms may appropriately be used. Nevertheless, because certain of them are limiting in meaning (for example, *ostinato variation* and *chaconne treatment* refer to subtypes within the main category), the name *harmonic variation* (or *harmonic plan* or *harmonic technique*) remains as the one best suited to describe the method as a whole.

Viecenz's description of the harmonic plan, the most comprehensive of any by the writers mentioned, is significant for showing that the true function of a bass theme is to represent a harmonic succession; in addition it stresses the complementary relationship which exists between this bass and its associated harmony, showing that if the bass is absent the harmony remains to represent it, and vice versa. Directing his initial discussion at the basso ostinato variations of the baroque period, he says:

Im Generalbasszeitalter war im wesentlichen nicht die Oberstimme das Agens der musikalischen Gestaltung, sondern die Basslinie, die den Verlauf der Melodiestimmen vorschreibt oder wenigstens inspiriert. Die einzelnen Töne der Basslinie stellen die Repräsentanten einer bestimmten vorgezeichneten Harmonienreihe dar. Die harmonische Ergänzung zum Akkord pflegte als geschlossene, aber abhängige Einheit dem Bass gegenüber zu treten, so dass beim Fehlen des realen Basses die Harmonie ideell immerhin als vorhanden gefühlt wird und ebenso umgekehrt . . . Ob die Basslinie als Harmonievertretung realiter oder idealiter in den Variationen vorhanden ist, ist völlig belanglos.[33]

Trans. In the thorough-bass period, it was not fundamentally the treble which was the agent of the musical fashioning, but rather the bass line, which prescribes the course of the melody parts, or at least inspires it. The individual tones of the bass line constitute the representatives of a definite, prescribed harmonic succession. The chord, as a harmonic complement, usually stood as a self-contained but dependent unity in relation to the bass, so that in the absence of the real bass the harmony, ideally speaking, is nevertheless felt to be present, and vice versa . . . Whether the bass line, as a representative of the harmony, is present actually or only ideally in the variations, is completely unimportant.

He goes on to say that in the chaconne the bass and related harmony maintain themselves in the variations, but admits that changes in the bass are possible by remarking, "Die Veränderungen des Basses geschiet zumindestens nur in Form melodischer Varianten." He then proceeds to the corollary, that the chief changes take place outside the ostinato bass:

Das Neue, was in den Variationen vor sich geht, besteht nicht im Verändern eines Gegebenen, sondern im Neuhinzuschaffen von etwas Anderem; es ist Ergebnis eines völlig freien und neuen Schöpferaktes, dem eine Einschränkung lediglich durch die vorgezeichnete Harmonienreihung erwächst.[34]

Trans.: The new features which appear in the variations consist not in the alteration of that which is given, but in the addition of something else; they are the result of a completely free and new creative act, which is limited solely by the prescribed harmonic succession.

It is this presence within the basso ostinato variation of extrinsic change (d'Indy's *l'ornement polyphonique*) which causes both Viecenz and d'Indy to group the basso ostinato variation with the cantus firmus variation, a classification objected to above (see pp. 15 f.). Finally, Viecenz points to the common bond existing between the basso ostinato variation and those variations which rest upon a constant harmony but are constructed sectionally (the nineteenth-century character variation, for example):

Die Spuren der alten Chaconne- und Ostinatobasspraxis sind bei weitem stärker, als gemeinhin angenommen zu werden pflegt. Was sind alle die Variationswerke, die an einem gegebenen Harmonieschema festhalten, anderes als Zyklen mit einem Basso ostinato![35]

Trans.: The traces of the old chaconne and ostinato-bass treatment are far stronger than they are generally acknowledged to be. What else are all the variations which hold fast to a given scheme of harmony but cycles with an ostinato bass!

Van den Borren's description of the harmonic plan is extremely brief:

On a bass which forms the subject and which remains unchanged the composer constructs a series of variations that are entirely confined to the other voices.[36]

More specific information regarding van den Borren's meaning may be had by examining his descriptions of certain harmonic variations, such as Byrd's *Malt's come downe*:

Malt's come downe carries us back to the field of pastoral music dear to Byrd. Here the bass follows a harmonic progression of quite a modern character, which implies without reserve the key of C major [*sic*]. . . :

Among the nine variations which the piece contains, there are three only in which the bass is adorned with figurations. The other parts are in free counterpoint. In variations 4 and 7 the rhythm of the bass is transferred to the upper parts, which are formed into successions of homophonic chords standing above a figured bass. *Malt's come downe* is an exquisite composition, in which all the qualities of Byrd appear, especially the poetical charm of the harmony, in which soft and gentle tones prevail.[37]

Here we see that van den Borren, like Viecenz, admits the possibility of ornamenting the given bass, and we learn that when he speaks in his definition of a bass subject "which remains unchanged" he means only that the salient outlines of the bass need be preserved, not its literal form. This is an important qualification, inasmuch as virtually all variations built on the harmonic plan show modifications of the original bass, at times incidental, at others more persistent and far-reaching.

In his analysis of another virginal variation, the *Galliard Ground* of William Inglott, van den Borren shows the possibility of modifying the strict harmonic plan by mixing it with other treatments:

Inglott offers an example of harmonic variation . . . in his *Galliard Ground* . . . This piece comprises five variations, and follows a somewhat complex plan . . . In the . . . [first three] variations the harmonic system is applied without restriction. In the last two the subject passes to the *superius*—all the other parts being free—and undergoes a slight figuration in certain passages of the repeats; we thus have the intervention of polyphonic and melodic elements.[38]

Were van den Borren using completely the terminology of this study he would say that in the last two variations the harmonic plan gives way to a modified cantus firmus treatment. Although in one sense Inglott's *Galliard Ground* is but another example of the way in which each separate technical plan is subject to the occasional intrusion of the others, it is nevertheless significant that many basso ostinato variations, especially those of the nineteenth century, show this particular mixing of harmonic and cantus firmus procedures.[39]

Other writers who discuss the harmonic plan add little to the ideas of Viecenz and van den Borren. It is a curious fact that all of them recognize this plan as underlying the basso ostinato variation, especially that of the baroque period, yet only a few refer to its presence in other types. This is a regrettable omission, for whereas it is true that the basso ostinato variation is perhaps the most significant early manifestation of the harmonic treatment, an equally important one came with the nineteenth-century character variations of Beethoven and Brahms. To understand such basic constructive similarities is to take an essentially broad view of variations as a whole, and to see, moreover, the way in which music, as it develops, invariably conserves and retains elements from the past.

Opposed to the foregoing structural plans is the free treatment, in which the component variations display a comparatively tenuous relationship to the theme, and where, in particular, the basic structure and harmony of the theme are substantially altered, if not actually abandoned. Incidental approaches to the free treatment appear throughout the history of the variation. Certain of the Spanish *diferencias* of the sixteenth century are extremely loose and unsystematic, notably Valderrábano's *Diferencias sobre la pavana real*, where in addition to coloration of the melodic subject are found pronounced harmonic and structural changes; and Cabezón's *Diferencias sobre el villancico, de quien teme enojo Isabel*, where the theme is developed by a free augmentation.[40] Equally definite though more subtle departures occur in the baroque chorale variations of Georg Böhm, J. G. Walther and J. S. Bach (see examples 46–49 in chapter iii). Here the method is often a free expansion of the theme structure by means of motival development, a handling referred to appreciatively by Vincent d'Indy as *l'amplification thématique*. In the character variation of the nineteenth century wide departures from the structure of the theme became increasingly numerous, a fact which makes it plain that the character variation is the true forerunner of the free treatment; the *Adagio* from Beethoven's *Quartet in E Flat*, Op. 127; Schumann's *Abegg Variations*, Op. 1, and *Symphonic Etudes*, Op. 13; Brahm's *Schumann Variations*, Op. 9; and Grieg's *Ballade*, Op. 24—all bona fide character variations—contain incidental use of the free technique.[41] During the closing years of the nineteenth century and the opening decade of the twentieth the free treatment attained a preponderant position in the hands of composers such as Dvořák, Franck, d'Indy, Elgar, Strauss, and Reger, and while not superseding completely the structural plans it did temporarily eclipse them.

There is no common terminology for variations exemplifying the free treatment. D'Indy includes such pieces in the category of *amplifying variations* (*les variations amplificatrices*); Stöhr names them *free variations*, Luithlen and Dejmek, *fantasy variations;* Goetschius says they belong to *the large* (or *higher*) *variation form.* Leichtentritt and Colles describe the species but do not name it.[42] Since none of the terms advanced is a technical one, there is little to recommend one above another. Nevertheless, a basis for choice may be had by examining the nature of the plans already discussed. It has already been shown that all three—the cantus firmus, the melodico-harmonic, and the harmonic—retain intact the structure of the theme; for this reason they are regarded in this study as belonging to the larger classification of *structural plans.* To this structural idea the variations of the late nineteenth century stand sharply opposed, since instead of conserving the structure of the theme, they often abandon it completely. Their nonstructural essence is well expressed by the term *free*, which, if viewed as representing the opposite of *structural*, is of specific technical meaning.

It is necessary to point out that this meaning of free variation is not universally accepted. The usage of Ebenezer Prout, which appears at first sight to follow that adopted here, is found upon closer inspection to be quite different. Assuming two opposing categories, the *strict variation* and the *free variation*, he defines the free species as one in which the outline of the theme "is widely departed from,"[43] yet his quoted examples—Beethoven's *Diabelli Variations*, Schumann's *Etudes symphoniques*, etc.—disclose that his conception embraces no more than the nineteenth-century character variation. There is perhaps reason for Prout to take a conservative view of what constitutes a free variation, inasmuch as when he wrote, in 1895, the relatively unfettered variations of Dvořák, Franck, and d'Indy were just becoming known. When, however, the same definition is seen to be perpetuated in contemporary manuals like the *Musiklexikon* of Hans Joachim Moser,[44] one can only conclude that Moser wrote it unthinkingly and perfunctorily. If, as Moser says, Brahm's *Handel Variations* represents the free variation, then the *Hiller Variations* of Reger would logically represent a super-free treatment, a palpable *reductio ad absurdum.*

Because the genuine free treatment is infinitely flexible in design, most writers tend to describe it in only general terms. Stöhr's account may be taken as an extreme example of this tendency:

Bis zu welchem Grade dieses Prinzip der *vollständig freien Variation* in der modernen Musik durchgedrungen ist, kann man bei dem grössten Meister moderner Variationstechnik, bei Max Reger bewundern, dessen Variationen in rein musikalischem Sinn nicht als solche auszusehen sind, da oft weder der harmonische noch der melodische Inhalt des Themas in ihnen auch nur andeutungsweise wiederkehrt. Man könnte daher sagen, dass hier wohl der geistige Inhalt des Themas den Umwandlungen unterworfen ist, die den Namen „Variation" rechtfertigen sollen.[45]

Trans.: The degree to which this principle of the completely free variation has established itself in modern music can be admired in the greatest master of modern variation technique, Max Reger, whose variations are not to be regarded as such in the strictly musical sense, since often neither the harmonic nor melodic content of the theme returns in the variations except in a suggestive way. One could therefore say that here, perhaps, the spiritual content of the theme is subjected to transformations which should justify the name *variation*.

But such a summary dismissal of the problem is unjustified, for the free treatment possesses tangible characteristics which may readily be described.

Its distinguishing mark, as mentioned earlier, is its refusal to accept the structural and harmonic control of the theme. In Luithlen's words, "Wird in den Variationen von den Grundprinzipien der Wahrung des Periodenbaues und der harmonischen Basis des Themas stark abgegangen, so entstehen 'Phantasievariationen.' "[46] Goetschius shows the necessity for this abandonment of theme outlines when he contrasts the aim of the *small variation form*, or structural variation, with the *large variation form*—the class which contains the free variation:

The leading purpose in the smaller grade is *technical* manipulation—"variation," with fairly direct reference to the Theme. In the larger grade the leading purpose is imaginative and *creative* manipulation—"elaboration," with only general allusion to the Theme . . . Such a creative process cannot always be carried on, with the necessary freedom, within the exact limits of the Theme. The confines of the latter must be broken through, its lines broadened, its scope widened, to make room for the unrestricted exercise of imagination, and to provide increased opportunity for free development.[47]

His further contention that these transformations of the design are effected through "insertions" is, however, too restrictive, inasmuch as it does not account for the construction of all free variations.

An aspect of importance is the development of motives taken from the theme. Leichtentritt appears to regard such development as the primary technique, for he emphasizes its presence in most of the free variations which he analyzes. Of Strauss's *Don Quixote* he says:

Die einzelnen Variationen sind vollkommen selbständige Charakterstücke, die nur insofern mit der Variationenform zusammenhängen, als die Motive des Themas in jede einzelne Variation mit hineinverwebt sind . . .[48]

Trans.: The individual variations are completely self-contained character pieces, which are connected with the variation form only so far as the motives of the theme are woven into every single variation ...

He calls Reger's *Hiller Variations* "eigentlich kontrapunktische Fantasien über Motive des Themas,"[49] and he points out that Schumann wrote on the title page of his *Carnaval,* which Leichtentritt regards as a free variation,"Scenes mignonnes sur quatre notes."[50] Although motival development within the free variation is closely related to that found in the classical sonata and symphony, the motives are derived from the theme in a much freer way. Instead of springing literally from the theme (the common practice in the sonata and symphony), they generally represent modified versions of the figures in the theme, being formed from the original figures through extensive alterations of rhythm, tempo, and dynamics.

Equally significant as a technical procedure is the transformation of themes, wherein large sections of a theme are radically altered in rhythm, tempo, dynamics, and so on, while the main outlines of the original melodic contour are preserved. Colles says that the *Variazione finale e coda* of Tchaikovsky's *Trio,* Op. 50, uses "a method which incorporates the transformation principle of Berlioz and Liszt . . . with Mozart's method of melodic variation."[51] D'Indy, similarly, views the thematic transformations of preceding nineteenth-century forms as influencing the free variations of Franck and his school:

Ainsi, par César Franck et son école, c'est en France que c'est conservée ... la tradition beethoveniénne, en matière de Variation. Sans doute, cette forme de composition appelée, croyons-nous, à un très grand avenir, ne peut, dans bien des cas, être examinée séparément, tant elle demeure intimement liée aux transformations thématiques que servent de base aux constructions *cycliques* ...: le rappel des *motifs conducteurs* que apparaissent dans l'œuvre de R. Wagner à partir de *Tannhäuser* et de *Lohengrin* (1845–1847), certaines dispositions employées par Liszt dans *Tasso* (1849), dans la *Faust-Symphonie* et dans la pièce pour piano intitulée *Sonate* (1853) pourraient aussi bien être qualifiés de Variations.[52]

Trans.: Thus it was in France, by César Franck and his school, that the Beethoven tradition of variation substance was conserved. Undoubtedly, this form of composition, destined, we believe, to have a very great future, often cannot be examined separately, so intimately does it remain linked to the thematic transformations which underlie cyclical constructions: the recurrence of leitmotifs, which appeared in the work of R. Wagner beginning with *Tannhäuser* and *Lohengrin* (1845–1847), certain usages employed by Liszt in *Tasso* (1849), in the *Faust Symphony* and in the piano piece called *Sonata* (1853) also might well be termed variations.

Whether the technical method employed is motival development or theme transformation, the connection with the theme is uniformly a melodic one. The significance of this melodic bond is clearly recognized by Goetschius, who says:

In the higher form of the variation . . . it is almost obligatory to adopt, and adhere to, the *melody-line of the Theme* (in a certain sense as if it were a Fugue-subject), as this is the only line of contact which will demonstrate with sufficient clearness the relation of the (quasi distorted) variation to its Theme.[53]

With the description of the free variation the classification of technical plans is complete. The four which have been discussed—cantus firmus, melodico-harmonic, harmonic, and free—are sufficiently comprehensive to explain all variations which fall within the scope of this study, *i.e.*, those written prior to the contemporary period. That they are not the only ones possible is obvious, and it is reasonable to assume that in the future others will be tried and perhaps generally adopted.[54] It also goes without saying that the explanation which they afford is a partial one, for to say that Beethoven's *Diabelli Variations* exemplify the harmonic treatment, or that Scheidt's chorale variations on *Warum betrübst du dich, mein Herz* use the cantus firmus technique, is to outline only the general approach which these composers have adopted. Beyond this it becomes necessary to fill in the foreground detail by showing the way in which the component variations of a series are integrated to form a satisfactory whole, by considering the employment of figuration, motival development, change of character, contrapuntal devices, and the like. In short, it is imperative to look into all characteristics which contribute to the *style* of the series in question. In this way one will be able to discover the factors which differentiate sets like Bach's *Goldberg Variations* and Brahms' *Haydn Variations*, which, although related through their common employment of the harmonic treatment, are in many respects quite dissimilar. The task of the following chapters is therefore to trace the four technical plans historically, and to attempt to show in this way the essential characteristics of the variations of successive historical epochs.

CHAPTER II

The Establishment of the Structural Techniques

THE PERIOD from 1500 to 1750 saw not only the first systematic beginnings of the instrumental variation but a development which, in significance and vitality, was rivaled only by that of the nineteenth century. The structural techniques, destined to remain the sole methods of construction until the latter half of the nineteenth century, had their origin in this epoch. Three important types—variations on secular songs, dances, and arias; on plain songs and chorales; and on basso ostinato themes—likewise arose in this period. Their writing, taken up as it was by most of the instrumental composers of the day, was widespread, and the variative principle, far from being limited to the variation form alone, found expression in such hybrid constructions as the variation suite and the variation ricercar.[1] So prevalent, in fact, did this principle become that the seventeenth century, the period of its greatest influence, has been called the "century of the variation."[2]

The variations written during these two hundred and fifty years followed a fairly restrictive plan. As we have seen, it was customary to preserve unaltered the formal structure of parts and phrases existing in the theme, and also to maintain the expression relatively unchanged. To achieve interest under such limitations was unquestionably difficult, just as today it is difficult to write an interesting strict canon, strict fugue, or movement in strict sonata form; yet Cabezón, Frescobaldi, Buxtehude, J. S. Bach, and their contemporaries wrote variations of genuine musical value while keeping within the bounds of the theme's structure and expression. That they were able to do so is obviously a tribute to their high technical skill and craftsmanship as composers. Moreover, the musical style of the period, with its emphasis upon counterpoint and its partial dependence upon modal harmony, was ideally suited to conceal the fact that the theme underwent little essential modification. Also tending to screen the lack of essential change was the diverse and often complex nature of baroque figuration. An outgrowth of renaissance coloration and diminution, it attained an early flowering under the English virginalists, and continued its multiform character until the time of J. S. Bach. Scale figures, syncopations, sequences, repeated notes, trills, broken chords, imitations, suspensions, cross rhythms, and still other types combine to provide the manifold textures found in the variations of this period.

Of the three main variation types introduced and developed during these two hundred and fifty years, the first was that built on secular songs, dances, and arias (called hereafter simply the song variation).[3] Making use, in turn, of all three of the structural techniques (cantus firmus, melodico-harmonic, and harmonic), its earliest occurrence was in Spain, where, under the name of *diferencias*, it appeared in books of lute tablatures by Luis de Navaréz (*Delfin para vihuela*, 1538), Alonso Mudarra (*Tres libros de musica*, 1546), and Anriquez de Valderrábano (*Silva de Sirenas*, 1547).[4] These early lute variations are often loose and unsystematic in construction and frequently present little more than colorations of the melodic subject, yet certain of them, notably the charming *Guárdame las vacas* of Navaréz, display surprisingly mature figuration and harmony. More important than the lute variations are the *diferencias* of Antonio de Cabezón (1510–1566), whose *Obras de musica para tecla, arpa, y vihuela* (Madrid, 1578) contain the first variations to be written for the keyboard.[5] The four-voice, quasi-polyphonic texture of the Cabezón *diferencias* is richer than that of the lute pieces, and the harmony is more varied and sure. Cabezón's style stands at the borderline between simple coloration and definite figuration, *i.e.*, between an embellishment which is essentially florid, ornamented, and irregular, and one which is essentially symmetrical and unified. The one piece where figuration is systematically carried out, *Otras diferencias de Vacas*, is striking and unusual for this period.[6]

From Spain the variation of secular melodies spread during the late sixteenth and early seventeenth centuries to other countries of western Europe, especially to England, Italy, the Netherlands, and Germany. The first real school of variation writing came with the virginal composers of Elizabethan England, chiefly William Byrd (*ca.* 1542–1623), John Bull (*ca.* 1562–1628), Giles Farnaby (*ca.* 1569–?), Thomas Morley (1557–*ca.* 1602), and Orlando Gibbons (1583–1625); these men and their associates made the song variation the most important type of early English keyboard music.[7] Their variations were probably somewhat influenced by those of the Spanish, yet the English pieces far outstrip the *diferencias* in range of treatment and richness of ideas. While in general they follow the earlier compositions in their use of counterpoint and modal harmony, they are more folklike than the Spanish variations; this is the result, in part, of a somewhat crude harmonic strength and, in part, of the greater rhythmic vitality and tunefulness of the English themes. Their figuration is diverse, often brilliant, and in the best works consistently and symmetrically applied. Here, in fact, is the most important single element in the style, for by means of strong, skillfully used figures the virginalists produced an early flowering of the decorative aspect of the variation.

Italy, like England, began to cultivate variations on secular songs and dances during the latter part of the sixteenth century. Unlike England, it produced no extensive school of writers but, instead, only a few relatively isolated figures. Among the earliest of these composers, all of whom wrote for keyboard instruments, were Antonio Valente (latter sixteenth century), G. M. Trabaci (early seventeenth century), and Ascanio Mayone (early seventeenth century) in southern Italy, and Andrea Gabrieli (*ca.* 1510–1586) in northern Italy;[8] the last and most important was Gerolamo Frescobaldi (1583–1644) in Rome.[9] The variations of these men, called by them *partite*, reflect the transition in musical style which was in progress at the time. Gabrieli's *Pass' e mezzo antico* shows typical renaissance qualities of modal harmony, strong yet simple figuration, repose, and restraint. Shortly after the turn of the century such features yield to the greater complexity and elaborateness of the baroque, and with the *partite* of Frescobaldi, beginning in 1614, the new characteristics mature. Frescobaldi's style is not only distinct from the comparatively sedate manner of Gabrieli and the early Spaniards but is notably different, as well, from the often florid constructions of the English. His figuration, rivaling the virginalists in its fantasy, is restless and complex. Irregular rhythms involving sudden changes of pattern, syncopations, and dotted values are characteristic and conspicuous. Figural imitations appear abundantly throughout the variations. Occasionally, long sweeping passages of embroidery recall the melodic flights of Frescobaldi's toccatas, and similarly, the many trill-like figures remind one of sixteenth-century Italian diminution. The harmony, making probably the first significant use of chromaticism in the variation, is colorful and varied. In general effect, the Frescobaldi variations are more sophisticated than those of the virginalists. For the folk spirit of the English pieces they substitute a refined complexity which, although bordering at times upon the bizarre, is always polished and suave. The rustic, open-air quality of the virginalists may be said to suggest Haydn, while Frescobaldi's elegant configurations presage Mozart.

In Germany the writing of variations on secular themes began somewhat later than in Spain, England, and Italy. Just as the Spanish *diferencias* had influenced composers in England and Italy at an earlier period, so now the methods of the English and Italian writers were transmitted to Germany. The intermediary between England and the continent was the Dutch composer J. P. Sweelinck (1562–1621), who, so far as is known, was the first to write variations in the Netherlands.[10] Through Sweelinck's German pupils, especially Samuel Scheidt (1587–1654), the variation was introduced into north Germany. In the south, the chief link may well have been J. J. Froberger (died 1667), who studied with Frescobaldi in Rome and later worked in Vienna. In addition to Scheidt and Froberger, the long line of composers includes Wolfgang Ebner (*ca.* 1610–1665), Alessandro Poglietti (died 1683), Johann Adam Reincken (1623–1722), H. F. Biber (1644–1704), Johann Philipp Krieger (1649–1725), Johann Pachelbel (1653–1706), F. X. A. Murschhauser (1663–1738), G. F. Handel (1685–1759), and many others.[11] The consummation of the German variation was attained with J. S. Bach (1685–1750), whose *Aria with Thirty Variations* (popularly called the *Goldberg Variations*) is one of the great variation cycles of all time.[12] Through the activity of these men Germany became, during the baroque period, not merely the chief country to foster variations on secular songs, dances, and arias, but the chief center of variation writing in general.

The secular variations of Sweelinck and Scheidt, like those of the virginalists, show vigor and strength, and while less rich in figural diversity than their English counterparts, they evidence the same freshness and interest in experimentation. Scheidt, especially, reveals an active curiosity, and occasionally introduces novel imitative effects such as the *imitatio violistica* and the *imitatione tremula organi* in simulation of the viol and organ respectively.[13] As the early baroque gave way to middle and high baroque a simpler texture appeared in German variation writing. The influence of the church modes, which had made for harmonic nuance and subtlety, was superseded during the course of the seventeenth century by the domination of the major-minor system and its more definite harmonic formulas; patterns of figuration became more regular; and the quasi-contrapuntal texture of the renaissance and early baroque variations gave way to a more homophonic style. It is this simpler style, the basis for the variations of Pachelbel, J. P. Krieger, Handel, and their contemporaries, which leads directly to the ornamental variation of the late eighteenth century. Against this style the *Aria with Thirty Variations* of J. S. Bach stands in sharp contrast. Its contrapuntal intricacy, its wealth of figuration, its manifold forms and devices (including canons, trios, duets, instrumental arias, a siciliana, a fughetta, and a French overture), and particularly its wide diversity of moods, from profound expressiveness to brilliant virtuosity, all serve to place this work quite apart from the current mode of easy superficiality.

The general design of the song variation is simple. In it the theme is followed by a moderate number of units, set off by cadences, which are arranged more or less progressively according to their rhythmic animation and degree of figural elaboration.[14] The growth in animation is not always steady, being interrupted from time to time by a return to quieter rhythms, yet by and large there is a noticeable increase in activity from the beginning of a set to the end. Aside from this somewhat desultory scheme of growth, the ordering of the separate variations is indefinite, for despite the frequent appearance of isolated pairs, more systematic groupings are rare.[15] The component variations keep unchanged the main outlines of the given subject, above all its structure, its tonality, and generally its meter and chief harmonic outlines. With regard to the retention of tempo and dynamics there is a lack of objective evidence, inasmuch as the early composers left few specific directions for performance in their scores. Nevertheless one may conjecture that from the earliest beginnings certain nuances of tempo were intended, and it is reasonable to believe that performers may have exploited dynamic contrasts to some degree, since on the organ and harpsichord it would have been natural to take advantage of the possibilities for contrasting registrations.[16]

Of the themes employed in the variation type under discussion, the most commonly used, particularly before 1650, is the popular song; Cabezón, Byrd, Frescobaldi, Scheidt, and their contemporaries wrote more variations upon this kind of subject than upon any other. The songs from which the themes were taken differ widely: some are lovesongs, others deal with nature; some are humorous, others sorrowful. In spite of this dissimilarity of subject, the melodies of the songs exhibit a prevailingly quiet movement that is seemingly little influenced by the diverse character of their texts.[17]

With the decline in the use of song themes after 1650 came a corresponding increase in the use of themes bearing the designation *aria*. In a sense, of course, the two types are one, for *aria* is the Italian equivalent for the English song, or *air*. Thus, when Frescobaldi writes *Partite sopra l'aria della Romanesca* he means only that his variations have as their theme the popular Romanesca melody or song. But the term *aria* was also used to denote themes which, instead of springing from the songs of the people, were written by the composer himself; the highly ornamented theme of Bach's *Goldberg Variations* is of this kind.[18] It should be noted that the term did not refer to an air from an opera; in the baroque period operatic themes were not used as variation subjects, although in the late eighteenth century they became very popular in this connection.

Dance tunes, although appearing less often than either the song theme or the aria, served as the basis for variations during the entire two hundred and fifty years. From Cabezón to Scheidt composers wrote primarily upon the pavane, galliard, allemande, and passemezzo; later writers chose as subjects the contemporary saraband, minuet, and gavotte. It is noticeable that none of these dances is fast; instead their movement ranges from the slow, solemn pavane and dignified saraband to the moderately paced galliard, passemezzo, gavotte, and minuet. The melodies of these dances are generally vocal in character, a fact which confirms an idea already suggested by the secular song and aria melodies, namely, that renaissance and baroque variation composers sought melodic subjects which were primarily songlike rather than those which were of an instrumental nature.[19]

A peculiarity of the epoch which can be observed in connection both with song melodies and dance tunes is the use of common themes by different composers. The Romanesca melody, sometimes bearing the additional title *O guárdame las vacas*, was used not only by Navaréz, Mudarra, and Cabezón, but also by the Italian composers Mayone and Frescobaldi.[20] The dance melody which appears in Cabezón's *diferencias* as the *Pavana italiana* recurs in a set by Bull as the *Spanish Paven* and in a series written jointly by Sweelinck and Scheidt called the *Paduana hispania*.[21]

It may be noted in passing that popular song and dance themes had a bearing upon the basso ostinato variation. The typical four-note descending subject of the passacaglia and chaconne may well have been suggested by the Romanesca melody referred to above,[22] and two other basso ostinato types, the folia and bergamask, were constructed upon dance basses (see pp. 66 f.). It is plain, therefore, that it is sometimes difficult to draw a line between dance variations which employ the harmonic technique and basso ostinato variations built upon dance basses. In this study the distinction is made on the basis of continuity. Sets like Frescobaldi's *Partite sopra follia* (Tagliapietra, IV, 45 ff.), built on the harmonic plan and having no joining of the separate variations, are held to be dance variations; whereas sets like A. Scarlatti's *Variazioni sulla follia di Spagna* (*ibid.*, VIII, 112 ff.), also built on the harmonic plan but showing a continuous structure, are held to be basso ostinato variations.

The melodies of these different theme types—song, dance, and aria—are invariably presented in conjunction with other voices, the union of melodic subject and supporting parts forming the variation theme.[23] All three types are normally brief. Many of the sixteenth-century themes consist of but one or two phrases, and those of the baroque period, although frequently cast in the more lengthy binary form, are not extensive. Their conciseness is matched by an equally pronounced structural symmetry, most of them showing a regular division into one-, two-, and four-measure groups; this structure obtains in the following typical themes:

Navaréz, *O guárdame las vacas*, 4 + 4
Byrd, *John come kisse me now*, 4 (1 + 1 + 2)
Frescobaldi, *Aria detta Balletto*, ‖: 4 :‖: 2 + 2 + 4 :‖[24]

Both qualities, brevity and symmetry, were destined to remain attributes of variation themes as late as Brahms, although not always to the degree illustrated here.

The vocal nature of the themes may explain in part the way in which they were treated. Lacking any pronounced motival organization, they did not often encourage composers to a development of theme motives; instead, they lent themselves readily and most naturally to an elaboration based upon independent figures. It is historically significant that the use of nonthematic figures is characteristic of pre-nineteenth-century variations as a whole, and that only beginning with Beethoven did the development of theme motives attain prominence within the form. In the song variation the figural handling is both *imitative* and *linear*. As the terms suggest, imitative figuration has to do with patterns which echo one another in different voices (example 1). In linear figuration,

Example 1. Byrd, *O Mistris Myne.*[25]
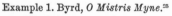

on the other hand, the patterns are confined to a single voice, or presented in concurrent voices without imitative interplay (example 2).

Example 2. Bach, *Goldberg Variations.*[26]

Not only does the song variation reveal the figural practice of pre-nineteenth-century variations generally, but also it presents a complete view of the three structural techniques: the cantus firmus, melodico-harmonic, and harmonic. Further discussion of the song variation will relate directly to each of these plans in turn.

The cantus firmus technique underlies many song variations written prior to 1625.[27] In this treatment, it will be recalled, the literal or nearly literal melodic subject occupies different voices in successive variations; the supporting parts, meanwhile, provide new contrapuntal settings. The artless *Wehe, Windgen, wehe* of Samuel Scheidt, in which the melody, after remaining in the soprano for three variations, passes to the bass in variation 4 and to the tenor in 5, shows the method clearly:

Example 3. Scheidt, *Wehe, Windgen, wehe.*[28]

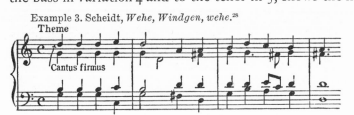

In addition to such normal changes of position the cantus firmus occasionally shifts its location within a single variation. This shifting may occur in such an irregular, haphazard way that the melody is virtually lost, as in the excerpt from Byrd's *Walsingham* (example 4).

Example 4. Byrd, *Walsingham.*[29]

Or, as happens more frequently, the changing may coincide with well-defined structural units, the purpose of the transfer being to present repeated parts or phrases of the theme in a different guise. Such modified repetition within a variation (generally called double variation) is achieved in Scheidt's *Est-ce Mars* through the unusual expedient of employing invertible counterpoint (example 5). In both examples the

Example 5. Scheidt, *Est-ce Mars.*[30]

result is an increased variety and subtlety of effect as compared with the normal practice of maintaining the cantus firmus in a single part for an entire variation.

The voices which surround the melodic subject are highly figured, all of them, as a rule, participating simultaneously in the figural play. The chief figural means is that of imitation, with the patterns weaving in and out of the accompanying voices and directing attention to the several parts in quick succession. Normally the texture consists of short stencil figures, as in example 1 (see p. 34), but longer patterns also appear, such as the sixteenth-note figures of example 8 (see p. 37). Ordinarily, as in the examples just cited, a figure enters as a preceding one finishes, *i.e.*, without overlapping; now and again ingenious stretto treatments present themselves, and even short canonic fragments may be discovered, as in the two lowest voices of example 6.

Example 6. Byrd, *John come kisse me now.*[31]

Most of the figures employed lack thematic relationship to the cantus firmus, but some of them, exceptionally, are derived from it, normally by taking over a characteristic feature of the theme "head." The derived figures (often referred to in this study as *motives* because of their thematic origin) spring from the cantus firmus with little change. Many of them are literal transcripts of a fragment of the subject, as in the eleventh variation of Byrd's *Walsingham* (example 7, *a*); others present the theme fragment in a simply embellished form (example 7, *b*). This

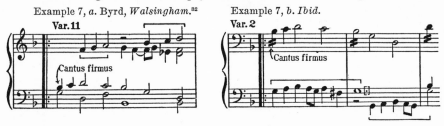

Example 7, *a*. Byrd, *Walsingham*.[32]   Example 7, *b*. *Ibid.*

close following of the thematic material contrasts sharply with the radical transformations which appear in many nineteenth-century variations and which are discussed at some length in chapter v (see pp. 96 ff.).

Whether the figuration is derived from the cantus firmus or is independent of it, a figure introduced at the outset of a variation does not, as a rule, persist throughout. Instead, the common plan is for a variation to present a succession of figures, one giving way to the next at a point of structural cleavage, or even, for no seeming reason, during the course of a phrase.[33] Sometimes the figures used in the later course of a variation are no more than variants of the one employed initially; at other times the later figures are distinctly new. Both procedures appear in the second variation of Scheidt's *Soll es sein*, portions of which are quoted in example 8. A possible reason for this figural diversity is the

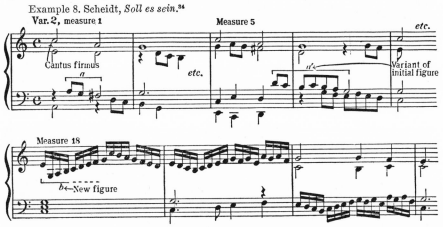

Example 8. Scheidt, *Soll es sein*.[34]

apparent desire on the part of composers of cantus firmus variations to secure, within the separate variations, internal variety and plasticity;

it is obvious, from the many excerpts akin to example 8 which might be offered, that they believed it important to treat the successive phrases, sections, and parts of the theme differently. Nor did the early composers confine this aim to cantus firmus variations alone, for melodico-harmonic and harmonic variations of the period show the same general intention; indeed it may be said that the attainment of inner variety and plasticity has been one of the common concerns of variation composers of all periods.[35]

Linear (*i.e.*, nonimitative) figuration in the cantus firmus variation is less common than the imitative kind but plays, nevertheless, a prominent role. A frequent procedure, especially with Sweelinck and Scheidt, is the addition of a single line of figuration to the cantus firmus to produce a two-voice piece, or *bicinium*, as in Scheidt's *Est-ce Mars* (example 9). Also common is the employment, in connection with a three- or

Example 9. Scheidt, *Est-ce Mars.*[36]

four-part texture, of a figured soprano or bass (example 10); in this use there is often an exchange of the figuration between the extreme parts in successive variations to form a pair, or at the midpoint of a single

Example 10. Byrd, *The Woods so Wild.*[37]

variation to produce the effect of double variation. It was shown in chapter i that these alternations between the soprano and the bass are an especial characteristic of the melodico-harmonic variation, and, although they are by no means confined to that plan—for they appear with frequency in the harmonic variation and even, as pointed out here, in the cantus firmus variation,—the presence of the alternation in other plans normally represents melodico-harmonic intermixture or influence (see pages 17, 41 f., and 52 f.). Such a view is supported by the preponderantly homophonic aspect of the variations containing alternate figuration, since their simplicity of texture again suggests melodico-harmonic practice. Byrd's *The Woods so Wild* affords a typical example of this essentially melodico-harmonic style within the cantus firmus variation (example 10).

From time to time another kind of linear figuration presents itself, in which two or more voices undergo figuration simultaneously, the figured parts proceeding ordinarily in parallel thirds, sixths, tenths, or successive first inversions, and employing identical rhythms. Considerable richness of harmony may sometimes result from this figural means, as in the first variation of Scheidt's *Est-ce Mars* (example 11).

Example 11. Scheidt, *Est-ce Mars.*[38]

Just as a variation is often built upon more than one figure, so it sometimes shows an alternation of imitative with linear figuration. Obviously such alternation is a further means, and an important one, of securing inner variety. Its effect may be judged from the Sweelinck excerpt (example 12), where it is used to give a different treatment to the second of two identical phrases in the theme.

Example 12. Sweelinck, *Mein junges Leben hat ein End.*[39]

Another problem of importance in the cantus firmus song variation is that of harmonic change. Theoretically the degree of possible change in cantus firmus variations in general is limited only by the fancy of the composer and the necessity of harmonizing the cantus firmus; the actual practice in the song variation, however, is fairly conservative.[40] As a rule all cadences are preserved, and occasionally a series will go so far as to maintain the entire harmonic outline with little change; this is true, for example, in Inglott's *The Leaves bee Greene*, where the frequent appearance of the cantus firmus in the bass tends to stabilize the harmony. Nevertheless, incidental chord substitutions are common in all cantus firmus song variations, and virtually complete recastings of single phrases appear from time to time. Such changes may be observed even in the more exceptional example of the Inglott piece referred to above, for in the eighth variation (example 13) there is a noticeable deviation from the original harmony.

Example 13. Inglott, *The Leaves Bee Greene.*[41]

Because the cadences are ordinarily preserved more tenaciously than any other portion of the harmony, most variations which exhibit conspicuous harmonic departures tend to do so at the beginnings of phrases rather than at phrase endings, and they often show especial predilection for changing the initial measure of a theme. The degree to which phrase beginnings sometimes vary harmonically may be judged from the quotations from Byrd's *Walsingham* (example 14), which give in a compara-

Example 14. Byrd, *Walsingham.*[42]

tive manner the opening bass lines of six out of the twenty-two variations. A quotation in score from the same composer's *John come kisse me now* (example 15) will make graphic the importance of such harmonic changes in imparting flexibility to a cantus firmus series.

Example 15. Byrd, *John come kisse me now.*[43]

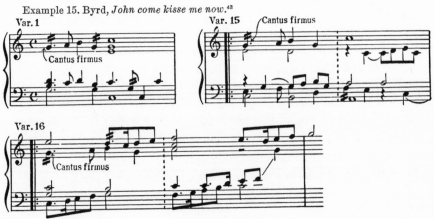

The foregoing discussion of the cantus firmus song variation shows that the cantus firmus treatment has much inherent interest, exhibiting figural richness, harmonic variety, and a capacity for polyphonic elaboration. However, even when this type of variation was being written most prolifically, in the late sixteenth and early seventeenth centuries, the heyday of cantus firmus practice in music generally was already past; essentially, therefore, the cantus firmus variation technique must be regarded as a reactionary rather than a progressive treatment, one better suited to the requirements of modal polyphony than to the new harmonic feeling of the seventeenth century. With this new style the other two structural techniques were more in keeping.

In the melodico-harmonic song variation the theme melody, instead of appearing literally or nearly literally in different voices in turn, is altered or disguised, especially through figuration, and is generally restricted to the soprano; the basic harmony stays unchanged; and the texture is less complex, on the whole, than that of the cantus firmus type.[44] For these reasons the variations follow the theme closely and display an unusual transparency as well. The melodic subject becomes in this technique a conspicuous center of interest, owing to its figured guise and its prominent position in the soprano voice. The bass, too,

Example 16. Bull, *The Spanish Paven.*[45]

emerges as a conspicuous figured part, although secondary in importance to the soprano. During one or more variations in a series it receives a continuous, figured treatment similar to that normally given to the melodic subject, at which times the latter temporarily assumes its original, simple form. This change in the position of the figured part is often the basis for small groups of variations, especially of pairs, the same pattern decorating the melodic subject in the first variation, the bass in the second, and sometimes two parts in a third. Example 16 illustrates the application of this specifically melodico-harmonic means.

Even more common than the foregoing practice, in which the bass is figured for an entire variation, is the alternation of the embellishment between soprano and bass within a single variation. William Byrd demonstrates the flexibility of this procedure in his graceful *Callino Casturame* (example 17).

Example 17. Byrd, *Callino Casturame.*[46]

The prominence given to figurations of the melody and the bass in this treatment suggests at once the desirability of comparing these figured versions with their simple prototypes in the theme. In figurations of the melody one may distinguish a wide divergence. Some represent little more than a mechanical overlaying; others are more free, while still showing the thematic outlines with clearness; finally, there are those which virtually abandon the melodic subject and which tend, thereby, to take the variation of which they are a part out of the melodico-harmonic realm into the harmonic.

The figuration described above as a mechanical overlaying possesses, as may be expected, relatively little intrinsic interest, for it shows an almost supine dependence upon the essential tones of the theme. Such dependence is likely to arise whenever, as in example 18, the pitch and

Example 18. Handel, *Gavotte* from *Eighth Suite* (Second Collection).[47]

rhythmic location of the melody tones are copied without change in the variation. Embellishments like these are comparatively uninteresting because, once the listener perceives the theme and the embellishing figure, he can foretell with unfortunate exactness what is to follow. Happily, such figuration is not abundant. For one thing, few themes have a simple enough structure to make it possible, and a more important consideration is that composers as a whole must surely have sensed its lack of artistic validity. Most melodic figurations, therefore, display much wider departures from the theme than those of the Handel quotation above.

Greater freedom of melodic figuration is attained chiefly in two ways: through shifting the rhythmic location of the given theme tones, and by subjecting them to octave transpositions. The rhythmical shifting of the theme tones means, in effect, that their entrance in the figural pattern is slightly anticipated or delayed. A good example of the way in which this simple device works to produce new interest may be had from the second variation of Munday's *Robin* (example 19), where, de-

Example 19. Munday, *Robin*.[48]

spite its close following of the theme, the figuration achieves a noticeable independence as compared to Handel's treatment. Equally effective are the slight modifications in the second variation of Farnaby's *Pawles Wharfe* (example 20), where similar rhythmical shiftings are embodied

Example 20. Farnaby, *Pawles Wharfe*.[49]

in a broken-chord figuration. It will be noted at once that an important element in the Munday and Farnaby embellishments is a more flexible use of the chosen figure as compared with example 18, and it may well be asked if the rhythmical shiftings spoken of above are not, in fact, incidental to the creation of these more pliant figurations. Which of the two effects—rhythmical shifting of theme tones or the flexible use of figures—is to be considered the cause and which the result need not be determined; the significant thing is that the two occur side by side.

The second device important in producing freedom of melodic figuration, octave transposition, often gives the figuration a contour which differs noticeably from that of the theme. Thus, in the Ebner quotation (example 21) a relatively narrow melodic phrase is expanded upward,

Example 21. Ebner, *36 Variations on an Air*.[50]

with the result that the contour of the subject is materially altered and at the same time a point of climax is secured for the variation as a whole. A similar expansion of range, this time downward as well as upward, occurs in the variation by Reincken (example 22), which shows,

Example 22. Reincken, *18 Partite diverse sulla "Meyerin."* [51]

in addition, that octave transpositions are not confined to broken-chord figurations but may appear in a prevailingly scale-wise context as well. In both examples, especially that of Reincken, the octave transpositions are combined with rhythmical shiftings, and in the Ebner quotation an irregularity in the use of the sixteenth-note pattern contributes its share to the general interest of the figuration.

From the pliant embellishments just described it is but a step to those figurations which maintain only an occasional and incidental contact with the melodic subject. That step consists in covering up certain tones of the melodic subject by relegating them to inner voices of the variation or in omitting them entirely. The variation sets of Ebner and Reincken just referred to are a rich source of these quasi-harmonic treatments; from these sets typical excerpts appear in examples 23 and 24. Example 23 shows, in its last two measures, a complete loss of

Example 23. Ebner, *36 Variations on an Air.* [52]

Example 24. Reincken, *18 Partite diverse sulla "Meyerin."* [53]

melodic contact between theme and variation, because the tones of the melodic subject pass at this point into lower voices. In example 24, likewise, there is a melodic figuration so free as to produce a quasi-harmonic treatment; here the characteristic departures from the melodic subject include octave transpositions, omitted tones, and tones transferred to the alto voice.

Whereas the degree of correspondence between the melodic subject and its figured appearances differs greatly from one variation set to another, as the preceding discussion has shown, figurations of the bass tend to follow the theme in a more uniform way. The relationship may be described as a moderately free one, showing, as a rule, neither extreme strictness nor extreme license. Octave transpositions occur with great frequency, with the result that the contour of the theme bass is materially changed; hence it is reasonable to conclude that the given bass meant less to composers as a line than as an indication of the harmonies. Example 25 is typical of the degree of freedom normally attained.

Example 25 *a.* Farnaby, *Up T[ails] All.*[54]

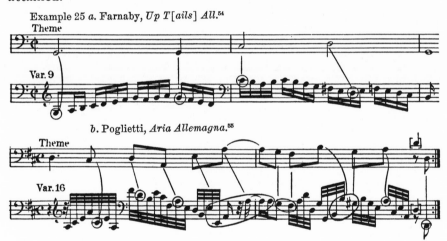

b. Poglietti, *Aria Allemagna.*[55]

Although figurations of single melodic lines are an important trait of the melodico-harmonic song variation, one occasionally finds isolated variations which stress the rhythmical recasting of the theme through change of meter, rather than the figuration of individual voices. The Frescobaldi excerpt of example 26 illustrates this less frequent type of

Example 26. Frescobaldi, *Aria detta Balletto.*[56]

alteration. Here the melodic subject remains relatively unornamented, as do the supporting voices; but the rhythmical design of the theme undergoes a pronounced change, outlining triple meter instead of duple. Rhythmical recastings such as this are obviously related closely to those found in certain sixteenth-century dance pairs, in which a duple-meter dance is transformed into a triple-meter variant, and they may well have entered the variation form from this source. Similar thematic metamorphoses occur in the seventeenth-century variation suite. Because all such changes modify the expression of the given theme or material, they may be regarded as anticipating the later character variation.

Up to this point we have seen that the melodico-harmonic song variation is characterized by the almost complete restriction of the melodic subject to the soprano voice, by a close adherence to the basic theme harmony, by a fairly simple texture, and, in particular, by the conspicuous figuration of the melodic subject and the bass. These features tend definitely to mark off this kind of variation from the cantus firmus type, despite their occasional, incidental appearance in the latter treatment. The melodico-harmonic song variation is further set apart from the cantus firmus species by its lessened emphasis upon imitative figuration. That such figuration is not incompatible with melodico-harmonic premises, even though its strict application demands unquestioned skill, may be seen from the beginning of the Farnaby variation in example 27. Nothing could be more delightful, and at the same

Example 27. Farnaby, *Up T[ails] All.*[57]

time more natural and unaffected, than the way in which the composer here leads his figure, built in conformity with the melodic subject, through a series of ingenious stretto imitations. Such a thoroughgoing imitative treatment is unusual, for the probable reason that its complexity, in comparison with the relative ease of figuring a single soprano or bass line, interfered with its wide adoption. Much more common is the somewhat casual kind of imitation which occurs in the Pachelbel quotation (example 28), wherein the brevity of the chosen figure, together with its less concentrated presentation, contrives to give the effect of a simply animated harmony.

Example 28. Pachelbel, *Aria sebaldina.*[58]

Finally, it may be pointed out that the figuration of the melodico-harmonic song variation is, on the whole, more homogeneous than that of the cantus firmus species. This does not mean that a figure used at the beginning of a variation invariably persists throughout, for the introduction of new figures and new figural treatments as a variation progresses does occasionally occur, as in the somewhat extreme example (29) of Tomkins. But it is nonetheless true that such an alternation of

Example 29. Tomkins, *Barafostus Dreame.*[59]

figures is opposed to the essentially linear and continuous spirit of the melodico-harmonic treatment, and that the progressive introduction of new figures is uncommon.

We come now to the harmonic treatment of the song variation.[60] In this technique, as in the two already discussed, the structural outlines of the theme are preserved, and, as in the melodico-harmonic variation, the basic harmony of the theme remains unchanged. The melody of the theme, however, is either abandoned completely or suggested in a wholly incidental way.[61] Because each variation of a series thus inaugurates a new melodic line, the treatment is unusually flexible in its effect.

It is of more than passing interest that the three structural plans represent three successive stages leading toward the abandonment of the melodic subject. In the cantus firmus variation the correspondence to the melodic subject is literal, save for occasional transient embellishment; in the melodico-harmonic variation the outline of the melodic subject is altered and obscured, generally through figuration; finally, in the harmonic variation, the melodic subject is replaced by totally new melodies. In the sense, therefore, that the harmonic plan is the only one in which the outlines of the melodic subject are completely disregarded, the problem which confronts the composer is unique.

It may be explained parenthetically that one difficulty in treating the harmonic song variation is that this species contains within it the superlative *Goldberg Variations* of J. S. Bach. The method of this study, that of finding the common practice or norm with respect to particular groups of variations, is based upon the supposition that the works consulted are of approximately equal aesthetic value, and so long as such an equality exists, the method works very satisfactorily. When, however, one work towers over the rest, a question arises about the validity of this leveling-off process, or method of the common denominator. The canonic treatments of the *Goldberg Variations* do not in the least represent common practice, yet manifestly they constitute a procedure of the highest interest. Similarly, the linear figurations of the *Goldberg* set differ greatly from those of other harmonic song variations, yet again they indicate a genuinely significant procedure. For these reasons it appears advisable to give to the *Goldberg Variations* a more prominent place in the following discussion than they would ordinarily receive as a single representative of the harmonic plan.

The harmonic song variation, like the cantus firmus species, is prevailingly contrapuntal and imitative in texture. Its imitative procedures are of two kinds: simple imitative figuration, and canonic and fugal writing. Simple imitative figuration is used here in much the same way as in the preceding techniques and may therefore be passed over briefly. Short stencil patterns occur abundantly, but with the significant difference that the figures are now at liberty to appear equally in all of the voices.[62] As before, new figures are often brought in as a variation proceeds, generally at points of structural cleavage; this greater care in the introduction of new patterns contributes a welcome struc-

Example 30. Frescobaldi, *Partite sopra l'aria della Romanesca.*[63]

tural clarity. Frequently, too, the later figures grow out of the initial one, as in the Frescobaldi example (30). Occasionally the figures are of much greater length, in which case the imitative handling is, on the whole, correspondingly less strict; and when the figures are especially long there tends to result a peculiar mixture of imitative and linear effect. This kind of mixed figuration—a specifically Italian device—may be seen in example 31, again from Frescobaldi.

Example 31. Frescobaldi, *Partite sopra Ruggiero.*[64]

Canonic and fugal treatments have not thus far been encountered, save for certain quasi-canonic strettos in the cantus firmus variation (example 6). Indeed, within the entire history of the form they appear but rarely, for apart from the *Goldberg Variations* the use of canon is restricted to chorale variations like Bach's *Vom Himmel hoch, da komm' ich her* and to incidental variations by Weber, Schumann, and Brahms;[65] and the use of fugue (or, more properly, *fughetta*) is confined to a few tentative approaches in the variations of Beethoven.[66] There are, of course, extensive concluding fugues in certain eighteenth- and nineteenth-century variations (see p. 93), but these true fugues are developed with complete freedom and lack any reference to the structural frame of the theme. On the other hand, the fughettas of Bach's *Goldberg Variations* maintain the binary plan of the theme, as well as its main harmonic outlines, with entire fidelity. The canonic variations of the *Goldberg* set consist almost entirely of trios, wherein the upper two voices present the canon and the bass supplies an independent part constructed from the bass of the theme; the one exception is variation 27, which, building directly upon the bass, consists of two canonic voices only. Variation 3 is a canon at the unison, variation 6 is a canon at the second, variation 9 is a canon at the third; in this regular way Bach proceeds to take in all the intervals of imitation up to that of the ninth, in variation 27. Two variations, number 12 at the interval of the fourth, and number 15 at the interval of the fifth, are in contrary motion. Despite the severity of the imposed restrictions Bach succeeds in imparting to these intricately contrapuntal pieces a feeling both of flexibility and naturalness. The extreme ingenuity of his handling becomes fully apparent only through a study of the score, yet examples 32 and 34 below are sufficient to suggest his extraordinary technical and musical mastery of the problems involved.

A noteworthy aspect of the canons, and, in fact, of the variations as a whole, is their strong individuality of mood, an individuality so striking as to warrant the name of character change. Thus, the flowing nature of variations 3, 6, and 27 contrasts with the serious tone of variations 9, 12, and 21; the vigorous eighteenth variation opposes the somber fifteenth and the dancelike twenty-fourth. Much of the individuality may be traced to contrasts inherent in the figuration, although differences in tempo and dynamics also play a part.

In spite of the figural diversity of the canons it is noticeable that they display a tendency toward sequence patterns of the most conjunct kind. Example 32 illustrates this clearly. Here the *dux* in the alto voice is

Example 32. Bach, *Goldberg Variations.*[67]

formed sequentially in two-measure units (measures 1 and 2, 3 and 4, etc.); the *comes*, entering in the soprano, imitates these patterns one measure later. The resulting combination of sequence and imitation is similar to that so often encountered in the episodes of Bach's fugues. In certain passages, surprisingly, as in the last three measures of example 32, the imitative effect is more visual than aural, for it tends to disappear in a keyboard realization of the score.

As we have seen, variations built on the harmonic plan make no attempt to follow the melodic subject but rely, instead, upon maintaining a correspondence with the harmony and structure of the theme. Because of the great technical difficulties imposed by a rigorous canonic style, it may well be asked to what degree Bach adheres to the given harmonic and structural fundament. Investigation reveals that the underlying binary plan of the theme is followed without exception but that the cadences are often passed over without rhythmic pause or emphasis; from this it appears that Bach saw the impracticability of reconciling the continuity demanded by a genuinely contrapuntal style with the theme's closely recurring cadential breaks.[68] With respect to the harmony one finds a closer adherence, for in general the bass part follows the main bass tones or harmonies, especially those at the beginnings and endings of the phrases. Sometimes, as in variation 12 (quoted in example 33), the intermediate harmonies of the separate phrases are likewise followed quite strictly; elsewhere, as in variation 9 (also quoted in example 33), they are handled rather freely. As a rule the bass exhibits the same lack of concern for the specific contour of the bass subject that is shown by the melodico-harmonic variation (see p. 45). The excerpts in example 33 are typical of Bach's range of harmonic correspondence.

Example 33. Bach, *Goldberg Variations.*

The bass is at all times definitely related in style to the canonic parts superimposed upon it; often it uses the same figural material, occasionally it even takes part in the imitative exchange. Example 34 shows such

Example 34. Bach, *Goldberg Variations.*

an imitative participation by the bass. This excerpt reveals again Bach's reliance upon sequential patterns, as well as a new type of harmonic departure (rare for Bach's day save in the basso ostinato variation) based upon change of mode, and utilizing a chromatic treatment of portions of the bass subject.

In contrast to the nine canonic variations in the *Goldberg* set there are only two which have fugal characteristics: variations 10 and 16. The first of these contains all the attributes of a complete, short fugue, or fughetta, for in it are a regular three-part exposition (measures 1–12), four entries on degrees other than the tonic or dominant (measures 13–28), and a concluding statement in the form of the answer (measures 29–32). The remarkable fact is that here, as in the canons, the fugal plan is superimposed upon the binary structure and the essential harmonies of the variation theme, and Bach further reinforces the already strong thematic correspondence by building the fughetta subject out of the opening bass phrase of the aria theme (example 35). Although the unusual structural symmetry of this fughetta, occasioned by its eight theme entries falling at regular four-measure intervals, is at variance with ordinary fugal practice, this fact does not detract from its completely satisfactory musical effect.

Example 35. Bach, *Goldberg Variations.*

The second of the two fughettas (last half of variation 16) shows the same completeness as the first but is more flexible, for not only are the entries disposed in a less symmetrical way, but also episodic passages and strettos contribute to its contrapuntal independence and vitality. In contrast to the preceding fughetta, the subject bears little relation to the theme of the aria; this is as one would expect since the subject begins, not in the bass, but in the soprano. The fresh, almost gay effect of the piece is delightful (example 36).

Example 36. Bach, *Goldberg Variations.*

The foregoing discussion of imitative procedures suggests their widespread occurrence in the harmonic type of song variation, and shows that in the *Goldberg Variations* they assume new and complex guises. Linear writing is used less often; nevertheless, it appears conspicuously from time to time and, in common with imitative writing, attains new distinction in the *Goldberg Variations.* Many of the practices involving linear figuration have their analogues in the melodico-harmonic variation. Thus, the melodic subject is occasionally replaced, throughout an entire variation, by a single line of figuration, as in the ornate *seconda*

Example 37. Picchi, *Pass' e mezzo antico.*[60]

parte of Picchi's *Pass' e mezzo antico* (example 37). Here the correspondence between figuration and melodic subject is wholly incidental and quite possibly fortuitous; hence we see the consummation of the trend toward melodic freedom observed above in examples 21 to 24. Often the figuration appears alternately in the extreme parts within a single variation, as in the *Pass' e mezzo antico* of Andrea Gabrieli.[70] In Byrd's *Malt's come downe* we see still another feature of the melodico-harmonic species: the figuration of the soprano in one variation, of the bass in a second, and of two parts in a third. This practice, however, is rare.

More significant and original than any of the procedures just enumerated are the simultaneous linear figurations of the *Goldberg Variations*. Alternating with the richly imitative canons, fughettas, and trios of this set stand what Donald Francis Tovey calls "brilliant duet variations" (numbers 1, 5, 8, 11, 14, 17, 20, and 23), the basis of which is simultaneous figuration in two parts constructed upon the harmony of the theme. Variation 1 (examples 38, 39) is a good example of their

Example 38. Bach, *Goldberg Variations.*

Example 39. *Ibid.*

general constructive scheme. Here, as Tovey points out, the two voices which make up the variation contain opposing material, with each four-bar phrase witnessing a free inversion of the voices or the introduction of a fresh idea. Thus, in the first phrase (measures 1–4) a flowing figuration for the right hand is opposed to a more sober, broken-chord figuration in the left hand; during the following phrase (measures 5–8) these figures are interchanged (example 38). Phrase 3 (measures 9–12) brings in a new figuration in the upper voice, while the lower voice reverts to essentially the same material it had at the outset; finally, phrase 4 (measures 13–16) reverses the figures of phrase 3 (example 39). These four phrases, embracing the first half of the variation, are enough to show Bach's method, inasmuch as the second half is similar in general design to the first. It will be seen that the kind of simultaneous figuration employed is richer, more contrapuntal, and more varied than that found in the two preceding treatments, for instead of proceeding in parallel intervals and identical rhythms it emphasizes the independence of the lines through the use of contrary motion, opposing rhythms, and the contrasts between linear and chordal writing. Nor should the importance of the phrase-by-phrase alternations of material be overlooked, since these varied restatements (a type of double variation) contribute much to the general richness of effect. Another point is that sequential patterns appear even more prominently than in the neighboring canonic variations.[71]

The preceding discussion of the harmonic song variation shows that, through its tendency toward complexity, often of a contrapuntal kind, the harmonic technique resembles the cantus firmus plan in general effect. Intrinsically, however, it is a deeper and more subtle treatment than either of the other two, and a medium in which the separate variations are able to develop with peculiar freedom and spontaneity.

When one considers the many features of the song variation perpetuated by later species its historical importance becomes clear. All three of the technical treatments discussed above became the bases of other seventeenth- and eighteenth-century types: the cantus firmus and melodico-harmonic plans were utilized in the baroque chorale variation; the harmonic plan served as the foundation of the baroque basso ostinato variation; the melodico-harmonic treatment became the basis for the eighteenth-century ornamental variation. Even in the nineteenth century, when the growing vogue of the character variation dictated far-reaching changes in the theme, many sets continued to adhere to the scheme of constant structure first formulated in the song variation; this is true, for example, of most of the important works of Beethoven and Brahms. The design of progressive rhythmic animation initiated by the song variation appeared with even greater force in the basso ostinato and ornamental variations. The discontinuous arrangement of the variations within a series also influenced later works, for aside from the basso ostinato variation and certain rhapsodic free variations (Franck's *Variations symphoniques*, for example), discontinuity has been the prevailing variation design of all periods. Finally it may be said that although the song variation represents, on the whole, a simple stage of development, yet the diversity of its basic plans, the contrapuntal realization of its harmony, and the vigor of its figuration often contrive to make it musically satisfying as well as historically interesting.

CHAPTER III

The Extension of the Structural Techniques to New Variation Types

INSTRUMENTAL VARIATIONS on ecclesiastical melodies and basso ostinato themes came into prominence later than those built on secular
songs, dances, and arias. During the last half of the sixteenth century and the first quarter of the seventeenth, when Spanish, English,
and Italian composers were actively engaged in writing variations on
pavanes, passemezzos, and popular airs, the variations on ecclesiastical
melodies and basso ostinato themes were still relatively uncommon; and
not until the late seventeenth and early eighteenth centuries did these
two newer types reach their culmination.

The variations on ecclesiastical melodies, based both upon plain-song
hymns and Protestant chorales, are identified almost exclusively with
the Protestant church musicians of central and north Germany.[1] The
presence of plain-song themes, with their implication of a Catholic
association, would appear to refute this statement; actually, however,
it does not, for plain-song hymns were common to both Catholic and
Lutheran services during the sixteenth and early seventeenth centuries.
Schering ascribes the origin of the variations on ecclesiastical melodies
to the early Lutheran practice of performing successive stanzas of a
hymn or chorale in alternation, the organ answering the choir or congre-
gation.[2]

Occasionally one finds variations on sacred melodies outside of Germany, especially in the early period. Two isolated examples appear in
the *Fitzwilliam Virginal Book*, both by John Bull (ca. 1562–1621); con-
temporaneously with Bull, J. P. Sweelinck (1562–1621) wrote plain-
song variations in the Netherlands. Bull's pieces have been called
"scholastic" and lacking in "real aesthetic interest,"[3] and this description applies with almost equal force to those of Sweelinck, whose
ecclesiastical variations lack the vigor and richness of his secular sets.
His favorite plan of presenting the chorale melody, as cantus firmus, in
uniformly long notes accompanied by rapid linear figurations in the
other voices is often mechanical and dull. For this reason it is difficult
to agree with Wilhelm Fischer when he calls Sweelinck the first great
representative of the chorale variation.[4]

Within Germany, in the period immediately following Bull and Sweelinck, the great name is that of Sweelinck's pupil, Samuel Scheidt
(1587–1654) of Halle, whose *Tabulatura Nova* (1624), outstanding in

[55]

early organ music, is devoted primarily to variations on plain songs and chorales. Scheidt's variations, in common with those of Bull and Sweelinck, are serious and restrained in style; they are, however, much more flexible and musical. In them the scholastic atmosphere which surrounds the work of the two earlier men disappears almost completely, and despite occasional stiffness, the music displays figural strength coupled with ingenious and varied harmony. Scheidt's plan of treating the successive phrases of the plain song or chorale as cantus firmus fragments, with the remaining voices providing an intricately imitative, contrapuntal setting, is so characteristic as to establish it as a type. This fact, together with the general maturity of style which the variations reveal, marks Scheidt, rather than Sweelinck, as the first great master of the ecclesiastical variation.

Following Scheidt, the foremost composers of variations on sacred themes were Georg Böhm (1661–1733) in Lüneburg, J. G. Walther (1684–1748) in Weimar, and J. S. Bach (1685–1750) during his Lüneburg and Leipzig periods. Others include Franz Tunder (1614–1667), Matthias Weckmann (1621–1674), Dietrich Buxtehude (1637–1707), Johann Pachelbel (1653–1706), and Johann Bernhard Bach (1676–1749). The style of these men is less homogeneous than that of the earlier composers. Alongside of variations which are intricately fashioned and contrapuntal, after the manner of Scheidt, stand those built upon a more homphonic plan, such as Pachelbel's *Ach was soll ich Sünder machen* and Walther's *Jesu, meine Freude;*[5] alongside of variations which preserve intact the structure of the theme (like the Pachelbel and Walther pieces just mentioned) stand those which incorporate intrinsic expansions of the chorale melody itself, such as J. S. Bach's *O Gott, du frommer Gott* and Böhm's *Christe, der du bist Tag und Licht.*[6] Such expansions represent, obviously, the influence of the free technique of variation writing; other works of Böhm show this influence even more conspicuously, some of them being so unfettered as to defy ready analysis; a case in point is his *Auf meinen lieben Gott.*[7]

Unlike the variations of the earlier period, which, as we have seen, were constructed impartially upon plain songs and German chorales, those of the post-Scheidt period abandon plain-song themes completely. An equally significant circumstance is that many of the later pieces were apparently intended for performance outside the church. According to Seiffert, the four chorale variations contained in Pachelbel's *Musikalische Sterbensgedanken* (1683) were intended for domestic rather than liturgical use;[8] likewise the marked dance rhythms of Buxtehude's *Auf meinen lieben Gott* and certain of the chorale variations of Böhm must surely have unfitted them for the church service.[9] One can occasionally assume a nonliturgical intention on the part of the composers prior to

1650, although the evidence is less plentiful; thus the plain-song variations of John Bull were evidently written for the harpsichord rather than the organ, and intended for the domestic circle rather than the religious ritual.[10]

Like the variation cycle based upon secular themes, the typical series based upon a plain song or chorale (hereafter called simply the chorale variation) is made up of a moderate number of variations separated by distinct cadences.[11] Apparently the character of the separate variations was sometimes influenced by the changing sentiment of the text;[12] in any case it may be said that there is little musical connection between successive members of the series. Even the pairing of variations, seen so frequently in the song variation, is absent from these pieces, although in a few of them, such as J. S. Bach's *O Gott, du frommer Gott*, successive variations are related through similar figuration.[13] Key and mode are preserved unchanged, and while deviations from the original meter are infrequent, the use of triple-meter variations by J. S. Bach, J. G. Walther, and others shows that composers did not hesitate to change, upon occasion, the basic duple meter of the chorale.[14]

The theme of the chorale variation has a distinctly sober cast; it is of about the same length, often, as the more tuneful secular song theme, but its tempo is somewhat slower and its rhythm more inelastic and square. Its melodic contour, formed of conservative, scale-wise progressions and narrow leaps, is unornamented and staidly vocal; its structure is balanced and clear.

Two primary techniques are used to develop these themes: the cantus firmus treatment, used by Sweelinck and Scheidt as the sole basis of their chorale variations and, less consistently, by many later composers; and the melodico-harmonic procedure, employed prominently by Pachelbel, Böhm, Walther, and J. S. Bach. As in the song variation, mixtures of the two techniques are common. In Scheidt's cantus firmus series *Warum betrübst du dich, mein Herz*,[15] for example, the chorale melody undergoes strong figuration in the concluding variation, after having been used literally up to that point; again, in J. S. Bach's *Sei gegrüsset, Jesu gütig*,[16] three cantus firmus variations (numbers 6, 9, and 10) are inserted into the prevailing melodico-harmonic plan. In addition to the two primary techniques, the free treatment makes its appearance from time to time in an incidental way.

The cantus firmus treatment of chorale melodies is similar to the cantus firmus treatment of secular songs, dances, and arias in that the melodic subject occupies different voices during the course of a series, is attended by new counterpoints in successive variations, and appears throughout in its literal or nearly literal form.[17] The chorale variatiosn are much more contrapuntal than the secular pieces, however, and

depart further from the basic harmony of the theme. Much of the polyphony is imitative, for rapid exchanges of short stencil figures occur
abundantly, and fuguelike beginnings based on relatively long theme
fragments are numerous. Even the strictest of imitative styles, the
canon, adapts itself to this technique, as may be seen in J. S. Bach's
remarkable *canonische Veränderungen* on the Christmas hymn *Vom
Himmel hoch, da komm' ich her,* to be described below (see pp. 60 f.).

An important departure from the cantus firmus treatment of secular
melodies lies in the expansion normally accorded to the theme. Within
the separate variations of the typical cantus firmus chorale series the
melody is usually presented fragmentarily. An imitative prelude leads
up to the first phrase; between the succeeding phrases stand interludes;
sometimes a postlude or an extension of the final cadence brings the
variation to a close. Such a drawing-out of the theme is completely
foreign to the secular-song variation; hence in its use of theme expansion the cantus firmus chorale variation is more nearly related to the
chorale prelude than to the secular variation. Its particular analogue
among chorale preludes is the one Schweitzer calls Pachelbel's "moti-
vistic" type, which is constructed in a series of fugal expositions built
upon the successive phrases of the chorale.[18]

A good example of this expansion within the cantus firmus chorale
treatment is the first variation of Scheidt's *Christe, qui lux es et dies.* It
begins with a fugue-like prelude based upon the opening chorale phrase
as "theme" (see example 40). This introduction is quite long, despite

Example 40. Scheidt, *Christe, qui lux es et dies.*[19]

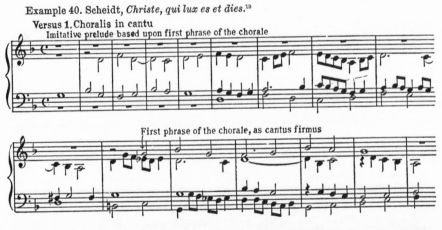

the stretto overlapping between the first two entries; it is succeeded by
the first phrase of the chorale, as cantus firmus. The entire scheme of
derived entries leading up to the announcement of the cantus firmus
may be traced back to the masses of Josquin and his contemporaries.
The interlude which follows (see example 41) is constructed imitatively

Example 41. Scheidt, *Christe, qui lux es et dies.*

upon a diminished fragment of the second cantus firmus phrase. In distinction to the five-measure "theme" of the opening section, Scheidt uses here only a one-measure motive; for this reason the interlude is very short in comparison with the opening prelude—a characteristic, incidentally, of interludes generally within these pieces. Because the imitative play continues past the entrance of the cantus firmus, the motive serves the double role of foreshadowing the chorale and, thereafter, of providing a rich and organic accompanimental web. The derivation of the next interlude (beginning of example 42) is less plain,

Example 42. Scheidt, *Christe, qui lux es et dies.*

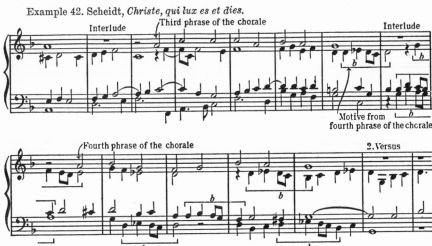

although the motive employed may possibly be traced in a free way to the two opening notes of the cantus firmus. The construction of the final interlude (example 42, end of first score) is much like the first. The underlying motive is a freely diminished form of the chorale phrase which follows. As before, the motive persists after the chorale melody enters.

Although the design of the Scheidt variation just analyzed is thoroughly typical, many cantus firmus chorale series reveal individual departures. Those of J. G. Walther tend to apply the fugal treatment exemplified in the opening of the Scheidt variation (example 40) to each of the chorale phrases in turn; Walther's *Erschienen ist der herrliche Tag*[20] carries through the fugal plan with especial fidelity, the preludes and interludes alike being intricately imitative and of substantial length. Bach's *Vom Himmel hoch da komm' ich her*, and many separate variations within the chorale series of Walther employ canonic treatments. Those of the Bach work are unusually elaborate. In the first four variations the chorale melody, as cantus firmus, is accompanied by two-part canons at various intervals of imitation (octave, fifth, seventh), together with an additional free part in variations 3 and 4. The canon in variation 4 is developed by augmentation; in variation 5 the chorale melody itself is imitated canonically in contrary motion, accompanied by free parts. Throughout, Bach displays his exceptional command of counterpoint; the whole piece is a compositional tour de force akin to the *Goldberg Variations* and *The Art of the Fugue*, though on a smaller scale. A fragment from the beginning of the fourth variation (example 43) will show

Example 43. Bach, *Vom Himmel hoch da komm'ich her*.[21]

the complexity of the imitative procedure, as well as the use of material that is independent of the theme. Walther's canonic writing is less abstruse. His common plan is to treat the chorale itself in canon, accompanied by free parts, as in the excerpt from *Ach Gott und Herr* (example 44).

The consistent expansion of the chorale theme by means of episodic preludes and interludes, seen in all examples thus far cited, effectually distinguishes the cantus firmus chorale variation from the baroque song variation and basso ostinato variation. The value of this structural expansion is partly that the inserted preludes and interludes, by possess-

Example 44. Walther, *Ach Gott und Herr.*[22]

Var. 1 (after 5 measure prelude)

First phrase of the chorale

ing a certain individuality of their own, set off the chorale melody to advantage, and partly that they contribute to the form an element of unpredictability which the structure of the average pre-nineteenth-century variation so conspicuously lacks. Although the expansions do not represent the free technique of variation writing (for they leave unchanged the intrinsic arrangement of phrases and parts within the theme), they constitute an approach to this more flexible treatment.

Individual variations of a cantus firmus chorale series occasionally lack the expansion provided by episodic preludes and interludes. The opening variation of Walther's *Christus der ist mein Leben* (example 45)

Example 45. Walther, *Christus der ist mein Leben.*[23]

First phrase of the chorale

Var. 1

Second phrase of the chorale

shows this more concise plan. Here the chorale melody, as cantus firmus, appears continuously in the uppermost voice. Because the figure used initially in the supporting voices persists throughout, the variation has a more obvious unity than that found in the "expanded" cantus firmus type. In passing it may be stated that Bach, in his *Orgelbüchlein*, wrote many chorale preludes showing this construction.

After its application to chorale themes, the cantus firmus variation-technique disappeared almost completely. Musically rich, it was without important influence in the ensuing classic and romantic periods. Its strength was its abundant capacity for many kinds of change—harmonic, structural, figural. Its weakness, in the baroque period, was that the contrapuntal style, without which a true cantus firmus variation is impossible, was currently in decline.

The melodico-harmonic chorale variation[24] is more transparent and graceful than the complex cantus firmus type. The theme melody is confined mainly to the soprano voice, where it generally appears in figured form;[25] the basic theme harmony undergoes little change; and the texture, although often involved, is less contrapuntal than that of the cantus firmus chorale variation. At times the bass becomes the chief figured part while the chorale melody in the soprano resumes its original, simple form; through such alternations the outer voices tend to complement one another, as in the melodico-harmonic song variation.[26] Despite the frequent linear figuration in soprano and bass, the emphasis is upon imitative, stencil-like patterns, a natural consequence, possibly, of the innate seriousness of the theme.

Probably the most significant technical innovation in the melodico-harmonic treatment of chorale themes is what Vincent d'Indy calls *l'amplification thématique*.[27] In the cantus firmus chorale variation the theme was generally expanded by means of episodic preludes and interludes; here it is sometimes amplified through essential enlargements of the chorale melody itself. Spitta, who attributes the first use of the method to Georg Böhm,[28] describes the means employed as a kind of development:

. . . each separate line . . . is thematically exhausted by the disseverance of its principal melodic ideas, and by their repetition, dissection, modification, and various recombination. . . . Nor was he [Georg Böhm] bound as in variations strictly speaking, by the harmonic and rhythmical conditions of the theme, but could create new proportions and phrases, building up a composition all his own. . . . He must have been the first composer who availed himself in instrumental music of that development of the melodic constituents of a subject— using them as independent themes and motives to form the component elements of a tone structure on a larger scale—which played a principal part in the musical art of Beethoven's time.[29]

The simplest examples of amplification are those in which the melodic line is constructed from literal repetitions of small thematic fragments. Most of these repetitions take the form of dynamic echoings, frequently

Example 46. Bach, *O Gott, du frommer Gott*.[30]

presented in conjunction with octave transpositions, as seen in Bach's *O Gott, du frommer Gott* (example 46). Bach's *Christ der du bist der helle Tag* (see example 47) typifies a somewhat more complex practice, that of stating the opening notes of a phrase and then, after an interlude, of

Example 47. Bach, *Christ, der du bist der helle Tag.*[31]

Example 48. *Ibid.*[32]

repeating these notes and completing the phrase. Still more involved is the thematic development which consists of successive restatements of a melodic motive upon different degrees of the scale (see example 48). One can observe this usage in both Böhm and Bach; to a remarkable degree it anticipates the developmental methods of the nineteenth century.

The device of amplification is often coupled with a species of ostinato bass, called by Spitta and Riemann *basso quasi ostinato.*[33] Spitta credits

Böhm with being its originator and has a clear description of its construction:

He [Böhm] constructs an ornate series of notes, forming two or three bars, to introduce the piece, usually in the bass, and then repeats the whole or portions of it as often as is feasible between the lines, using it even as counterpoint to them, and allowing it to reappear once more *solo* at the close.[34]

That this bass is not a true ostinato is evident from the freedom of its recurrence, for, although the general outline of the initial bass phrase is preserved, its length is freely altered and transitions to new keys are common. Bach uses the *basso quasi ostinato* as the means of forming the first variation of his early chorale partitas, very probably taking over the technique from Böhm during their association at Lüneburg.[35] (See example 49.)

Example 49. Bach, *O Gott, du frommer Gott.*[36]

When applied to chorale themes, the melodico-harmonic treatment is thus more intricate than when it is used to vary secular songs, dance themes, and arias. Indeed, one may safely say that this straightforward technique, the simplest in the category of structural treatments, attains its culmination in the chorale variation, for although it was subsequently much utilized in the variations of Haydn, Mozart, and certain nineteenth-century composers (see chapter iv), it never again evinced such a manysided aspect. Not alone in its contrapuntal tendency and figural richness but also in its ability, through *l'amplification thématique*, to unfold a theme, the melodico-harmonic technique here assumes a new seriousness and depth.

Looking at the chorale variation as a whole, one is impressed by the anomalousness of its position. A hybrid type, combining traits of the secular song variation with those of the chorale prelude, it exhibits characteristics which are in some respects more advanced than those of the pure variation types; among these characteristics are the conspicuous expansion of the theme and the relatively consistent use of figures derived from the theme. Surprisingly, it effects these innovations not through the harmonic plan (intrinsically the freest and historically the most productive among the three structural techniques), but rather by means of the ancient cantus firmus treatment and the simple and unpretentious melodico-harmonic method. Finally, in spite of its undeniable inherent interest, the chorale variation had little immediate influence upon the course of variation technique as a whole. Rather, its cultivation ended with the baroque period; and the innovations introduced, instead of being transmitted to rococo and classic variations, were left to be explored by the musical historian and theorist of a later century.

The harmonic technique, neglected by the writers of chorale variations, became during the baroque period the basis for the multiform basso ostinato variation.[37] Except for isolated early examples, such as the *recercadas* of Diego Ortiz (see p. 19), the instrumental basso ostinato variation began with the English and Italian keyboard composers of the late sixteenth and early seventeenth centuries. In England it underwent little immediate development but in Italy it became firmly established during the course of the seventeenth century. There, Gerolamo Frescobaldi (1583–1644), Andrea Falconiero (born during the latter sixteenth century), Biagio Marini (died *ca.* 1660), G. B. Vitali (*ca.* 1644–1692), Arcangelo Corelli (1653–1713), and their contemporaries wrote basso ostinato pieces which show harmonic clarity, figural restraint, and continuity of structure, characteristics destined to influence many subsequent composers. In the second half of the century the basso ostinato variation was taken over by the French and Germans, and at the same time English composers evinced a new interest in it. In France it showed little vitality, tending to merge with the rondo form; this fusion is apparent in the *passecailles* and chaconnes of the French clavecin composers, among them J. H. d'Anglebert (1635–?) and François Couperin (1668–1733), whose pieces differ from those of the Italians through their plenitude of graceful *agréments*.[38] The basso ostinato variations of the contemporary English writers, John Blow (*ca.* 1648–1708) and Henry Purcell (1658–1695), although pleasant and skillfully made, exhibit few new traits.[39] In Germany, on the other hand, the basso ostinato compositions of J. K. Kerll (1627–1693), Georg Muffat (1635–1704), H. F. Biber (1644–1704), Johann Pachelbel (1653–1706), J. K. F. Fischer (*ca.* 1670–*ca.* 1738), G. F. Handel (1685–1759), and especially those of Dietrich Buxtehude (1637–1707), and J. S. Bach (1685–1750) display conspicuous innovations. Although the German pieces show at times the homophonic simplicity of the Italians and at other times the ornamented, quasi-rondo structure of the French, they tend in general to be more elaborate and contrapuntal, especially when designed for the organ.

Basso ostinato variations from this period appear under five chief names: ground, folia, bergamask, passacaglia, and chaconne. Although it is customary to speak of each type as having distinct characteristics, there is considerable overlapping among them. Such ambiguity is especially apparent in the passacaglia and chaconne, whose interconnection is historically very close. It can also be seen in the name *ground*, which is sometimes used generically to include all basso ostinato variations, sometimes to refer to a specific English variation type, sometimes to denote the bass subject itself; when *ground* is used to denote the bass subject itself the word is synonymous with *ground bass*, or *basso ostinato*. All five species, save the English ground, may be traced back to prototypes in dance music. The exact relation between dances and variations is in all species obscure; the most definite connection exists in the folia and bergamask, both of which are constructed upon the basses of the original dances, and sometimes upon the melodies as well.[40]

The ground, using the name in its more restricted sense to mean a definite English variation type, dates from the sixteenth century. Van den Borren says that at the time of the virginalists the term referred to two different types of compositions, one having a subject which passed from part to part in succeeding variations, the other a subject which remained in the bass throughout;[41] of these two, it is obvious that only the second can be considered a basso ostinato variation. During the seventeenth century the variation with a subject consistently in the bass gradually superseded that with a movable subject, and by the time of Blow and Purcell it made use of strikingly individual basses, as example 50 shows.[42]

Example 50. Purcell, *Ground*.[43]

The folia (*follia, follia di Spagna, folies d'Espagne*) was originally an ancient Portuguese dance. Melodies titled folia are on record as early as 1577,[44] and it is upon the bass of one of these tunes that most folia variations are constructed (example 51). Some folias, like A. Scarlatti's *Variazioni sulla follia di Spagna*, utilize only the first half of the bass quoted in example 51.[45] Others are built upon the melody, as well as the

Example 51.

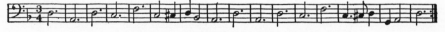

bass, of this ancient dance, but such pieces, examplifying the melodico-harmonic treatment, cannot be regarded as true basso ostinato variations. Corelli's twelfth solo violin sonata, one of the most celebrated of all folias, is of this type.[46]

The bergamask began as an Italian dance. During the seventeenth century it was widely used, especially in violin literature, and occasionally formed the basis of variations.[47] Nettl quotes many bergamask melodies from this period, most of which have the harmonic fundament shown in example 52. The bergamask variations are much less numerous

Example 52.

than other basso ostinato types and apparently were confined mainly to Italy. Like the folia variations, they are built at times upon the melodico-harmonic principle rather than the harmonic.

Of far greater importance than any of the preceding varieties are the passacaglia (*passagaglia, passagallo, passecaille*) and chaconne (*ciaconna, ciaccona*). Music theorists and historians have long attempted to distinguish between them but their results show little agreement. Litterscheid points out that even authorities like Johann Mattheson and J. G. Walther, who lived when the ostinato variation was at its height, fail to concur in their definitions of these two types.[48] Hence it is not unlikely that the terms passacaglia and chaconne were used loosely and even interchangeably by the later baroque composers.[49] The connection between these types and their dance ancestors is slight, for unlike the folia and bergamask variations, which conserve the basses of the early dances quite strictly, the passacaglia and chaconne maintain this relationship only in a rhythmical sense. The triple meter of the ancient passacaglia and chaconne dances appears in all but a very few of the basso ostinato variations bearing those names, and the accented second beat of the old chaconne frequently manifests itself in the rhythm of a quarter note, dotted quarter, and an eighth. Probably the earliest example of these types is in Frescobaldi's *Toccate e partite d'intavolatura di cimbalo e organo* (Rome, 1614).[50] While in Italy they appeared alongside the folia and bergamask, in Germany they became the main basso ostinato pieces to be employed.

In both countries, as well as in France, composers wrote most of their passacaglias and chaconnes upon a few stock basses. By far the most usual of these is a four-note series descending from tonic to dominant (example 53). Another is the reverse movement, upward from

Example 53. J. K. F. Fischer, *Chaconne*.[51]

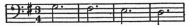

tonic to dominant (example 54). Four-measure variants of both are frequent, such as those of example 55. Longer themes, too, may often

Example 54. Pachelbel, *Chaconne.*[52]

Example 55, *a.* Vitali, *Passagallo.* [53]   *b.* Biber, *Passacaglia.*[54]

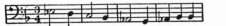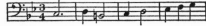

be traced to the simple patterns of examples 53 and 54. Thus, the Handel theme of example 56, *a*, is composed of the descending series followed by ascending movement, and the Muffat theme (example 56, *b*) is made up of two statements of the ascending series. Even the bold and striking subject of Bach's *Passacaglia* in C minor (example 56, *c*) may be said to bear a free resemblance to these four-measure patterns by virtue of the opposition of movement shown in its two phrases.[55]

Example 56, *a.* Handel, *Ciaccona.*[56]

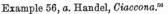

b. Muffat, *Passacaglia.*[57]

c. Bach, *Passacaglia.*[58]

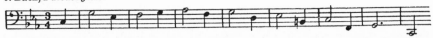

As the excerpts quoted in examples 50–56 show, the basso ostinato theme is usually brief, and is generally, though not invariably, in triple meter. Its structure is most often that of a single phrase ending on the dominant, sometimes that of a pair of phrases ending on the tonic. Many basso ostinato themes are constructed entirely from notes of equal value, as in Handel's *Ciaccona* (example 56, *a*), or upon a single rhythm, as in Bach's *Passacaglia* (example 56, *c*). The presentation of the unharmonized bass is rare; generally the bass is accompanied from the outset by its harmonic realization. This harmonic superstructure is equal in importance to the bass itself in providing the foundation for the variations which follow.

One of the most striking characteristics of the basso ostinato theme is its lack of melodic individuality. As the result of its slow speed, its prevailingly conjunct movement, and its quietly monotonous rhythm, the ostinato bass has a neutral, sometimes even a drab effect, as in the descending tetrachord pattern of example 53. Although its lack of individuality is explainable in part by the fact that the theme is in the bass, not all of its indecisiveness is so attributable, for baroque basses in general are alive and interesting; in greater part its lack of intrinsic interest appears to stem from the almost complete absence of figuration.

Because the basso ostinato theme is quite brief, the number of variations in a set is generally greater than that in the song or chorale variation. Twenty or thirty statements of the theme are frequent, and an even larger number is sometimes encountered.[59] Among these pieces of greater length are L. Couperin's *Passacaglia in G Minor*, with thirty-nine appearances; J. P. Krieger's *Passacaglia in D Minor*, with forty-five; and the *Passagallo* of G. B. Vitali, with sixty-five.[60]

A most important distinguishing trait of the basso ostinato variation is its continuous structure; the separate members of a series, instead of being detached from one another, as in most variations on chorales and secular songs, are connected to form an unbroken chain of movement. It is true that one occasionally encounters pieces such as Frescobaldi's *Partite sopra follia*, or B. Pasquini's *Partite diverse di follia*, which carry basso ostinato names but lack a continuous structure; these, however, are better thought of as belonging to the category of dance variations.[61] As example 59 demonstrates (see page 70), continuity in the basso ostinato variation is brought about largely through the forward compulsion of the dominant half-cadence which ends most basso ostinato themes. Melodic bridging of the cadence measure has a similar binding function, and is of especial importance in variations whose subjects lack the forward impetus of a dominant ending. Bach makes systematic use of such bridging by anticipating the figure of the coming variation.

Example 57. Bach, *Passacaglia*.[62]

Related to structural continuity is the tendency of the basso ostinato variation to provide an increase of rhythmic movement as the series advances; already shown to exist in the secular-song variation, such progressive animation is often more conspicuous in the basso ostinato pieces. The acceleration commonly takes place in successive stages, as in Buxtehude's *Ciaconna in E Minor*.[63]*

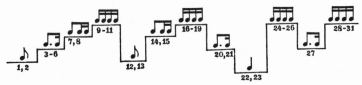

Occasionally the rhythmic level attained in the first rise is maintained with little change throughout the remainder of the variations. Bach's C-minor *Passacaglia* exemplifies this less usual arrangement:

Some basso ostinato variations show little or no acceleration of movement but these are confined mainly to the early history of the type.[64]

Within the general scheme of progressive growth, the basso ostinato series is usually divided into small variation groups. The organization of these groups sometimes resembles that of the song variation, wherein the soprano is figured in one variation, the bass in a second, and often two parts are figured simultaneously in a third. Alessandro Scarlatti's *Variazioni sulla follia di Spagna* shows this arrangement conspicuously.[65] A commoner plan is to build the second of a pair of variations from the first. Taking the first as a temporary "theme," the composer immediately writes a variant, using either simple figural embellishment, as in Louis Couperin's *Passacaglia in G Minor* (example 58), or

Example 58. L. Couperin, *Passacaglia*.[66]

using inversion of parts through double counterpoint, as in Buxtehude's *Passacaglia in D Minor* (example 59). Sometimes the figural

Example 59. Buxtehude, *Passacaglia*.[67]

patterns initiated by the first variation of the group are carried on almost identically, without change of part or further elaboration. Bach provides clear examples of this device in his *Chaconne* for solo violin:

Example 60. Bach, *Chaconne*.[68]

Underlying all these different groupings is the evident desire of the composer to secure a degree of unity and cohesiveness greater than that obtainable through the use of constantly new ideas. The transfer of figuration from the soprano to the bass probably contributes least to this end, since the prominent relocation of the figured part tends to emphasize the position of the cadences, and thus interferes with true continuity. The other procedures call attention to the cadences less conspicuously, and hence succeed more fully in achieving an uninhibited flow.

In some pieces there are also larger groupings based upon contrasting keys and modes. Buxtehude, in his D-minor *Passacaglia*,[69] divides the twenty-eight variations into four sections having contrasting keys; between the sections stand short, modulatory episodes. The plan, in outline, is:

D minor	F major	A minor	D minor
(1–7)	(8–14)	(15–21)	(22–28)

A somewhat similar scheme underlies Falconiero's *Ciaccona in G*.[70] In the *Passagallo* of G. B. Vitali is an altogether novel design based upon a series of modulations along the circle of keys; beginning in E flat, the piece moves successively to B flat (variation 9), F (variation 17), C (variation 25), G (variation 33), D (variation 41), A (variation 49), and finally to E (variation 57), where it ends.[71] A more common plan than any of the foregoing is exemplified by J. K. F. Fischer's *Chaconne in G*,[72] which contains three main divisions in opposing modes:

G major	G minor	G major
(1–10)	(11–20)	(21–36)

This three-part design, based upon change of mode rather than change of key, appears occasionally from the time of Louis Couperin (*ca.* 1626–1661) onward, and finds perhaps its best-known application during the baroque period in Bach's *Chaconne* for solo violin.

Notwithstanding the implication inherent in the term *basso ostinato*, that the bass line is adhered to rigorously, one finds frequent departure from the literal bass in these variations, and only exceptionally, as in Pachelbel's *Ciaconna in D Minor*,[73] is the literal bass used throughout a piece. It is plain, therefore, that the designation *basso ostinato* does not fit all continuous variations of the baroque period with equal accuracy. The degree of change in the bass line varies greatly. On the one hand, the bass may be dissolved into linear figuration, may participate in imitative figuration, or may undergo slight rhythmic modifications or minor changes in contour, all without losing its clear relationship to the original theme. Thus, in the excerpts from Kerll's *Passacaglia in D Minor* (example 61), the descending tetrachord subject remains plainly

Example 61. Kerll, *Passacaglia* in D minor.[74]

visible despite chromatic interpolation in variation 6, figuration in variation 8, and figuration and partial transposition in variation 38. On the other hand, the ostinato bass may be almost completely abandoned in favor of a new bass growing out of the harmony of the theme, as in the twenty-fourth variation of Buxtehude's *Ciaconna in E Minor* (example 62). This type of bass change is clearly more extreme than those

Example 62. Buxtehude, *Ciaconna* in E minor.[75]

illustrated in example 61, yet so long as it appears incidentally, the basso ostinato character of a piece is not seriously disturbed.

In pieces built on the descending tetrachord theme, one frequently encounters what may be called a basic variant, the ascending line from tonic to dominant, similar to that in example 54. Obviously, the presence of two basic forms of the theme within a single composition again runs counter to the classical meaning of a basso ostinato; nevertheless the ascending line appears so often as a substitute for the original descending form as to suggest that baroque composers may have conceived it as another, thoroughly satisfactory way of attaining the dominant half-cadence. It would appear, in other words, that these composers may consciously have had in mind the writing of pieces built upon a pair of *bassi ostinati* rather than a single theme. J. K. F. Fischer's *Ciacona* from the *Suite in A Minor* (example 63) shows this underlying

Example 63. Fischer, *Ciacona* from *Suite* in A minor.[70]

dualism with especial clarity. Here, it will be observed, the descending line forms the basis of variations 1, 2, 3, 4, and 7; the ascending line the foundation for variations 5, 6, and 8. All of the basses exhibit slight rhythmic modifications of the stock forms shown in examples 53 and 54; in addition, variation 7 presents a chromatic alteration of the descending pattern, variation 8 a partial transposition of the ascending version.

Frequently there are even wider departures from the initial bass. The *Passacaglia* from Pez's *Concerto pastorale*, for example, contains variants which are unusually numerous and diversified. Example 64 gives

Example 64. Pez, *Passacaglia* from *Concerto Pastorale*.[77]

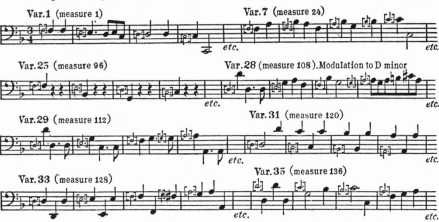

a representative sampling of the different bass forms employed and, for comparison, the two stock patterns from which they appear to have sprung (indicated by the notes in brackets). The bass form of the opening (variation 1) recurs in variations 2 to 6; thereafter each variant normally appears twice, with the result that the entire *Passacaglia* shows a pronounced pairing of the variations. The fact that the harmony implicit in certain of the variants (notably 7 and 35) is distinct from that of the two stock basses is further proof of the unorthodox nature of the changes.

The inflexibility of the bass line may further be relaxed by a transient shifting of the theme to another voice, or by having it appear temporarily on new scale degrees; obviously, transpositions such as these constitute still another violation of the strict basso ostinato principle. Couperin's *Passacaglia in G Minor* (example 65) contains several of

Example 65. L. Couperin, *Passacaglia*.[78]

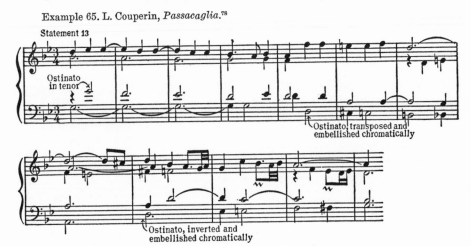

these changes. The familiar four-note descending theme, normally in the bass, appears at the thirteenth statement in the tenor, while the bass remains immobile; it next is transposed down a fourth and modified chromatically; finally, it is used in ascending movement, again with chromatic alteration. Occasionally the theme is transferred to the soprano voice, as in J. S. Bach's *Passacaglia in C Minor*, but since the average ostinato bass is rhythmically and melodically monotonous, its appearance in the uppermost part is likely to be ineffective. Buxtehude, whom Spitta acknowledges to be Bach's equal in the writing of passacaglias and chaconnes,[79] does not employ this device in any of his independent basso ostinato pieces for clavier.

The preceding discussion of bass treatments has shown that the basso ostinato theme, instead of being maintained literally throughout a composition, normally undergoes modifications which extend from simple figurations to marked alterations of contour; further, that the theme occasionally leaves the bass to take up a position in another voice, or, while remaining in the bass, sometimes appears temporarily on new scale degrees. Alongside of this wide array of bass changes there comes, as has been suggested, a corresponding range of harmonic deviations. When the ostinato is closely followed, the harmonic departures are ordinarily slight. In Bach's organ *Passacaglia*, a work in which the theme is used throughout in its literal or simply figured form, the modifications are limited to incidental substitutions and interpolations; the same is true of Buxtehude's *Passacaglia in D Minor*, where again the theme appears almost literally throughout. Even these slight recastings may produce an expressive and subtle result, as the excerpts in example 66 demonstrate.

Example 66. Buxtehude, *Passacaglia* in D minor.[80]

But there are also compositions, such as Pachelbel's *Ciaconna in D Minor* and Fischer's *Chaconne in G*, which, while adhering closely to the ostinato, exhibit more consistent and striking harmonic departures. The Pachelbel *Ciaconna* (example 67) employes, in systematic alternation

Example 67. Pachelbel, *Ciaconna* in D minor.[81]

from the beginning of the piece to the end, two contrasting "harmonizations" of the literally used ostinato, the one entirely in minor, the other making a brief transition through the relative major. The harmonic changes within the middle section of the Fischer *Chaconne* (example 68) are so conspicuous as to make it seem that the composer,

Example 68. Fischer, *Chaconne* in G.[82]

possibly stimulated by the imposed restrictions of a fixed bass and cadence scheme, seized every means of circumventing the natural implications of such a scheme, a completely fixed and rigid harmony. The most striking of these changes takes place at the seventeenth statement, where there appears a series of transitions through new keys, paralleling the stepwise descent of the ostinato.

One has finally to take account of those harmonic departures inspired by radical modifications of the ostinato theme itself. Such departures have already been suggested by examples 63 and 64; an excerpt from Georg Muffat's *Passacaglia in G Minor* (example 69) will serve as a more complete illustration. This work shows, as the result of French influence,[83] a rondo-like structure, the theme recurring literally in variations 6, 12, 18, and 24. Between these recurrences, the original bass is

Example 69. Muffat, *Passacaglia*.[84]

occasionally figured (variations 10 and 14) or simplified (variations 3, 16, and 17); frequently it is almost completely abandoned (variations 5, 7, 8, 11, 15, 19, 20, 21, and 23). In the first half of variation 4 (as in the corresponding portions of variations 5, 9, 14, and 22), the normal, ascending bass line is supplanted by the descending variant; over this variant stands a harmonic succession notably different from that of the theme, despite their identity of cadential objective.

Thus it is that no absolute rule can be given regarding the extent of harmonic change in the basso ostinato variation, any more than one can be laid down concerning the extent of modification within the bass theme itself. A strict versus a free approach to the harmony is in no sense a matter of value, for one treatment may be as interesting as the other. It would seem reasonable that at times the choice of treatment may be attributable to the length of the chosen theme, since obviously the need for harmonic variety is more pressing with a short theme than with a longer one. But short themes are not invariably handled freely, nor longer ones handled strictly; hence it remains true, as suggested above, that the choice of treatment is primarily a matter of the composer's personal temperament and inclinations.

Generalization regarding the extent of harmonic changes, and of changes in the bass theme itself, is made difficult because the basso ostinato variation apparently meant different things to different composers; as we have seen, men like Buxtehude and Pachelbel took an inherently strict view of the type, while men like Muffat and Fischer conceived it in a much freer way. The fundamental aesthetic question upon which these groups divide is whether the basso ostinato variation should be rigorous, inflexible, and in very truth *obstinate*, or instead, should temper its inherent rigidity by means of occasional digression and contrast. This much is certain: by definition the basso ostinato variation is essentially rigorous and strict, and too great a relaxation of its strictness must necessarily give rise to a mixed treatment or a mixed form. Thus we observe that the harmonic deviations of example 68, carried out in conjunction with the nearly literal bass subject, show the influence of the cantus firmus technique; likewise, systematic modifications of the ostinato bass through the use of stock variants and other essential changes, as seen in examples 63, 64, and 69, tend to produce variations so free as to merit the name basso ostinato only partially.[85]

The figural dress of the basso ostinato variation is, in general, similar to that of the song variation and the chorale variation. Imitative figuration is widely used, often in the form of a quick succession of short, stencil-like figures, as in the fifth variation of Buxtehude's *Passacaglia in D Minor* (example 70). Imitative figuration such as this attains a

Example 70. Buxtehude, *Passacaglia* in D minor.[86]

high point of consistency and ingenuity in Bach's *Passacaglia in C Minor*. Statement 13 of this work (example 71), in which the ostinato

Example 71. Bach, *Passacaglia*.[87]

is transferred to the soprano, exhibits an especially powerful imitative treatment, the opposition of two different figures, together with occasional strettos, producing an unusual degree of contrapuntal intricacy.

Linear figuration also occurs abundantly in the basso ostinato variation, especially in the form of successive thirds, sixths, and tenths; this procedure is suggested in the first statement of Pachelbel's *Ciaconna in D Minor* (see example 67). In pieces built upon the descending tetrachord theme, linear figures are often employed sequentially; Bach's violin *Chaconne* is rich in examples of this kind. The excerpts taken from the *Chaconne* (example 72) show the diversity of Bach's treatment.

Example 72. Bach, *Chaconne.*[88]

Variation 9 suggests two voices by means of a single line (an effect called by Kurth *lineare Kontrapunkt*); variation 15 actually realizes the two-part effect by means of double stops; the eighteenth and twenty-first statements utilize elaborate scale fragments and broken-chord figures. In contrast to the foregoing variations, which carry out the sequence pattern strictly, variation 38 ingeniously disguises it through the use of imitations.

The foregoing analysis of the basso ostinato variation indicates that it is the most cohesive and at the same time the most flexible of the baroque variation types. Its cohesiveness is shown by its plan of rhythmical acceleration, its arrangement of the separate variations into groups, and above all by its continuous design. Its flexibility is evidenced not only by the lack of melodic ties between variations and theme but by the occasional new liberties taken with the harmony and the bass line. These traits, coupled with a wide variety of texture, extending from simple homophonic figuration to vigorous polyphony, make the baroque basso ostinato variation of particular aesthetic merit.

CHAPTER IV

The Structural Techniques under the Influence of Changing Styles

IF UP TO this point relatively little attention has been paid to the influence of changing musical styles upon the development of the variation, it is not because such influence was absent. One has only to compare the sober renaissance pieces of Cabezón and Byrd with the intricate baroque cycles of Frescobaldi and his successors to realize that the style change which took place around 1600 had important consequences within the song variation. It is not unlikely, indeed, that the transition from renaissance to baroque may have stimulated the rise of new types, since both the chorale variation and the basso ostinato variation first became conspicuous in the early seventeenth century. Technically, however, the results of this style mutation were not striking, for although the variation types of the baroque are more numerous than those of the renaissance, and more intricate and fanciful in their construction, they show no change whatever in basic techniques. The variations of J. S. Bach, no less than those of sixteenth-century composers, are built upon the cantus firmus, melodico-harmonic, and harmonic techniques.

Later style changes left a deeper imprint upon the variation, ushering in not merely new variation idioms and types, but alterations in the use of established techniques as well. The first of these more significant changes was the gradual simplification of style which took place beginning in the late seventeenth century. Even as baroque instrumental music was advancing to a culmination in the intricate works of J. S. Bach, the reaction toward a plainer style began to affect the variation. During the late seventeenth century the quasi-contrapuntal texture of the baroque variation gave way to a more tenuous and homophonic construction, earlier patterns of figuration, often so exuberantly irregular, became more symmetrical and restrained, and the diversity of the church modes was supplanted by the uniformity of the major-minor. The new style appeared first in the simple figuration and delicate rococo ornamentation of the French *noëls*, beginning with Nicolas le Begue (*ca.* 1630–1702) in 1676,[1] while shortly thereafter, in the closing decade of the century, a thinner texture began to permeate the long-established song variation in Germany.[2]

Eventually, under the influence of the more transparent style, the song variation became converted into a new and less elaborate type.

This was the ornamental variation of the eighteenth and nineteenth
centuries, a type standing midway between the baroque song variation
and the nineteenth-century character variation. Distinguished from the
song variation by its stereotyped plan and simple texture, and from the
character variation by its lack of sharp contrasts, the ornamental variation became identified at first with the Viennese classic composers,
Franz Joseph Haydn (1732–1809), Wolfgang Amadeus Mozart (1756–
1791), and Ludwig van Beethoven (1770–1827). It was later taken over
by Franz Schubert (1797–1828), Carl Maria von Weber (1786–1826),
Felix Mendelssohn-Bartholdy (1809–1847), and other romantic composers, in spite of the trend toward a more vigorous and dramatic idiom
in the early nineteenth century, and its last significant expression was
reached in the chamber music of Johannes Brahms (1833–1897).[3]

With the gradual conversion of the song variation into the ornamental species came other changes. Following the death of J. S. Bach
the vigorous basso ostinato variation fell into disuse for over a century,
and the intricate chorale variation disappeared entirely.[4] Equally important, the number of technical treatments was sharply reduced. Up
to this time the structural techniques had maintained their position;
beginning about 1750 they showed their first sign of decay. Of the
diverse techniques of the renaissance and baroque periods, the cantus
firmus and harmonic treatments were now abandoned, and only the
melodico-harmonic remained to form the constructional basis of the
new ornamental variation. The contraction of types and techniques, in
conjunction with the simplified style, suggests a period of variation
decadence, an impression heightened by the casual attitude which
composers frequently adopted toward the ornamental type. Many of
the late eighteenth- and early nineteenth-century keyboard variations
originated as *pièces d'occasion*, some the result of showy improvisations
upon well-known themes, others made purposely simple in order to
serve as instruction works or to gain the favor of amateurs.[5] Against
such minor evidences of triviality and display must be balanced the
growing incorporation of variation movements into cyclical forms, the
nature of which, on the whole, was distinctly more weighty and serious.
Whereas previously the use of variation movements in larger works had
been confined to an occasional place in such pieces as dance suites and
trio sonatas, in the Viennese classic period they were introduced into
the manifold forms of the sonata, symphony, divertimento, quartet, and
concerto. These incorporated variations, reflecting no doubt the more
serious attitude which composers entertained toward the larger forms,
have greater musical depth and interest than the independent sets. They
are important historically, moreover, in that they provide the first extensive use of the variation in connection with ensemble media.[6]

The new ornamental variation was constructed upon a relatively set and conventionalized plan. One indication of this is its uniform brevity; series with more than a dozen statements are exceptional, and many have fewer than six.[7] Further evidence is the stylized arrangement of the separate parts. The scheme of progressive rhythmic animation found in the baroque pieces still persists,[8] but is modified to include certain type contrasts. The first of these is afforded by a variation in the opposite mode, which, generally interrupting the rhythmic growth near the middle of the series, emphasizes harmonic subtleties rather than rhythmic movement.[9] It is convenient to refer to this contrasting statement as the minor variation, and while this term is not completely accurate, since a few ornamental cycles are written to minor themes and hence have major contrasting statements, its adoption will cause little confusion. Following the interruption occasioned by the minor variation, the rhythmic increase continues to a climactic *allegro* variation, sometimes to an *adagio-allegro* pair. These variations, based upon changed tempo rather than upon changed mode, constitute the other type contrasts. The *allegro* variation, often in changed meter, is usually enlarged by the addition of extensions, interpolated free cadenzas, or a short coda. The *adagio* variation, while not an inviolable rule in the ornamental species, is common in the clavier variations of Mozart and is used occasionally by other composers.[10] Like the minor variation, the *adagio* variation stands as a sharp contrast to the theme, and because of its juxtaposition to the concluding *allegro*, its place in the cycle is conspicuous.[11]

A structural peculiarity of the ornamental species is its occasional suggestion of other forms through the recurrence of the nearly literal theme. At times the recapitulation of the theme at the close is so marked as to create the impression of a three-part design, an effect clearly seen in the *Allegretto ma non troppo* of Mozart's *Quartet in D Minor*, K. 421, and in the variation movements of Haydn's *Quartets*, Op. 2, No. 6; Op. 17, No. 3; and Op. 30, No. 4. When, in addition to the *da capo* effect at the close, the theme recurs prominently during the course, the series is likely to simulate the rondo form. Paul Mies shows that the *Allegretto con variazioni* of Mozart's *Clarinet Quintet*, K. 581, has such quasi-rondo effect, variations one to three constituting the first contrast, and the *adagio* variation the second.[12] A similar resemblance to the rondo is sometimes occasioned by the use of two themes in parallel modes. Frequently identified with Haydn, the use of two themes is conspicuous in his *Andante con variazioni* for clavier. Here an opening theme in F minor is followed by a second theme in F major, after which come five variations built upon the two subjects in alternation. The entire arrangement is A B A' B' A'' B'' A''' Coda.[13]

The subjects used in the ornamental variation indicate clearly a growing trend toward the use of original themes, a tendency which was to become still more pronounced in the nineteenth-century character and free variations. Many of the finest sets, including most of those forming movements in cyclical works, rely upon themes of this kind. All but a few of the incorporated sets of Haydn and Beethoven, for example, are built upon original themes, and Mozart's incorporated variations employ them without exception.[14] Borrowed themes continue to include the dance piece and the popular song;[15] present in the variation for the first time, however, is the operatic excerpt. Used conspicuously by Mozart and Beethoven in their clavier variations, it consists of arias, concerted pieces, and instrumental interludes taken from favorite stage works.[16]

Example 73. Haydn, *Andante con Variazioni* in F minor.

All types of themes, original and borrowed alike, are notable for their simplicity and clarity. Most of them are fairly short (often sixteen measures), although a few are quite long.[17] Their structure, generally binary or ternary, is balanced and symmetrical; their harmony, more obvious than that of earlier periods, presents few surprises. Their chief departure from the themes of previous epochs lies in their melodic make-up. The quiet, vocal character of the renaissance and baroque melodies here becomes more lyrical and expressive, while in some themes a definite motival organization, new to variation subjects, can be traced. Both of these qualities are evident in the first subject of Haydn's *Andante con variazioni in F Minor* (example 73). Another characteristic of these simple themes is their marked predilection for the major mode: in the ornamental variation a minor theme such as that just quoted is a distinct rarity. The Mozart *Clavier Variations*, all fifteen of which are in major, strongly suggest the normal preference. The appearance of double themes, likewise new, has already been mentioned.[18]

In treating these subjects composers utilized the existing melodico-harmonic technique. As is seen in the melodico-harmonic pieces of the renaissance and baroque, the basic structural, melodic, and harmonic outlines of the theme are usually retained with little change. Figural manipulation of the melodic subject, accompanying harmony, and bass continue to provide the primary interest. The chief bearers of the figuration are the melodic subject and, to a lesser degree, the theme bass. Often these extreme parts are alternately figured in successive variations, thereby producing related pairs or groups.

In spite of the almost complete domination of the melodico-harmonic idea, there are occasional evidences of harmonic intermixture and influence. The extent of this harmonic effect varies from an incidental suggestion, as in Mozart's *Quartet in A*, K. 464, to a long interpolation, as in Beethoven's *La stessa, la stessissima*, and *Waldmädchen* sets. Cycles which form parts of larger works show greater reliance upon the harmonic procedure than those which are independent; Beethoven and Brahms, the two composers who favor it most, provide many examples of the mixed technique in their chamber works.[19] The infusion of the harmonic technique into the ornamental variation is interesting not only for the increased flexibility which it imparts, but also because it foreshadows the approaching return to an outright harmonic plan in the nineteenth-century character and basso ostinato variations.

Alongside its reliance upon constant harmony the ornamental variation exhibits, paradoxically, an occasional tendency toward harmonic freedom. This is most noticeable in the variations which undergo a change of mode, and is ordinarily confined, therefore, to one or two members of a cycle. Change of mode, itself a harmonic alteration of marked expressive effect, often gives rise in turn to still other modifications, the most important of which is the change of cadential objectives. Because the themes of the period often contain transient modulations to new keys, and since the modulations might produce a forced effect if carried over literally into the opposite mode, composers frequently lead them to new goals. A common situation, observable in the second variation from Haydn's *Symphony in G*, No. 94, is that in which a major-theme modulation to the dominant becomes, in the minor mode, a modulation to the relative key (see example 80). The converse, wherein a minor-theme modulation to the relative becomes, in the major mode, a modulation to the dominant, is also encountered, but because of the comparative scarcity of minor themes in this period it appears more rarely.

Sometimes, under the impetus of the changed mode, entire phrases of the theme are displaced to a new harmonic region. Chopin, in his pianoforte variations on Mozart's *La ci darem*, boldly shifts tonic to mediant at one point (see example 74), and later replaces dominant-centered harmony with harmony built around the submediant.[20]

Aside from change of mode, with its spur to increased freedom, harmonic departure in the ornamental variation is confined to occasional reharmonizations of the melodic subject. Reharmonization is used now

Example 74. Chopin, *La ci darem la mano*, Op. 2.

and again by Schubert,[21] and Beethoven employs it convincingly in his *Quartet*, Op. 18, No. 5 (example 75). Here, after three figural treatments of the theme, variation 4 returns to the original quiet style, but with new harmony.

Example 75. Beethoven, *Andante cantabile* from *Quartet*, Op. 18, No. 5.

A departure from earlier practice is the more frequent appearance of the melodic subject in the lower voices. It will be recalled that in previous melodico-harmonic usage the melody of the theme was generally restricted to the soprano; in the ornamental variation, on the contrary, it is often assigned to the alto, tenor, or bass during one or two variations in a cycle. Since the transferred melody is often stated quite literally, with the accompanying parts presenting new forms of figuration or assuming the role of independent voice lines, the procedure suggests at times a temporary return to the ancient cantus firmus attitude. The general plan of the *Poco adagio* in Haydn's *Kaiser Quartet*, Op. 76, No. 3, wherein the literal melodic subject appears in turn in all voices, is not unlike that found in the cantus firmus variations of Cabezón, Byrd, and Scheidt; and the simultaneous linear interest exhibited by the fourth variation of Mozart's *String Trio*, K. 563, is reminiscent of the cantus firmus treatment in Bach's *Vom Himmel hoch* cycle[22] (example 76).

Example 76. Mozart, *Andante* from *String Trio*, K. 563.

On the whole, however, the practice of transferring the melodic subject is less closely allied to cantus firmus procedure than the Mozart illustration would suggest. The average ornamental variation lacks the polyphonic involvement necessary for a true resetting of the given melody, and as a result attention centers upon the melodic subject instead of being diverted to the elaboration of accompanying parts. The new concentration of interest is clearly apparent in the graceful *Poco allegretto* from Brahms' *Quartet in B Flat*, Op. 67 (example 77), where the effect of the displacement is one of added color.

Example 77. Brahms, *Poco allegretto* from *Quartet*, Op. 67.

Intravariational change, commonly called *double variation*, attains exceptional prominence in the ornamental species.[23] The refinements resulting from its use were not unknown to earlier composers, but their employment of it was by no means so general as that of composers in the late eighteenth century and in the nineteenth.

Theorists have identified two kinds of double variation. The traditional type is the modified treatment, within a single variation, of literally repeated theme divisions. Writing of this type Ebenezer Prout says,

When ... the theme for variations consists of two eight-bar sentences, each of which is repeated, it is not uncommon to meet with what may be described as

Double Variations. In these, instead of the repetitions of each half being identical, a second variation of the first half precedes the first variation of the second half.[24]

Paul Mies, in his careful study of the Mozart variations, extends this simple conception to include the modified treatment of all *similar*, though not necessarily identical, divisions of the theme:

Diese Spiegelung tritt noch in anderer Weise auf: als Innen- oder Doppelvariierung. Unter diesem gelegentlich schon in der Literatur auftretenden aber nicht einheitlichen Begriff verstehe ich die verschiedene Variierung ursprünglich gleicher Teile des Themas innerhalb einer einzelnen Variation. Das betrifft vor allem die beiden Vorderglieder der Liedtypen, die Sequenzen und Wiederholungen der Fortspinnungstypen, Anfangs- und Endglied der dreiteiligen Liedformen.[25]

Trans.: This mirroring appears in still another way: as inner or double variation. By this concept, which is occasionally encountered in the literature of the variation, but not in a uniform way, I understand the contrasted varying, within a single variation, of parts of the theme originally corresponding. This affects, above all, the two opening phrases of the song types [*i.e.*, forms which have a symmetrical phrase design], the sequences and repetitions of the continuation types [*i.e.*, forms which show a progressive development], and the beginning and ending members of the three-part song forms.

It is plain that whereas the traditional view would limit the application of double variation to literally repeated "parts" in a theme, the newer conception would admit of its being applied, as well, to parallel phrases, balancing sections of single phrases and the corresponding beginning and ending of three-part themes. This enlarged view is much the more suggestive, and since it is especially helpful in explaining the construction of many ornamental variations it has been adopted for this study.

Several of the ways used to secure double variation in the ornamental cycles date from the renaissance and baroque. One of these is the transfer of figuration between soprano and bass;[26] another is the alternation of the literal melodic subject with its figured form.[27] The most important of the early procedures retained in the ornamental variation, however, is the transfer of the melodic subject to a new voice. A derivative of cantus firmus practice, and already observed in the Scheidt variations (see page 36), this method is generally applied to literally repeated "parts" of the theme. Its most impressive manifestations are those which involve an inversion of parts through double counterpoint, such as the third variation from Mozart's *String Trio*, K. 563, and the carefully wrought minor variation from Beethoven's *Sonata for Violin and Piano*, Op. 30, No. 1 (shown in example 78).

Example 78. Beethoven, *Allegretto* from *Sonata for Violin and Piano*, Op. 30, No. 1.

Among those double variation procedures which, instead of being handed down from the earlier period, originated within the ornamental variation itself, is the simple one of register change. Mozart applies it charmingly to modify parallel phrases in his *Sonata for Violin and Piano*, K. 379 (example 79). Beethoven, too, was aware of this means and often used it to advantage.[28]

Example 79. Mozart, *Andantino cantabile* from *Sonata for Violin and Piano*, K. 379.

Dynamic change, another type of double variation indigenous to the ornamental species, is often combined with other modifications, such as new figuration, or new counterpoint. Like the device of register change, it is usually applied to parallel phrases or to balancing sections of a single phrase. A striking example of dynamic change combined with altered harmony is the second variation of Haydn's *Symphony in G*, No. 94 (example 80). Many similar dynamic contrasts occur in Mozart,

Example 80. Haydn, *Andante* from *Symphony* in G, No. 94.

notably in the variation movements of his *Piano Sonata in A*, K. 331, and *String Quartet in A*, K. 464.

The manifold occurrence of double variation within the ornamental cycle indicates that composers were impelled by the general simplicity of the texture to work for unusual refinement and plasticity of structure. Unsatisfied with the practice of initiating changes only at the beginnings of the separate variations, the eighteenth- and nineteenth-century writers filled their sets with dozens of smaller modifications. In so doing they gave expression to a desire fairly common to variation composers of all periods, the desire to create flexibility and variety within each separate member of a cycle.

In two respects the ornamental variation anticipates the nineteenth-century character variation: through the use of character change and through the use of motival development. Character change appears only in an incidental way. Hermann Abert, writing of the Mozart variations, says that the normal principle involved is that of theme intensification rather than character change.[29] With equal truth he might have declared this principle to dominate the entire category of the ornamental variation. Nevertheless, by virtue of its set minor, *adagio*, and *allegro* variations, this species shows the nearest approach to a systematic use of character change prior to the character variation per se. Occasional dance styles—variations titled *minuet, mazurka, siciliana,* and *marcia*—add to the effect of such change, and sometimes variations wholly lacking in conventional superscriptions, such as the third variation of Schubert's *Death and the Maiden Quartet* (example 81), show character change unmistakably.[30]

Example 81. Schubert, *Andante con moto* from *Quartet* in D minor.

The development of theme motives takes place in an equally casual way, being confined like character change to random variations in a cycle. It appears with distinctness as early as Haydn, who, in the *Adagio* from the *Quartet in B Flat*, Op. 55, No. 3, begins the second variation with an imitative treatment of a motive taken literally from the head of the theme. A century later Brahms employs a somewhat freer type of motival development in his *Clarinet Quintet*, Op. 115 (example 82).

The ornamental variation has suffered both by comparison with the more complex types of the baroque and romantic periods, and by reason of its occasional superficiality. Its technical procedures are undeniably

Example 82. Brahms, *Con moto* from *Clarinet Quintet*, Op. 115.

restrictive, and its elaboration of the theme lacking in surprises. Because of its simple plan it is most at home within a larger work, where its homogeneity is an asset rather than a drawback. Essentially it must charm by its manner rather than by its content, yet to regard all ornamental variations as light or superficial would be erroneous. In the realm of multi-movement works, especially those of chamber music, the better ornamental variations occupy a position both of dignity and interest.

CHAPTER V

The Structural Techniques under the Influence of Changing Styles

(*Continued*)

IN CONTRAST with the ordered uniformity of variation writing in the latter half of the eighteenth century, the nineteenth-century variation displayed diverse and often conflicting tendencies. Whereas the general movement was toward the greater freedom of expression and laxity of formal restrictions associated with nineteenth-century musical romanticism, some composers exhibited, in opposition to this innovatory tendency, a proclivity for classical restraint; the result was a century of sharply contrasting types and techniques.

The change from the objectivity of the eighteenth century to the personalized expression of the nineteenth found immediate reflection in the idiom of variation writing. In contrast to the thinness and figural simplicity of the Haydn-Mozart style, the texture of variations now became thicker and more massive, and patterns of figuration more vigorous and individual. Toward the end of the century the harmonic scheme of the variation became more complex, with the chromatic element increasingly conspicuous, and about the same time a programmatic tendency began to appear.

The two types resulting most definitely from the new style were the character variation and the free variation, both of which exhibit marked divergence from the expression or character of the theme. Of these the free variation is the more typically romantic since, bearing little relation to the comparatively strict types of the past, it casts aside the structural restraints of the theme and indulges in an unfettered development of the given material. In contrast, the more conservative character variation is built on the old harmonic technique, whose return to prominence in the nineteenth century is mainly attributable to this type. Besides the establishment of these prevailingly romantic types, the century saw the revival of the basso ostinato variation, virtually unused since the time of J. S. Bach. The recurrence of this species, with its rigorous formal demands, strongly evidences a classical tendency; but just as the character variation is not wholly romantic, so the nineteenth-century basso ostinato variation is not completely classic, for it reveals at times extensive alterations in the expression of the theme. Like its baroque ancestor, and in common with the character variation, it stems from a harmonic treatment of the subject. The fourth type to be used was the ornamental variation; built upon the melodico-harmonic pattern and prevailingly classic in design, it was a carry-over from the eighteenth century.

The events which place the nineteenth-century technical procedures apart from those of the eighteenth are, then, the conspicuous return of the harmonic principle, as seen in the character variation and the basso ostinato variation, and the rise of a method hitherto seldom used—the free technique—in connection with the free variation. The resurgence of the harmonic treatment, of particular interest because it marks a further stage in the long history of the structural techniques, can be traced first in the character variation.

This type is a direct outgrowth of the eighteenth-century ornamental species, from which it is distinguished by its greater length and complexity, its lack of stereotyped plan, and above all, by its manner of setting off the component variations from the theme and from each other through sharp contrasts in expression.[1] Visible as early as 1790 in Beethoven's *24 Variations on Viene Amore by V. Righini*,[2] the character variation flourished chiefly in the first three-quarters of the nineteenth century, attracting the interest of such composers as Robert Schumann (1810–1856), Felix Mendelssohn-Bartholdy (1809–1847), Johannes Brahms (1833–1897), Camille St. Saëns (1835–1921), and Edvard Grieg (1843–1907), in addition to Ludwig van Beethoven (1770–1827) himself. During the closing years of the century it was superseded in great part by the free variation, yet despite the encroachment of the newer type it persisted well after 1900, numbering among its last prominent manifestations Reger's *Variations and Fugue on a Theme by Mozart* and *Variations and Fugue on a Theme by Telemann*, written at the beginning of the First World War.[3]

Among the composers named above, three were preëminent for the quality of their character variations: Beethoven, Schumann, and Brahms. At a time when the free variation was in the air, the steady preference of these men for the structural technique is noteworthy, for although it is true that all three, and especially Beethoven and Schumann, made incidental use of the free technique, none of them can be credited with writing an outright free variation.[4] The more outstanding examples of character variations include, from Beethoven, the variations in the *Eroica Symphony*, Op. 55, the *Adagio molto* from the *Piano Sonata*, Op. 111, the variation movements in the *String Quartets*, Op. 127 and 131, and the *33 Variations on a Waltz by Diabelli*, Op. 120; from Schumann, the *Etudes symphoniques*, Op. 13; and from Brahms, the *Variations on a Theme by Handel*, Op. 24, and *Variations on a Theme by Haydn*, Op. 56a. The most celebrated of these pieces is unquestionably Beethoven's *Diabelli* cycle, a work which has repeatedly evoked the highest praise. Hugo Leichtentritt calls it the greatest masterpiece of the character variation;[5] Hans von Bülow says that it constitutes a microcosm of Beethoven's genius;[6] and Donald Francis Tovey ranks it alongside the *Goldberg Variations* of Bach.[7] All the compositions named, however, are significant works, so that if at times we may wish the literature of the type were larger, we can have no reason to complain of its quality.

The rise of the character variation was attended by the renewed importance of the keyboard as a medium for variation performance. In the latter eighteenth century the finest variations had been those incorporated into cyclical works for ensemble groupings, and those for clavier had, as a class, been trivial and shallow in comparison. In the nineteenth century the incorporated ensemble pieces, while still of high quality, lack the sweep and power of the independent cycles for piano solo. Because of keyboard works like Beethoven's *Diabelli* set, Schumann's *Etudes symphoniques*, and Brahms' *Handel Variations*, the piano can justly claim to be the most important medium of the character variation.[8]

The general plan of the character variation is one of comparative flexibility. The changes undergone by the theme, being more vivid than those found in earlier types, have the effect of cutting up the cycle into sharply contrasting segments. Sometimes a set will exhibit a continual flux from beginning to end, each variation being set off from those which surround it; Schumann's *Etudes symphoniques* exemplifies this arrangement.[9] Again, the plan may be that of single variations alternating with variation groups, as in Beethoven's *Diabelli* set,[10] or it may consist entirely of opposing groups, as in Brahms' *Variations on an Original Theme*, Op. 21, No. 1.[11] Obviously, therefore, the ordering of the constituent variations is not bound to a formula as it is in the ornamental variation but is determined entirely by the fancy of the composer. A further deviation is that strong changes are not necessarily reserved until late in the cycle, as are the minor and *adagio* variations of the ornamental type. On the contrary, the initial variation sometimes contrasts forcefully with the theme. The new procedure emerges conspicuously in Beethoven's *Diabelli* cycle, where the waltz subject is followed immediately by a strongly contrasting *Marcia;* also in Brahms' *Variations on a Hungarian Song*, Op. 21, No. 2, where a major theme is followed at once by a group of six variations in minor. Still another innovation is the emphasis given to the concluding section. Not only are coda developments of greater length than those of the ornamental variations but several important works make use of intricate, independent finales. Schumann's *Etudes symphoniques* concludes with an ample, rondo-like *allegro;* Brahms' *Haydn* set ends with a basso ostinato section, a type of conclusion entirely new to the variation form. The plan of closing with a fugue, seen first in Bach's *Passacaglia and Fugue in C Minor*, reappears in the nineteenth century with Beethoven's *Fifteen Variations with Fugue*, Op. 35, and thereafter can be found in works by Schumann, Brahms, and Reger.[12]

Despite these pronounced differences from the ornamental species, the character variation retains many characteristics of the earlier type. The correspondence is greatest in those variations which constitute movements of larger works, since there the length of the cycle is moderate[13] and the use of character change limited;[14] but throughout the character variation generally the sparing employment of key change,[15] the appearance of double variation,[16] and the occasional intrusion of melodico-harmonic practice[17] all point to an intimate relationship between the two types.

There is evidence that composers of this period were more conscious than their predecessors of the need for selecting good themes. Schumann repeatedly advocated using only subjects which possessed musical worth, and cautioned against those which, because of their complexity, were already too variation-like. As Werner Schwarz says, in his study of the Schumann variations:

Bei Besprechungen von Variationswerken bringt er seine Einstellung zur Variationsform als solcher klar zum Ausdruck. Bezeichnend für seine ganze Auffassung ist schon, was er von einem zu variierenden Thema verlangt: „Gegen Themas war ich von jeher sehr streng, weil sich der ganze Fortbau darauf gründet". . . . Oder: „Schon an der Wahl des Themas erkennt man seinen Mann. Je mehr Erinnerungen sich an dieses knüpfen, je beziehungsvoller, tiefsinniger werden die Gedanken darüber ausfallen. . . . Themas, die Nachahmungen zulassen, eignen sich bekanntlich am besten zum Variieren.". . . Er beklagt sich über Themen, die „weder poetisch noch sonst was seien, aber auch formell nichts taugten.". . . Gegen das Material des Themas, das ihm Hauptmann von Fricken mit Variationen darüber geschickt hat, wendet er ein, dass es „schon zu Variationsmässig" sei; er wünscht es „in einer einfacheren, in der Ur-Gestalt," ändert es dementsprechend um und komponiert dann seine symphonischen Etüden darüber.[18]

Trans.: In discussions of variation works he [Schumann] expresses clearly his attitude toward the variation form as such. Characteristic of his whole conception are his demands with respect to a variation theme: "Toward themes I have always been very strict, since the entire structure which follows depends on them." . . . Or, "One can judge a composer by his choice of theme alone. The more reminiscences that are connected with it, the more relevant and profound will the thoughts concerning it turn out to be. . . . Themes which permit of imitations lend themselves most readily to variation, as is well known." . . . He complains of themes which "are neither poetic nor anything else, and which are even worthless from a structural standpoint." . . . Regard-

ing the material of the theme which Hauptmann von Fricken sent him, along
with variations on it, he raises the objection that it is "already too variation-
like"; he wishes it in a simpler form, in the basic one, changes it accordingly
and then composes his *Symphonic Etudes* on it.

Similar counsel occurs in the mid-nineteenth-century treatise, *Die
Lehre von der musikalischen Komposition* by Adolph Bernhard Marx,
the author emphasizing that the musical content of a theme, and not
its current popularity, should govern its acceptance.

Das Thema muss also der Bearbeitung werth sein. Wir setzen hinzu, dass das
Interesse in dem musikalischen Inhalte des Thema's, nicht etwa in äusserlichen
Beziehungen desselben liegen muss. Irgend ein Satz—ein Tanz, Lied, Marsch
u.s.w. kann für uns zufälliges äusserliches Interesse haben; wir können die
Gattung oder den Komponisten lieben, ein Lied kann uns um des Textes willen,
als volksthümlicher oder patriotischer Ausdruck, um der Erinnerung an früher
Erlebtes willen lieb sein. Dass Alles hat sein Recht, aber nur ein äusserliches;
es kann zu Wiederholungen reizen, nicht aber eben so sicher zu künstlerischer
Bearbeitung wecken. Namentlich werden Komponisten sehr oft durch die
Beliebtheit eines Liedes oder Opernsatzes irregeleitet; ja es ist eine Zeit lang
förmlich Mode und Metier gewesen, jede eben beliebt gewordne Oper in allen
einzelnen nur irgend loszureissenden Stücken variationenhaft zu zerarbeiten,
bloss in Spekulation auf die Gunst des Hauptwerks, ohne Rücksicht auf innere
Angemessenheit der einzelnen Aufgabe. Dergleichen lässt denn freilich kein
künstlerisches Gelingen hoffen, sondern gereicht nur zur Profanation des
Hauptwerks, das man zerreisst und stückweis' abnutzt. Wer selber hofft und
strebt, jemals ein würdig Kunstwerk hinzustellen, sollte sich weder durch Un-
bedacht noch äussern Vortheil zu so üblem Dienst gegen andre Künstler und
gegen das Publikum verleiten lassen.[19]

Trans.: The theme must therefore be worthy of treatment. We add to this that
the interest must inhere in the musical content of a theme, not, shall we say, in
its external relationships. Any piece at all—a dance, song, march, or the like—
can have for us a chance external interest; we may like the type or the composer; we may like a song for the sake of a text, as a popular or patriotic expression, or for the sake of a remembrance of earlier experiences. All this has
its place, but only in an external way; it can stimulate repetitions but cannot
as certainly call forth artistic treatment. Especially are composers very often
led astray by the popularity of a song or an operatic piece; for a time it was the
actual fashion and practice to make variations on all the individual pieces
which could be torn loose from an opera just risen to popularity, simply trading
upon the good will of the parent work without regard for the inner suitability
of the separate assignment. Such treatment can, of course, hope for no artistic
success; instead, it only contributes to the profanation of the opera as a whole,
which is dismembered and used up piecemeal. Whoever hopes and strives at
any time to set down a worthy work of art must not permit himself to be mis-
led, either through thoughtlessness or external advantage, into such an evil
service toward other artists and toward the public.

That many nineteenth-century composers held a point of view akin to that of Schumann and Marx is suggested by the relative absence, within the character variation, of dull or trivial subjects.

In accordance with the new attitude, composers tended increasingly to write their own themes.[20] Beethoven, in particular, favored the original theme, his *Piano Variations*, Op. 34 and Op. 35, the variation movements in the *Piano Sonatas*, Op. 109 and Op. 111, and those in the *Quartets*, Op. 74, Op. 127, and Op. 131 all stemming from this source. It is significant that in their search for productive themes composers rejected as unsuitable two sources hitherto widely popular. Neither the secular song, in use within the variation for almost three hundred years, nor the operatic aria, so conspicuous in the late eighteenth century, found any important place in the character variation. In their stead came excerpts from instrumental works such as suites and sonatas, together with instrumentally conceived subjects furnished by members of the composer's own circle. Borrowed themes of this kind serve as the foundation for such compelling works as Schumann's *Etudes symphoniques* and the *Handel* and *Haydn* series of Brahms. Beethoven's *Diabelli Variations* is also written on a borrowed subject though, contrary to the rule, the theme is trite; Beethoven, in his willingness to use such material, here stands apart from other composers of character variations.[21]

The technique by which these themes are developed has its foundations in the ancient harmonic procedure, made so familiar by the English virginalists and seventeenth-century Italians and Germans in their song variations and basso ostinato compositions. After lying dormant from the time of J. S. Bach, save for incidental use in the ornamental variation, the harmonic treatment returns in the nineteenth century in altered guise, for as used in the character variation it is more heterogeneous than it was in the earlier types. Often it contains an incidental admixture of the melodico-harmonic treatment, probably as a carry-over from the eighteenth-century pieces. At other times it anticipates the free cycles through its incorporation of variations departing widely from the harmony and structure of the theme.

The gradual reappearance of the harmonic technique can be plainly traced in the character variations of Beethoven. His earliest examples, the *Righini* set and the *Six Variations*, Op. 34, follow the melodico-harmonic pattern of the ornamental species. In the *Fifteen Variations with Fugue*, Op. 35, the harmonic scheme shows itself conspicuously, but in conjunction with the melodico-harmonic; in the last movement of the *Eroica Symphony*, Op. 55, the free treatment is introduced alongside the other two. The harmonic plan finally becomes predominant in the late-period works: the *Andante* from the *Sonata in E*, Op. 109; the *Diabelli Variations*, Op. 120; the *Adagio* from the *Quartet in E Flat*, Op.

127; and the *Andante* from the *Quartet in C-Sharp Minor*, Op. 131. Here the admixtures of melodico-harmonic and free techniques, when present, are wholly subordinate to the general harmonic design.

Practically all succeeding composers follow the plan established in the late-period works of Beethoven. A few, it is true, fall back upon the prevailingly melodico-harmonic procedure of his early work. Mendelssohn, in the *Variations sérieuses*, Op. 54, and Saint Saëns, in the *Variations for Two Pianos on a Theme by Beethoven*, Op. 35, follow the simpler scheme, but they are exceptional. The character variations of Schumann, Brahms, Grieg, and Reger, all stem from the late Beethoven procedures. Some, like Schumann's *Abegg Variations*, Op. 1, and *Symphonic Etudes*, Op. 13; Brahms' *Schumann Variations*, Op. 9; and Grieg's *Ballade*, Op. 24, follow the lead of Beethoven's Op. 127 by incorporating in an incidental way the free technique. Others follow the more conservative pattern of Beethoven's Op. 109, 120, and 131, in which free influence is completely renounced and the technique is either totally harmonic or predominantly harmonic with melodico-harmonic infusions. Included in this group are Schumann's *Impromptus on a Theme by Clara Wieck*, Op. 5; Brahms' *Variations on an Original Theme*, Op. 21, No. 1, *Variations on a Theme by Handel*, Op. 24, *Poco adagio* from the *String Sextet in G*, Op. 36, *Variations on a Theme by Haydn*, Op. 56a, and *Andante* from the *Piano Trio in C*, Op. 87; and Reger's *Mozart Variations*, Op. 132, and *Telemann Variations*, Op. 134.

An important aspect of the character variation is what German theorists call *thematische Arbeit*, that is, the development of motives derived from the theme.[22] Hugo Leichtentritt gives a clear idea of the process involved in his analysis of the *Diabelli Variations*, showing how in each variation Beethoven takes a new motive, derived from some characteristic of the theme, and leads it through the given harmonies:

Für jede Variation wird ein ganz neues Motiv erfunden, und dieses Motiv wird auf die wesentlichen Harmonien des Themas hindurchgeführt.... Die Motive der einzelnen Variationen haben zum grössten Teil kenntliche Beziehungen zum Thema. Irgendeinen charakteristischen Punkt des Themas wählt Beethoven für seine Variation aus und führt ihn in der Variation ausführlicher durch, entwickelt die Variation aus einem Keime im Thema.... Der Beginn des Themas bietet eine Anzahl charakteristischer Punkte.... Die Vorschlagsfigur [a] benutzt Beethoven in Variation 9 ... 11 ... 27 ... 31.... Mit dem Vorschlag verwandt ist der Triller, auf den Beethoven mehrere Stücke basiert, wie Variation 6 ... 12 (Langsamer Triller) ... 21.... Auf dieser Tonwiderholung [b] beruhen ausserdem Variation 2 ... 10 ... 25 ... 32 ... 33.... Aus den ersten fünf Noten des Themas, zumal die letzte Auftaktnote und den Quartensprung im zweiten Takt betonend: [c] gewinnt Beethoven das Motiv für Variation 1.... Der absteigende Quartenschritt wird wichtig in Variation

5 . . . 15 . . . 17 . . . 20 . . . 22 . . . 24. . . . Diese Beispiele mögen genügen, um zu zeigen, welche Fülle unterschiedlicher Motive ein Meister aus einem unscheinbaren Thema zu schöpfen versteht.[23]

Trans.: For each variation an entirely new motive is invented, and this motive is carried out with attention to the essential harmonies of the theme. . . . The motives of the individual variations have, for the most part, recognizable relationships with the theme. Beethoven chooses some characteristic aspect of the theme for his variation, and, in the variation, develops it more completely; he develops the variation out of a germ idea from the theme. . . . The beginning of the theme offers a number of characteristic points. . . . Beethoven uses the grace-note figure [a] in variation 9 . . . 11 . . . 27 . . . 31 . . . Related to the grace note is the trill, upon which Beethoven bases several pieces, such as variation 6 . . . 12 (slow trill) . . . 21. . . . Upon this tone repetition [b] are founded, in addition, variation 2 . . . 10 . . . 25 . . . 32 . . . 33. . . . Beethoven obtains the motive for variation 1 from the first five notes of the theme, particularly by emphasizing the last upbeat note and the leap of the fourth in the second measure. [c] The descending-fourth leap becomes important in variations 5 . . . 15 . . . 17 . . . 20 . . . 22 . . . 24. . . . These examples may suffice to show what a wealth of diverse motives a master composer is able to draw out of an insignificant looking theme.

Implicit in Leichtentritt's description is the fact that the motives spring from the beginning, or head, of the theme; and further, that they generally constitute a modified form of some easily recognized feature of it.

Leichtentritt's definition of the conditions under which motival development operates is substantiated by other theorists. Otto Klauwell, again referring to Beethoven's *Diabelli Variations*, describes the procedure as a metamorphosis achieved through the rhythmical transformation of the beginning notes of the theme.[24] Werner Schwarz, speaking of Schumann's method, calls it an improvisation upon a definite figure, rhythm, or characteristic harmonic succession from the theme.[25] Victor Luithlen points out that motival treatment constitutes an important element in the Brahms variations, and says that the motives used are at times clearly related to the theme, at others only faintly so.[26]

A study of representative scores reveals the greatest diversity in the motives employed. Some consist of but two or three tones, others extend to several measures; some are quiet in rhythm, others active; some cover a narrow range, others a wide one. The manner in which the motives are derived from the theme is of the highest significance, and again shows divergent procedures. In general, the method of Beethoven is to use short motives taken over from the theme with relatively little change. Schumann and Brahms, on the other hand, prefer to use fairly long motives whose relationship to the theme is often subtle and complex.

Among the more obvious modifications applied to the theme material are embellishment, simplification, and inversion. By far the most common of these is embellishment, a process which explains the construction of Beethoven's shorter motive forms, such as the first two given in example 83. Occasionally, as in the last two quotations from the same

Example 83. *a*, Beethoven, *Righini Variations*; *b*, Beethoven, Op. 127, *Adagio*; *c*, Schumann, Op. 13; *d*, Beethoven, Op. 109, *Andante*.

example, embellishment results in longer motives; the excerpt from Beethoven's Op. 109 is especially instructive in showing the degree of elaboration sometimes attained by this means. In all quotations the relationship between motive and theme is clear and definite. It may be noted that the motive of the *Righini Variations* derives, exceptionally, from the bass of the theme rather than from the soprano melody.

Simplification and inversion of the theme material, although more rare, are sometimes present, especially in the variations of Brahms. Simplification, in the sense used here, consists in divesting the theme of its figuration, as illustrated in Brahms' *Handel Variations* (example 84).

Example 84. Brahms, Op. 24.

Inversion, properly speaking, is usually not a means of constructing the motive but, rather, a way of manipulating it. Nevertheless, in some variations the inverted form of the motive is used so consistently as to compel our acceptance of the inversion as the norm. A case in point is Brahms' *Variations on a Hungarian Song*, Op. 21, No. 2, variation 3 (example 85, *a*), where a free inversion of the opening notes of the theme

Example 85. *a*, Brahms, Op. 21, No. 2; *b*, Reger, Op. 134; *c*, Schumann, Op. 13.

becomes securely established in the first half of the variation; and a somewhat similar usage occurs in Reger's *Telemann Variations*, Op. 134, variation seventeen (example 85, *b*). Still more convincing is the first variation of Schumann's *Etudes symphoniques* (example 85, *c*), where a motive resulting from the simultaneous inversion and embellishment of the head of the theme—and deviating widely, therefore, from the theme—is used throughout in the inverted position.

Opposed to these generally simple alterations stand several which are more complex; of these the most important are reduction and expansion. Reduction, like embellishment, is a frequent means of creating motive forms. Now and again the procedure is one of simple diminution, as in the following Brahms quotations (examples 86, *a*, *b*). but as a rule

Example 86. *a*, Brahms, Op. 21, No. 1; *b*, Brahms, Op. 24; *c*, Fauré, Op. 73 ; *d*, Schumann, Op. 41, No. 3, *Assai agitato; e*, Beethoven, Op. 127, *Adagio*.

the reduction is carried out in a much freer manner, similar to that of the excerpts from Fauré, Schumann, and Beethoven (examples 86, *c, d, e*). In these motives the rhythm of the theme is completely ignored, and individual tones of the theme are occasionally repeated or suppressed. It is plain that such changes are more radical than any single alteration thus far discussed.

The changes brought about by expansion are even more complicated. Generally they involve the introduction of some new material, as well as the alteration of the old. Often there is a spinning out of the chosen fragment, as in the sixth variation of Beethoven's *Diabelli Variations* (example 87, *a*). Again, the original subject matter may be freely re-

Example 87. *a*, Beethoven, Op. 120; *b*, Brahms, Op. 24; *c, ibid.*

arranged and extended, as in the intricately fashioned motives from Brahms' *Handel Variations* quoted in example 87, *b, c*.

A final alteration belonging to the category of complex changes is change of meter. Less common than reduction and expansion, its transforming effect is equally impressive (example 88).

Example 88. *a*, Beethoven, Op. 120; *b, ibid.; c*, Beethoven, Op. 109, *Andante.*

The foregoing catalog of changes is comprehensive enough to explain the derivation of most motive forms. There are, of course, occasional motives so free in their construction as to bear little recognizable connection with the theme. These, in one way, are among the most interesting of all, since in spite of the fact that they defy ready analysis, the

aura of the theme often surrounds them. That this is so may indicate
that the relationship we have difficulty in perceiving was plain to the
composer and that these motives, like the rest, actually spring from the
theme. Schumann's *Etudes symphoniques* is particularly rich in motives
of this kind. The three shown in example 89 appear at first glance to be

Example 89. Schumann, Op. 13.

markedly different from the head of the theme, yet reveal upon closer
examination that each may have originated in the basic triad form
which initiates the subject.[27]

The many motives thus far described have one element in common.
Whether closely connected with the theme or only distantly related to
it, they exhibit almost without exception a change in the original theme
rhythm. To use Otto Klauwell's description, they are rhythmical transformations (*rhythmische Umbildungen*) of a portion of the theme. This
fact establishes a striking difference between motival development as
used in the character variation and that employed in other instrumental
forms. The most obvious comparison is with the nineteenth-century
sonata and symphony, especially those movements containing formal
development sections. Here we find that the developmental procedure,
unlike that of the character variation, is marked by a close adherence to
the rhythmic shape of the theme motives. In the first movement of
Beethoven's *Pastorale Symphony*, for example, most of the development
is built upon a motive taken literally from the second bar of the principal theme. Much the same situation can be found in the fugues of
Bach, where the episodic developments usually maintain the rhythmic
integrity of the chosen theme fragments. It would appear that the
rhythmic transformations which distinguish the motives of the character variation are unique in eighteenth- and nineteenth-century absolute
music and that their nearest parallel is to be found in the leitmotif
transformations of Richard Wagner's music dramas.

The peculiarity of motival development within the character variation is, then, the way in which it makes over the material of the theme.

This reshaping of theme fragments, representing as it does a kind of variation art in miniature, sets apart the motival development of the character variation far more than the manipulation of the motives once they are formed, for the manipulation itself conforms in the main to that found in the sonata and fugue. One important though obvious difference must be mentioned, namely, that in the variation the development is strictly conditioned by the plan of parts and phrases existing in the theme, whereas in the other forms the development is essentially free. The controlled freedom of the *Adagio* from Beethoven's pianoforte *Sonata*, Op. 111 (example 90) illustrates this difference clearly.

Example 90. Beethoven, *Arietta* from *Piano Sonata*, Op. 111.

In spite of the prevalence of motival development within the character variation, most sets fall back upon figural treatments from time to time. The line between these two procedures is extraordinarily hard to draw, for there are many border-line techniques. The extreme examples, however, are clear, and show unmistakably the existence of two opposing methods. A comparison of the tenth variation of Mendelssohn's *Variations sérieuses* with the thirteenth indicates at once the reality of the distinction; whereas the one develops a motive from the head of the theme, the other is entirely decorative (example 91). The amount of purely figural decoration in the character variation is surprisingly large and establishes plainly the close relationship between this type and those which preceded it.

Equal in importance to motival development as a distinguishing feature of the character variation is the device to which the type owes its name: change of character or expression. This kind of change appeared in the variation form long before the nineteenth century, but at no former period was it employed with consistency. In the renaissance and baroque eras, wide departures from the expression of the theme were entirely sporadic and incidental, despite occasional works which, like Poglietti's *Aria allemagna* and the *Goldberg Variations* of Bach, strikingly forecast the nineteenth-century attitude. Again in the Viennese

Example 91. Mendelssohn, *Variations sérieuses*, Op. 54.

classic period, the dominating idea was mood continuity rather than character change, notwithstanding the pronounced departures which were occasioned in the ornamental variation by its minor, *adagio*, and concluding *allegro* members.[28] In the nineteenth century, on the contrary, character change attained the position of a dominating principle and, far from being confined to the type which bears its name, it appeared with equal conspicuousness in the free variation and even influenced to some degree the nineteenth century basso ostinato pieces. It is therefore of importance to inquire into the nature of this change and try to determine the ways in which it was produced.

In its broadest sense the problem ot character change is infinitely complex, for it amounts to nothing less than the search for the underlying causes of style changes in general. The differences between the motet and the madrigal, or between the *adagio* and *scherzo* of the symphony, or between the style of Hindemith and that of Bartók—all these are questions which a thoroughgoing study of character change might reasonably be expected to answer. Although nothing so exhaustive can be attempted here, it is quite possible to suggest the main causes of character change within the variation form itself.

We must bear in mind that the *expression* of the variation theme is different from theme attributes such as melody, harmony, and rhythm,

even though it is definitely related to them. Proof of the difference lies
in the fact that whereas we may change the harmony of a theme while
preserving its melody, or alter the figuration while preserving its harmony, we can change none of these elements without modifying to
some degree its expression. The expression, or character of a theme is
actually the resultant of the theme's more tangible qualities: its melody,
harmony, rhythm, and so on. From this it follows that some degree of
character change must be present in all variations, regardless of their
particular type or period. The reason we are not always conscious of the
change prior to the nineteenth century is that the theme modifications
which contribute to it are generally slight, and often act singly rather
than in combination. Character change, in other words, has a quantita-
tive aspect, for it is obvious that a wide modification of an element—
rhythm, let us say—has greater effect upon the expression of the theme
than a narrow one; and equally obvious that the modification of a single
element, such as rhythm, is less potent than the modification of several,
such as rhythm, harmony, and texture.

In whatever period character change has appeared in the variation
it seems to have been the result primarily of three factors: change of
rhythm, change of tempo, and change of dynamics; other factors, while
occasionally important, have been subordinate to these three. In the
renaissance and baroque periods, such character change as then existed
was chiefly the result of altered rhythm and tempo. The dancelike
variations within the cycles of Frescobaldi, Scheidt, Ebner, Reincken,
and J. S. Bach can be accounted for in this way, as can also the virtuoso
displays of Bull and others. In the eighteenth-century ornamental type
the contrasts produced by the *adagio* and concluding *allegro* variations
show the continued utilization of changed rhythm and tempo, while the
novel effect of the minor variation demonstrates that a harmonic device,
change of mode, had also become important. Dynamic change, too, received new emphasis in this type, although its application was less
conventionalized in that no stereotyped *forte* variation resulted. In the
character and free variations of the nineteenth century the same basic
changes were still at work, especially those of rhythm and dynamics.
With the growing use of the orchestra in the latter part of the century
coloristic changes added their effect, and throughout the entire romantic
period character change was heightened now and again by polyphonic
contrasts, chromaticism, and change of mode.

The transforming power of rhythm, tempo, and dynamics can be
appreciated most fully if we observe first the variations from which
these changes have, in large measure, been withheld. Lacking sharp
differentiation from the theme, such variations provide relief from their
more highly individualized neighbors in the series. A case in point is

Brahms' *Handel Variations*, where variations 11 and 12 oppose both the energetic vigor of the tenth and the somber expressiveness of the thirteenth (example 92).

Example 92. Brahms, *Variations and Fugue on a Theme by Handel*, Op. 24.

Rhythmic change, perhaps the most significant cause of changed expression, is brought about primarily through altered figuration. Diversity of rhythm and diversity of figuration, in short, are generally synonymous. It would be natural to expect, therefore, that periods of vigorous figural creation should be those in which character change should flourish most, and this is actually true. The energetic figuration of the baroque, rhythmically more vital than the placid diminution of the renaissance, helped make possible the *Goldberg Variations;* the complex motive forms of the nineteenth century, surpassing in rhythmic interest the graceful figures of the late eighteenth, opened the way to the *Diabelli Variations* and its successors. Within the history of the variation form, the baroque period and the nineteenth century show the greatest figural and rhythmic boldness; and it is more than a coincidence that the most notable examples of character change should fall within these two periods.

The transforming power of changed tempo in conjunction ·with changed rhythm appears conspicuously in the tenth variation of Grieg's *Ballade* for pianoforte, Op. 24, where the jogging thirds, off-beat accompaniment, and lively pace strongly modify the dolorous *andante* theme (example 93). Often, as here, the result is a dance style. Certain of

Example 93. Grieg, *Ballade*, Op. 24.

Beethoven's *Six Variations*, Op. 34, and *Diabelli Variations*, Op. 120, employ the superscriptions *menuetto* and *marcia;* the fifth variation of Schumann's *Impromptus*, Op. 5, has a scherzo quality; and the fourteenth variation of Brahms' *Variations on a Theme by Robert Schumann*, Op. 9, is waltzlike. At other times the union of changed tempo and rhythm leads to more tranquil moods, as in the occasional *adagio* variations, the nocturne-like eleventh étude of Schumann's *Etudes symphoniques*, and the ghostly unreality of the twentieth variation of Beethoven's *Diabelli Variations* (example 94).

Example 94. Beethoven, *33 Variations on a Waltz by A. Diabelli*, Op. 120.

Change of dynamics in conjunction with change of rhythm, seen in the dramatic eighth variation of Schumann's *Impromptus* (example 95), is an equally striking means of effecting alterations of mood. Now and again entire cycles-rely principally upon the combination of changed rhythm and dynamics for new expression, and neglect tempo change

Example 95. Schumann, *Impromptus*, Op. 5.

almost completely; this is true of Beethoven's *Righini Variations*, the *Handel Variations* of Brahms, and especially of those variations which, like the *Allegretto* from Beethoven's *Quartet*, Op. 74, form parts of multimovement works.

But, important as are the foregoing means of attaining character change, the most striking manifestations are those brought about by combinations of all three of the basic factors, augmented at times by still other alterations. The example par excellence of this tripartite union is Schumann's *Etudes symphoniques*, all members of which, save études I and II exhibit the combined action of changed rhythm, tempo, and dynamics. The brilliant tenth étude (example 96) shows this association unmistakably.

Example 96. Schumann, *Etudes Symphoniques*, Op. 13.

The remaining factors which contribute to altered expression in the nineteenth century include change of mode; the contrast between homophony and polyphony, or between diatonic and chromatic writing; change of instrumental tone color; and change of register. These factors are no less striking in their effect than the three previously discussed; their subordinate position is the result solely of their less frequent use. At times the presence of one of these subordinate factors will augment the already considerable transformation brought about by combined action of rhythm, tempo, and dynamics, as in the fuguelike variation in Beethoven's Op. 109 or the major études of Schumann's Op. 13. Again, one of these less-used factors will add its effect to that of rhythm alone, or to the rhythm-tempo or rhythm-dynamics alliance.

It is plain that there can be no one formula for character change. Not only the degree of its employment but also the manner of its production varies with different composers, and even with different works of the same composer. Essentially, however, it is the result of a complex of separate modifications, of which rhythmic change is a kind of common denominator and tempo and dynamic changes are the main accessories.

Viewed as a whole, the nineteenth-century character variation is seen to be diverse, elaborate, and vigorous, a type which embodies the most complex use of the harmonic technique to be found in any period, apart from the *Goldberg Variations* of Bach. Through its sharp contrasts and occasional virtuoso display it reflects the romanticism of its time, yet because of its continued use of the structural principle and its emphasis upon a symphonic concentration achieved through motival development, it shows definite classic qualities. Its plan of motival construction not only brought the type into agreement with the practice of post-Bach instrumental music as a whole, but gave it an organic unity superior to that of most preceding variations. The essence of the character variation is only partly its freedom of expression; even more its nature depends upon its new-found manipulation of thematic fragments.

The reintroduction of the basso ostinato variation came early in the second half of the century. Foreshadowings of its return were visible earlier: Beethoven's variations in the *Eroica Symphony* (1804) and *32 Variations in C Minor* (1806), Schumann's *Impromptus on a Theme by Clara Wieck* (1833), and Franz Liszt's *Spanish Rhapsody* (1845) all showed definite basso ostinato influence. With Liszt's *Variations on a Theme by J. S. Bach* (1866) the reappearance of the true basso ostinato variation was unmistakable, and from that time to the present it has been in fairly constant, though limited, use. The nineteenth-century type of basso ostinato variation may be said, however, to end about the time of Max Reger's *Introduction, Passacaglia, and Fugue* for organ, Op. 127, written in 1913.

These later works are more homogeneous than their seventeenth-century forerunners. Aside from an incidental use of the folia theme in Liszt's *Spanish Rhapsody*, stock basses play no part, and the designations folia, bergamask, and ground are no longer applied. That dance influence still persists, however, is evidenced by the frequency with which the chaconne-like, accented second-beat rhythm continues to appear (see last half of example 100).

Among the composers of the nineteenth-century type Reger is the most prolific, Brahms the most important. Reger, because of the Bach-like character of his figuration and the strictness with which he retains the ostinato, is essentially conservative; Brahms, in contrast, shows more progressive traits. The master work of the period is unquestionably the *Allegro energico* from Brahms' *Fourth Symphony;* but the finale from Brahms' *Haydn Variations*, Liszt's *Variations on a Theme by J. S. Bach*, and Reger's *Introduction, Passacaglia, and Fugue*, Op. 127, also deserve careful study.[29]

Unlike the baroque basso ostinato variations, most of which were independent compositions, the nineteenth-century pieces ordinarily form parts of multimovement works, or are united organically with other forms. Some of the combinations effected are without historical precedent. Brahms' Op. 98 records the first appearance of a basso ostinato movement in a symphony,[30] his Op. 56a, probably the first use of a basso ostinato construction as the finale of a character variation. The plan of Liszt's *Bach Variations* is likewise novel, and consists of a passacaglia concluding with a chorale. Reger's favorite plan of joining passacaglia with fugue can, of course, be traced back to J. S. Bach, but Reger often enlarges upon the original by adding a weighty introduction.

Although the themes used in these pieces ordinarily follow the conventional four- and eight-measure plan of the baroque subjects, they occasionally depart from this symmetrical structure. Brahms, in the finale of his *Haydn Variations*, has a five-measure theme (see example 97), and Reger, in his *Chaconne for Violin Alone*, uses one of seven

Example 97. Brahms, *Variations on a Theme by Joseph Haydn*, op. 56a.

measures. The nineteenth-century subjects are also marked by an increased chromaticism, a characteristic which suggests the influence of the baroque vocal basso ostinato. Liszt builds his *Bach Variations* upon the chromatic and expressive *Crucifixus* theme from Bach's *Mass in B Minor*. Reger's themes, although original, likewise display at times a strongly chromatic quality. The rather extreme example (98) is from his *Introduction, Passacaglia, and Fugue for Two Pianos*, Op. 96.

Example 98. Reger, *Introduction, Passacaglia, and Fugue for Two Pianos*, Op. 96.

In spite of the essentially classical nature of the basso ostinato variation, the late manifestations show unmistakably the influence of nineteenth-century musical romanticism. Brahms, especially, gives to his two basso ostinato pieces a romantic flavor, coupling dramatic intensity with quiet lyricism. The imaginative opening statements of the *Allegro energico* from his *Fourth Symphony* well illustrate the greater expressive range of the nineteenth-century treatment compared with the more restrained emotion of the baroque type; the vigorous *fortissimo* heralding of the subject gives way to a sonorous echo in the brasses and *pizzicato* strings, which in turn leads to a sustained and lyrical treatment by the woodwinds[31] (example 99). Equally striking is

Example 99. Brahms, *Allegro energico* from *Fourth Symphony*, Op. 98.

the pronounced change of expression beginning with the thirteenth recurrence of the theme, where the 3/2 augmentation results in an extended *adagio* interlude. The four statements comprising this section have the effect of delicate miniatures, variations 13 and 14 being traced by the solo woodwinds, and variations 15 and 16 exploiting the solemn tones of the *pianissimo* trombones (example 100). The emphatic char-

Example 100. Brahms, *Allegro energico* from *Fourth Symphony*, Op. 98.

acter changes revealed in the foregoing excerpts mark a new trend for the basso ostinato variation; for while certain contrasts of expression had appeared in the baroque prototype, chiefly as the result of changed mode, no such far-reaching changes had hitherto been employed.

Further romantic influence upon the nineteenth-century basso ostinato variation reveals itself in a heightened color usage. Certain of the coloristic effects in the concluding movement of Brahms' *Fourth Symphony* have already been pointed out, and although these are due in large part to the possibilities inherent in the orchestral medium, composers who wrote basso ostinato variations for solo instruments often show a similar tendency. Reger's organ *Passacaglia*, Op. 127, calls for extensive contrasts in registration, ranging dynamically from *ppp* to *fff*; his *Chaconne for Solo Violin*, Op. 117, No. 4, opposes *pizzicato* with *arco* in the fifteenth and sixteenth statements of the theme, and exploits the G string in the twenty-second. Throughout both pieces there is much chromaticism, a quality which is also apparent in Liszt's *Bach Variations*. Chromaticism had, of course, been utilized incidentally by baroque basso ostinato composers, but the chromatic usage of Liszt and Reger is much more persistent than that of the earlier writers.

A structural feature of the nineteenth-century pieces is the greater freedom accorded the subject to invade the upper voices. This is especially true of Liszt's *Bach Variations* and the *Allegro energico* from Brahms' *Fourth Symphony*. The Liszt work clearly goes beyond earlier pieces in its transference of the theme, for no less than one-fourth of the total appearances of the subject are in upper voices. If under such circumstances the name basso ostinato appears scarcely accurate, still less does it fit Brahms' *Allegro energico*, where not only is the theme given out initially in an upper voice (see example 100), a wholly un-orthodox procedure, but where well over half of the total theme state-ments occur outside of the bass. These examples, it must be granted, are extreme; yet few nineteenth-century basso ostinato pieces forego trans-ferred presentations entirely. Most of them, furthermore, contain one or more appearances of the ostinato subject in the soprano voice, a practice rarely followed by baroque composers.

Viewed as a whole, the nineteenth-century basso ostinato variation well exemplifies the underlying stylistic conflict of the period. Basically it is a classic type, whose conservative tendencies show themselves in its plan of continuous movement and broad groupings, its proclivity for the ancient chaconne rhythm, and its avoidance of extreme con-trasts. But while it thus retains the salient traits of its baroque pred-ecessor, it evidences equally definite romantic traits by reason of its increased harmonic richness, its occasional wide departures from the expression of the theme, and its greater freedom in using the ostinato outside of the bass. That it did not achieve wider prominence may be attributed more to the disinclination of late nineteenth-century com-posers to adhere to strict forms in general than to any paucity of con-structional and emotional possibilities within the type itself.

CHAPTER VI

The Emergence of the Free Technique

THE TRUE free variation dates from about 1875. At this time variations began to be written in which the free treatment, instead of being incidental, was preponderant. Among the earliest of these pieces were Anton Dvořák's *Pianoforte Variations*, Op. 36 (1876) and *Symphonic Variations*, Op. 78 (1877); P. I. Tchaikovsky's *Variations on a Rococo Theme for 'Cello and Orchestra*, Op. 33 (1878), and the variation movements in his *Piano Trio*, Op. 50 (1882), and *Third Suite for Orchestra*, Op. 55 (1884); and César Franck's *Variations symphoniques* (1885). In all but the last the influence of the character variation is plainly visible, for not only are the component variations separated by distinct cadences but the beginning members of each cycle retain the structural plan of the theme. With Franck's *Variations symphoniques*, however, virtually all structural resemblance to the character variation disappeared. In this work there are no longer any interruptions between variations; there are few easily recognized indications of where one variation ends and another begins; the plan of sections and phrases contained in the given thematic material has been abandoned, for the most part; and the ensuing elaboration is, to use H. C. Colles's words, "rhapsodic" and "generally in the nature of a free development."[1]

In the closing years of the century the continuous flow and uninhibited development which mark Franck's *Variations symphoniques* became more and more the rule. Furthermore, composers tended increasingly to write their variations for orchestra, and in keeping with the *fin de siècle* propensity for descriptive music, began supplying them with programs. Thus was evolved the programmatic orchestral variation, a type which, in its formal elasticity and descriptive intent, is almost indistinguishable from the symphonic poem. To this class belong works like Vincent d'Indy's *Istar* (1896), Richard Strauss's *Don Quixote* (1898), and Frederick Delius's *Appalachia* (1902).

The period from about the turn of the century to the beginning of the First World War saw the return of more conservative practices. Sir Edward Elgar's *Variations on an Original Theme* (1899), commonly called the *Enigma Variations*, although descriptive in character, retained the traditional *caesurae* of earlier variations; and the discontinuous plan was again followed in such works as Alexander Glazounov's *Pianoforte Variations*, Op. 72 (1901), Sergei Rachmaninov's *Variations on a Theme of Chopin* (1903), Karol Szymanowski's *Variations on a Polish Folksong* (1904), Max Reger's *Hiller Variations* (1907), and M. E.

Bossi's *Orchestral Variations* (1908). Furthermore, most of these later variations reverted to the ideals of absolute music, as did Ralph Vaughan Williams' *Fantasia on a Theme by Thomas Tallis* (1910), a continuous variation. Thus the free variation shows a complete cycle of development, in which two procedures stand opposed: the discontinuous and generally nonprogrammatic works typified by Dvořák, Elgar, and Reger, and the uninterrupted and often descriptive compositions typified by Franck and d'Indy.

The recognition of these contrasting procedures has more than an academic significance, for the presence or absence of *caesurae* has a direct bearing upon the general design. The discontinuous free variation, as may be expected, is more closely related to previous variation types than the continuous free variation.[2] It bears an unmistakable resemblance to its parent, the nineteenth-century character variation, in several ways. One of these is its economy in the use of new keys. Dvořák's lengthy *Symphonic Variations* introduces but four new keys (variations 18, 19, 25, and 26); Elgar's *Enigma Variations* only two (variations 5 and 9). The plan in Reger's *Hiller Variations* of having the tonality change from variation to variation is quite unusual, and on the whole the introduction of new keys is purely nominal. The predilection of the discontinuous free variation for coda-like finales is another resemblance to the character variation. Exceptionally these finales are fugal, as in Reger's *Hiller Variations;* more often they resemble, in their free working-out of theme fragments, the codas of nineteenth-century sonatas and symphonies. Then too, the discontinuous free variation recalls the character variation through its pronounced departures from the mood of the theme. Usually each variation contrasts forcefully with its predecessor, after the manner of Schumann's *Symphonic Etudes.* Such a juxtaposing of markedly dissimilar variations may be seen prominently in the *Tema con variazione* of Tchaikovsky's *Third Suite* (all of the specifically free variations, numbers 5 and 7–12, show pronounced character change); and even more conspicuously in Bossi's *Orchestral Variations*, where the sharp differentiation of the variations leads to set styles—scherzo, zingaresca, alla marcia, pastorale, chorale, and recitative.

The continuous free variation, on the other hand, bears little connection with previous variation types.[3] Indeed, its closest similarity is to forms outside the variation field, its loosely knit and quasi-improvisatory style approximating that of the fantasia, rhapsody, and symphonic poem. Even its name is not always an immediate clue to the composer's intention to write variations, for descriptive names like *Istar* and *Appalachia* often take precedence in the title over the designation *variations*. Because of the unsystematic nature of its thematic development, the continuous free variation can be described much less definitely than the discontinuous type. The internal organization of a descriptive piece such as d'Indy's *Istar* is, of course, controlled in some measure by the program; but the design of nondescriptive works is wholly unpredictable. In all of them, however, there is marked freedom of key and reliance upon character change.

Of the many types considered thus far the free variation shows the greatest expansiveness. One reason is that most free variations are independent works rather than constituents of larger forms, and as such are relieved from the obligation of being scaled to neighboring movements.

Example 101. Strauss, *Don Quixote*, Op. 35.

Another is the fact that each component variation is free to continue indefinitely, quite without regard to the length of the theme. As a result, a relatively small number of variations can easily produce a lengthy work. Strauss's *Don Quixote*, for example, has but ten variations, yet the time of performance is well over half an hour.

The themes of the free variation resemble, in their brevity, those of previous species. Brief two- and three-part forms still prevail; occasionally less conventional patterns are encountered. Some themes are concise unions of but two or three phrases, as in Dvořák's *Symphonic Variations*, Elgar's *Enigma Variations*, and Glazounov's *Pianoforte Variations;* on the other hand, the initial theme of Franck's *Variations symphoniques* is lengthy and structurally indefinite. The Franck work is built on two themes instead of one, and a similar dualism occurs in Strauss's *Don Quixote*. The character of the various subjects alternates between the traditional lyricism of earlier themes and a fragmentary, motival construction which here appears prominently for the first time. The newer approach is evident in the Elgar and Franck themes (see examples 103, 146, and 150), and even more in the themes of Strauss's *Don Quixote*, the texture of which is a mosaic of contrasting motives (see example 101). Most of the themes are original with the composers, but borrowed themes still persist. The use of folk songs is continued in Szymanowski's *Variations on a Polish Folk Theme* and Delius' *Appala-*

chia, the latter based on an American negro melody. In addition, themes borrowed from other composers underlie Rachmaninov's *Chopin Variations*, Reger's *Hiller Variations*, and Vaughn Williams' *Fantasia on a Theme by Thomas Tallis*. Themes in the minor mode (rare in the ornamental variation and more common in the nineteenth-century character variation) appear frequently.

In the working out of these themes two technical procedures outweigh all others: motival development and theme transformation. Motival development, described in connection with the character variation, is used here in much the same manner as in the earlier type. Most of the motives, however, spring quite freely from the theme (see example 102),

Example 102. *a*, Parry, *Symphonic Variations; b*, Rachmaninov, *Variations on a Theme by Chopin*, Op. 22; *c*, Delius, *Appalachia; d*, Glazounov, *Pianoforte Variations*, Op. 72.

and recall in this way the more extensive motive transformations of Beethoven's *Diabelli Variations* and Brahms' *Handel Variations* quoted in examples 87 and 88. Furthermore, the development of the motives is now completely uninhibited, for instead of having to follow the structural outline of the theme and of having to conform to its length and principal cadences, the course and extent of the development are, in the truest sense, free. For the first time in the history of the variation, a motival development comparable with that used in the fugue and sonata is consistently applied.

Theme transformation, the second of the two technical methods, consists in retaining the essential contour of the melodic subject but in altering radically other elements of the theme—rhythm, tempo, dynamics, and the like. It is not always easy to distinguish from motival development. In both, the connection with the theme is primarily a melodic one, with the remaining thematic elements—harmony, structure, and so forth—abandoned at will. The principal difference between the two is that whereas motival development utilizes only short fragments of the melodic subject, theme transformation applies itself to larger excerpts, sometimes even to the melodic subject in its entirety. In both methods the melodic material of the theme is drastically modified; yet, whereas the creation of motives is but the first act in a process of manipulation, the transforming of themes tends to become an end in itself. It is obvious that theme transformation, because of its more extensive contact with the melodic subject, is somewhat less flexible as a compositional device than motival development.

Unlike motival development, which is used with much consistency in the nineteenth-century character variation, theme transformation appears in earlier variations only sporadically. Foreshadowings of its use within the free variation occur in the related forms of the early dance pair and variation suite; they may also be seen in certain baroque song variations (such as Frescobaldi's *Aria detta Balletto*, quoted in example 26) and in occasional variations from the eighteenth and nineteenth centuries (such as the concluding variation of Mozart's *Je suis Lindor*, in which the duple-meter theme becomes a minuet). It is doubtful, however, if this casual prior usage had any important influence upon the theme transformations of the free variation. Instead it seems probable that the late nineteenth-century variation writers were consciously emulating the theme metamorphoses found in the symphonic poems of Berlioz and Liszt.

A clear picture of the way in which theme transformation operates within the free variation may be had from the opening of Elgar's *Enigma Variations*. The theme is a fragmentary one, beginning as in example 103. Each of the first four variations modifies this line rhyth-

Example 103. Elgar, *Variations on an Original Theme*, Op. 36.

mically (see example 104). Variation 1, while adhering to the original 4/4 meter, is syncopated and continuous. The following three change to triple meter: variation 2 is smooth-flowing, variation 3 shows a fragmentary pattern like the theme, and variation 4 is a continuous version of the original line formed by the simple expedient of removing the quarter-note rests (example 104). It will be noted that the rhythmic

Example 104. Elgar, *Variations on an Original Theme*, Op. 36.

changes are often coupled with alterations in tempo and dynamics, and that the result of the several changes is, in each variation, a melodic line which differs markedly from the original in expression.

Transformation may affect all or only a part of the melodic subject. When, as in variation 4 above, the entire subject is transformed, the structural design of the theme is necessarily followed rather closely; nevertheless variety can often be obtained by the use of expansions and extensions. Elgar here enlarges the sixteen-measure theme to thirty-two measures, the A B A′ (6 + 4 + 6) design of the theme becoming A B A′ A″ A‴ (6 + 8 + 6 + 4 + 8). Transformations which, like this one, affect the theme in its entirety, lend themselves most readily to the discontinuous type of free variation; yet occasionally they appear in the continuous type as well.

Much more common than the modification of the complete theme is the transformation of separate parts or phrases, a handling exemplified in variations 1 to 3 of the *Enigma* and shown with special clearness in variation 2. A characteristic of these partial transformations is their association with motival development, a union which results in a comparatively wide departure from the original design of the theme. In Elgar's second variation, a motive taken from the head of the theme is developed into an animated background which persists throughout (see example 105). Against this restless accompaniment is heard, in the eighteenth measure, the transformation quoted earlier (example 106).

Example 105. Elgar, *Variations on an Original Theme*, Op. 36.

Example 106. Elgar, *ibid.*

The variation concludes, as it began, with the background figuration alone, and to this degree preserves the ternary plan of the theme; it involves, nevertheless, a marked alteration of the original design, as is evident from a simple comparison:[4]

Theme	Variation 2
A (6)	Episodic prelude on motive from A (17)
B (4)	Transformation of A (26)
A (6)	Episodic postlude on motive from A (14)

As the transformed theme segments are reduced more and more in size, it becomes increasingly difficult to distinguish between transformation and motival development. A case in point is the section of d'Indy's *Istar* written in 15/8 meter, where two measures of the slow-moving theme undergo the pronounced transformation shown in example 107.

Example 107. d'Indy, *Istar*, Op. 42.

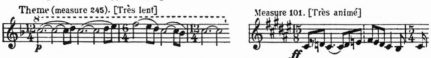

Since the altered fragment serves, in its entirety, as the basis for the development which follows, it possesses the characteristics not only of a transformed theme but of a motive as well.

Not all thematic transformations are as straightforward as those of the Elgar and d'Indy quoted in examples 104 and 107. Toward the close of Strauss's *Don Quixote* the Don's theme (given in example 101) appears in the form shown in example 108. The opening two measures

Example 108. Strauss, *Don Quixote*, Op. 35.

of this transformed melody are obviously an outgrowth of the first motive of the theme (marked *a* in example 101), but the derivation of the remainder is less clear. A transformation such as this recalls the freely contrived motives of Schumann's *Etudes symphoniques* discussed in the preceding chapter, with their challenge to the imagination. Equally far-reaching transformations may be seen in Delius's *Appalachia*, at the first entrance of the theme in minor (beginning measure 143); also in the nineteenth variation of Dvořák's *Symphonic Variations*.[5]

In both motival development and theme transformation the connection with the theme is primarily a melodic one, as has already been pointed out. A supplementary means of maintaining melodic contact with the theme consists in quoting a theme fragment intermittently, in the manner of a leitmotif. D'Indy's *Istar* is rich in this usage; in it a three-note descending motto, anticipating the first three notes of the theme, is used periodically to herald new variations or sections (see example 109).[6] A peculiarity of d'Indy's treatment is his insistence upon the same tones—G, F, and D flat— in each statement of the motto, regardless of the changing tonal context. A similar usage appears in Strauss's *Don Quixote*, where the themes and motives depicting the three chief characters—Don Quixote, Sancho Panza, and Dulcinea— recur almost literally as guides to the dramatic action.

Example 109. d'Indy, *Istar*, Op. 42.

The techniques of motival development and of theme transformation are admirably suited to the free variation, with its propensity for escaping the structural control of the theme. Doubtless it is this failure to conform to the theme *in extenso* which gives to the type its feeling of great license; yet over and above this structural divergence is the fact that one has to do here with a more eclectic method than in any previous species, since few of the techniques employed in the free variation are actually indigenous to it. Motival development in the free variation is appropriated from earlier instrumental music; theme transformation is taken over from the nineteenth-century symphonic poem. There are in the free variation, moreover, remnants of the structural procedures used in previous variation types. Separate members of a cycle may revert to the cantus firmus treatment, as in the second variation of Dvořák's *Symphonic Variations*, or may follow the equally ancient melodico-harmonic practice, as in the opening variation of Tchaikovsky's *Trio*, Op. 50. These incidental manifestations of the structural techniques are generally limited to the discontinuous free variation, where they appear early in the cycle;[7] but a notably complete representation of them occurs in Franck's *Variations symphoniques*, a work lacking *caesurae* (see Appendix, p. 150 f.).

The free variation, even more than the character variation, reflects the spirit of nineteenth-century musical romanticism, with its dramatic conflicts, its looseness of design, and its emphasis upon color and virtuosity. Foremost among the attributes of the free variation are its continuous construction and its freedom from the structural pattern of the theme. Of these qualities continuity is the less significant, for although it is important in combating what is conceded to be a drawback of variations generally, their regularly recurring perfect cadences, not all free variations are written in the continuous manner. The crux of the free type is its abandonment of the structure of the theme. This innovation gains for it two definite advantages: the avoidance of the monotony engendered by a constantly repeated structural pattern, and the opportunity to secure an untrammeled development of the theme material. While structural license is not beneficial in all its results, since the increase in flexibility is offset by the loss of the clear outlines possessed by simpler variations, it is nevertheless the characteristic to which free variations owe their pronounced individuality and their appeal to late nineteenth-century composers.

In a sense, the free variation was a historical postulate. For over three hundred years the variation form had been structurally conceived, and it was inevitable that sooner or later variations should be written in a nonstructural manner. The free variation, the first to consolidate the new technique, has for this reason an assured historical position. In the period since the death of Reger composers have occasionally reverted to structural practices, as Arnold Schönberg's *Orchestral Variations*,[8] Aaron Copland's *Piano Variations*,[9] and the basso ostinato variations of Paul Hindemith[10] indicate. Nevertheless, it seems improbable that composers of the future will renounce completely the flexibility shown to exist in the free technique by the men of the preceding generation.

CHAPTER VII

An Aesthetic of the Variation

To ATTEMPT a synthesis of the principles at work in the variation form is a hazardous task, for the many kinds of variations, by their very diversity, seem to preclude common laws. Nevertheless, this study would be incomplete without at least a preliminary search for basic formulas. As already shown, the variation theme is a complex of separate, though interdependent, musical elements; and the technique of variation consists in changing these elements, now singly, now in combination, now radically, now in moderation. While potentially there exists for each element a corresponding change, and while theoretically, therefore, any factor of the theme is as susceptible to modification as the next, actually not all of the many possible alterations are of equal importance. Generally speaking, those elements which are the most conspicuous, and hence the most easily and quickly comprehended, demand change the most insistently; conversely, those elements which are relatively inconspicuous demand little, if any, change. For, as George Santayana points out,

When . . . repeated impressions are acute, and cannot be forgotten in their endless repetition, their monotony becomes painful. The constant appeal to the same sense, the constant requirement of the same reaction, tires the system, and we long for change as for a relief. If the repeated stimulations are not very acute, we soon become unconscious of them; like the ticking of the clock, they become merely a factor in our bodily tone, a cause, as the case may be, of a diffused pleasure or unrest; but they cease to present a distinguishable object.[1]

Obviously it becomes important to find out which elements in the theme give rise to "acute impressions" in order to understand how best to avoid monotony.

For this purpose it is convenient to regard the theme complex as consisting of three main parts: the chief melody, or *melodic subject*; the supporting harmony and over-all structure, the two together constituting the *harmonico-structural frame*; and the *character-giving elements* most responsible for the expression of the theme—rhythm, tempo, dynamics, and so forth. It is this last group which calls for initial consideration.

The most strongly apprehended of any factor within the theme is its rhythm. Because the constant recurrence of a given rhythmic pattern would result in intolerable boredom, it is essential that each component variation attempt in some measure an independent rhythmical life of its own. This it achieves primarily through new figurations. Whether the figurations which introduce the new rhythms are derived from the theme motivally or take their rise independently, whether they oppose the theme sharply or present only a quiet embellishment, it is essential that they contrive to dispel the monotony which would accrue from a too-literal rhythmic recurrence. The discontinuous structure shown by most variations has doubtless facilitated the introduction of figural changes, yet the fact that continuous variations also present a diversity of figural patterns would indicate that the conferring of a rhythmical autonomy upon the separate members of a cycle is an inherent attribute of all variation writing.

But while rhythmical independence among the members of a variation series is indispensable, under no circumstances can it be maintained that a cycle must necessarily incorporate outright change of character. It is true that the individualization of separate variations often attains the status of a pronounced character change, either through figural deviations which are unusually emphatic, or through the supporting action of altered tempo and dynamics; but this is not always the case. Furthermore even in nineteenth-century romantic music, where character change flourishes most abundantly, its presence is no assurance of artistic excellence. Beethoven's *Six Variations*, Op. 34, is a less intense work, in spite of its pronounced character changes, than his earlier *Righini* or *Waldmädchen* sets which exemplify more subtle handlings of the theme material. Brahms seemed to feel the subordinate position which character change occupies, for while it forms an integral part of his variation technique, he used it with reserve; of the eight variations in his *Haydn Variations*, for example, pronounced character change is confined to the scherzo-like fifth variation, the siciliana-like seventh, and the minor eighth variation. It may be said that a composer who changes the character-giving elements does so for personal and stylistic reasons, not because of the aesthetic demands of the variation form, and that aside from change of rhythm—the invariable attribute of all variations—the alteration of these character-giving elements must be regarded as accessory and incidental.

The melodic subject is probably the most conspicuous and hence the most sensitive and critical factor in the theme complex apart from rhythm. Just as the leading tone, aptly called *la note sensible* by the French, is a sensitive factor in the harmony of common practice, not admitting of over-use in a chord which contains it, so the literal melodic subject in the variation form will not admit of over-emphasis. The means of changing the given melody are already familiar. In the melodico-harmonic variation it is figured and embellished; in the harmonic variation it is replaced by other melodies which, although containing possible motival connections with the original, are distinctly new creations; in the free variation it undergoes far-reaching transformations and developments. Only in the cantus firmus variation, with its recurrence of the relatively unchanged melodic subject, is there an apparent exception to the rule; but in reality this type of variation conforms, as do the others, to the larger principle of securing relief from the melody of the theme, inasmuch as the contrapuntal elaboration of the other voices here contends with the cantus firmus for the attention of the listener.

The least conspicuous and sensitive portion of the theme complex is unquestionably the harmonico-structural frame. In the history of the variation form this aspect of the theme was the last to undergo extensive alteration; until the advent of the free variation the structure was generally retained with little change, and (excepting in the cantus firmus variation) the harmony was also carefully preserved. The abandonment of the harmonico-structural frame in the free variation must be regarded, therefore, not as the outgrowth of inexorable aesthetic demands, but rather, like the employment of character change, as the result of the proclivities and desires of individual composers.

Within the structural techniques, therefore, the harmonico-structural frame assumes the role of a fundamental bond between theme and variations. This bond is not invariable, for, as we have seen, the cantus firmus variation was not committed to harmonic constancy; nor is the bond necessarily a literal one, for structural variations of all types and periods have displayed incidental modifications of the underlying harmony and structure. In general, themes with indefinite or irregular phraseology—plain songs, chorale melodies, and some of the secular songs of the sixteenth and seventeenth centuries—have given freer play to such modifications than themes with more definite or more regular phraseology, such as most secular songs, dance themes, and themes of instrumental origin. Even in these last, one finds alterations of detail; the separate variations, while remaining faithful to the broader harmonic and structural outlines, show no such concern for the smaller components. Thus it has been common at all periods to supplant chords in fundamental position by their inversions, or the reverse; or to deviate slightly from the harmony through the use of substitute chords and embellishments. Likewise it has occasionally been the practice to alter the balance of phrases within a part, or of measures within a phrase, or to make small extensions or contractions in a single variation.

Despite such changes of detail, the harmonico-structural frame may, by virtue of its prevalent retention, be regarded as the essential substance of the theme. Prior to the time of the free variation the great variation masters—Byrd, Frescobaldi, Bach, Beethoven, Brahms—all show a singular attachment to the given structure and (except for the cantus firmus variation) to the given harmony. With Brahms the attachment was conscious, as may be seen from a letter he wrote in 1869 to his friend Schubring:

> ... bei einem Thema zu Variationen bedeutet mir eigentlich, fast, beinahe nur der Bass etwas. Aber dieser ist mir heilig, er ist der feste Grund, auf dem ich dann meine Geschichte baue. Was ich mit der Melodie mache, ist nur Spielerei oder geistreiche—Spielerei. Ich denke mit Schrecken an:

> Variere ich die Melodie, so kann ich nicht leicht mehr als geistreich oder anmutig sein oder, zwar stimmungsvoll, einen schönen Gedanken vertiefen. Über dem gegebenen Bass erfinde ich wirklich neu, ich erfinde ihm neue Melodien, ich schaffe....²

Trans.: A theme for variations actually means to me little more than the bass. This, however, is sacrosanct; it is the firm foundation upon which I then construct my story. What I do with the melody is only child's play or sophisticated trifling. I regard with horror things like: [see the illustration above]. If I vary the melody, it is hard for me to be more than ingenious or graceful, or to deepen a beautiful idea, even though I give it a nice atmosphere. On the given bass I really invent anew, I invent for it new melodies, I create.

Inasmuch as the melodic subject demands change insistently, whereas the harmonico-structural frame may generally be retained without incurring monotony, and since, exceptionally, the melodic subject may be kept as a cantus firmus provided there is sufficient compensating change in the accompanying voices, a principle, valid for the structural techniques, emerges. *The melodic subject and the harmonico-structural frame are complementary phenomena: alterations of the melodic subject are balanced by a relatively close adherence to the harmonico-structural frame; conversely, the literal retention of the melodic subject is offset by harmonic departures within the harmonico-structural frame, as well as by figural or contrapuntal involvement of the supporting voices.*

Consideration of this principle brings one to a better understanding of the comparative merits and limitations of the three structural treatments. The melodico-harmonic variation faces the constant danger that its rather limited modification of the melodic subject will not be sufficient to offset its steadfast retention of the harmonico-structural frame; for this reason it is not merely the strictest but also the most difficult of the three techniques to handle satisfactorily. The harmonic variation stands at the opposite extreme, possessing the most favorable construction of any; as in the melodico-harmonic treatment, its retention of the harmonico-structural frame provides a definite bond with the theme, but the substitution of ever-new melodies in place of the original one creates a vitality and diversity not always present in the simpler species. The cantus firmus variation is a compromise. Its employment of the literal melodic subject runs counter to what is evidently an aesthetic principle of importance within the variation form as a whole, yet its contrapuntal elaboration of the voices accompanying the cantus firmus, together with its relaxing of harmonic ties with the theme, contrive to give it satisfactory balance and progressive interest.

The appearance of counterpoint within the cantus firmus variation provides a clue to the role of counterpoint within the variation form as a whole. Although the different variation types are not wholly contrapuntal after the manner of the canon and the fugue, individual sets often employ a musical fabric composed entirely or in part of counterpoint. As intimated above, those variations which preserve the melodic subject most literally demand contrapuntal treatment most urgently. It is a necessity in the cantus firmus type; it is desirable, to some degree, in the melodico-harmonic variation and in those free variations which use quotations of the literal theme melody; and only in variations of the harmonic family can it be omitted with comparative safety. The fructifying effect of counterpoint within the texture of accompanying parts may be seen by comparing the melodico-harmonic song variations of the English virginalists with those written by German composers of the late baroque, such as Johann Christoph Bach, F. X. A. Murschhauser, and Johann Mattheson. The variations of both groups adhere quite closely to the essential contour of the given melodic subject, yet the quasi-contrapuntal imitations and figurations of the virginalists supply an interest not matched by the broken-chord embellishments of the German composers. Counterpoint, by directing attention away from the melodic subject, makes literal or nearly literal repetition of the melody tolerable, whereas the association of the embellished or figured subject with a flat harmonic accompaniment results in superficiality. As Vincent d'Indy says:

En étudiant les maîtres palestriniens ... , nous avons eu l'occasion d'admirer déjà les plus belles manifestations vocales de *l'ornement contrapontique* ... Mais, avec les errements *harmoniques* qui supplantaient peu à peu les vieux usages *polyphoniques*, avec la *virtuosité* qui se propageait de plus en plus aux dépens de l'*expression musicale*, la Variation, issue du Contrepoint, devint bientôt méconnaissable. ... Alors apparaissent et pullulent ces recueils dits *Thèmes variés* ou *Airs variés*, dans lesquels les formules contrapontiques, désormais désséchées et racornies, ont revêtu l'aspect de petites vignettes harmoniques que nous avons comparées précédemment ... aux figures régulières qui décorent certains édifices. ... Ce que nous avons appelé les *éléments intangibles* du Thème ne consiste plus guère que dans le *nombre de mesures* (généralement *quatre* ou *huit* de ses périodes avec leurs harmonies plates, leur immutable *monotonie* et les notes initiales de chacune d'elles, véritable "poteau indicateur," "guide-âne" de l'auditeur bénévole.[3]

Trans.: In studying the sixteenth-century masters . . . , we have already had occasion to admire the exquisite vocal manifestations of contrapuntal embellishment . . . However, with the harmonic vagaries which gradually supplanted the old polyphonic methods, with the virtuosity which was cultivated increasingly at the expense of musical expression, the variation—outgrowth, as it was, of counterpoint—shortly became unrecognizable . . . Then appeared and multiplied those collections called *Thèmes variés* or *Airs variés*, in which the contrapuntal formulas, henceforth dry and shriveled, have assumed the guise of small harmonic ornaments, which we have previously compared . . . to the regular figures which adorn certain buildings. What we have called the intangible elements of the theme occasionally consists only in the number of measures in its phrases (generally four or eight), with their flat harmonies, their unchanging monotony and the beginning tones of each one of them—the true signpost or guidebook of the well-disposed listener.

Against the principle of balance which governs the structural techniques, the free variation opposes the idea of free development—a development, that is, which acknowledges no responsibility to the structural outline of the theme. Such handling of theme material has much to recommend it, especially to a composer of romantic leanings, for it enables him to mold the theme in accordance with his every caprice, it leads readily to a continuous design, and it avoids the short-breathed effect of the structural variations by permitting the indefinite extension of each component member. It may, of course, be questioned if the free variation is as variation-like, as truly a variation, as the members of the structural category. The distinction between the two is not that one possesses development whereas the other lacks it, for all good variations contain development and only inferior ones are content with paraphrase. The distinction is rather that the development of the structural variations is a controlled development, in opposition to the uninhibited manipulation possible in the free type. The freer a variation cycle becomes, through its indulgence in unfettered development, the more it enters the realm of free composition and the less it resembles genuine variation. In short, the truest variations would seem to be structurally conceived—to follow the theme *in extenso*, not necessarily in a literal manner, but always in a way which treats progressively the successive units of the theme. Composers of free variations have recognized that an unreserved allegiance to the free treatment does not produce the most characteristic variations, for normally they temper its extravagances by mixing with it the more conventional structural practices.

In any case, the primary task of all variations is that of securing unity within a manifold; and it is to the successful accomplishment of this task that both the structural and the free variations are necessarily committed. Actually, the problem is nothing less than the eternal quest of all art; yet because of the peculiar nature of the variation form, wherein given material is subject to continuous restatement unrelieved by digression, the problem is here defined in its simplest and most direct terms. In the structural variations and those portions of the free variation which are structurally conceived, the problem is solved by establishing a balance between changes in the melodic subject and those in the harmonico-structural frame. In the specifically free portions of the free variation it is solved by applying the methods of motival development and of theme transformation exploited in the eighteenth and nineteenth centuries by composers of fugues, symphonies, and symphonic poems. Because motival development and theme transformation are borrowed from other forms rather than indigenous to the variation, the concept of balance originating in the structural techniques remains the unique contribution of the variation to the fundamental problem of tonal organization. The use of this concept assures the variation an understandable relationship among its parts and at the same time parries the incessant threat of monotony inherent in the terms of its construction.

APPENDIX

Appendix

THE PLAN of this study has been to describe the techniques of variation writing by means of examples chosen from a wide array of compositions. Such a plan has the advantage of providing a cross section of the technical practices of many composers, but at the same time the disadvantage of not presenting comprehensive pictures of individual works. To compensate for this drawback, four variation sets will be analyzed in their entirety during the following pages. The sets have been chosen so as to exemplify each of the basic technical plans in turn, and to represent, as far as possible, different variation types and contrasting historical periods. The list comprises:

1. Cantus firmus technique: Antonio de Cabezón, *Diferencias sobre el canto del Caballero*, a sixteenth-century song variation (analyzed following this listing).

2. Harmonic technique: J. K. F. Fischer, *Chaconne in G*, a late seventeenth-century basso ostinato variation (analyzed beginning p. 134).

3. Melodico-harmonic technique: J. S. Bach, *Sei gegrüsset, Jesu gütig*, an early eighteenth-century chorale variation (analyzed beginning p. 140).

4. Free technique: César Franck, *Variations symphoniques pour piano et orchestre*, a late nineteenth-century free variation (analyzed beginning p. 147).

1. CANTUS FIRMUS TECHNIQUE

Antonio de Cabezón's solidly constructed *Diferencias sobre el canto del Caballero*,[1] for organ, was published posthumously by Cabezón's son Hernando in the year 1578, as part of Cabezón's famous *Obras de musica para tecla, arpa, y vihuela*. It commands interest not only as a representative of the early Spanish school of variation writing and of the cantus firmus treatment, but also because of its intrinsic musical value; for coupled with its sober and restrained style is an admirable contrapuntal and harmonic vitality.

The tune which serves as the cantus firmus was apparently well known in Cabezón's day.[2] As used in the *diferencias*, in the transposed Ionian mode, it consists of two balancing phrases, the first cadencing on D, the second on F (see example 110). Its melodic contour is severely conjunct.

Example 110.

Diferencia 1 (measures 1–16) presents this melody in the soprano voice. A quietly moving scale figure[a] weaves through the three support-ing voices, especially during the second phrase. Since this variation is the one which will be referred to as "theme," it is quoted in its entirety (example 111). It will be noted that the cadences (measures 8–9 and

Example 111.

16–17) are bridged by figuration, a characteristic of all the later ca-dences as well. In this way the five *diferencias* which compose the piece are bound into one continuous whole.

In the second *diferencia* (measures 17–32) the cantus firmus, appear-ing once more in the soprano voice, receives at two points a slight em-bellishment. At the beginning of the first phrase it assumes the form seen in example 112. At the start of the second phrase it undergoes the change shown in the opening measures of example 113. Such incidental

Example 112.

Example 113.

decorations of the cantus firmus are not unusual, and indicate that com-posers were more concerned with producing an artistic result than with following pedantically a set formula. The accompanying voices of the second variation become somewhat more animated; the figuration, although not completely unified, makes considerable use of a quick, turning figure,[b] and another resembling it, but slower.[c]

An important element in the unstudied naturalness of the *diferencias* is their freedom from a rigid harmonic pattern. This freedom is not absolute, for in all the variations except the fifth the cadence forms established in the first variation are carefully preserved; nevertheless, between the cadences the substitutions and departures are constantly in evidence. That the harmony of variation 2 changes materially as compared with variation 1 may be seen by contrasting example 113 with measures 9–12 of example 111.

With the third *diferencia* the cantus firmus is transferred to the tenor voice. The figuration of the accompanying voices is much the same as that of the preceding variation, except that a new, dotted-note figure[d] is introduced; nevertheless the general effect of this *diferencia* is somewhat less animated. These characteristics are clearly shown in example 114. During the first half of the variation the cantus firmus is stated virtually without change, but in the second half it receives the most extensive decoration encountered in the entire piece (see example 115).

Example 114.

Example 115.

Measure 41

Moreover, the form which it exhibits at the close (measures 44–46) is retained for the two remaining variations.

The last two *diferencias* carry forward, with little alteration, the features already described. In *diferencia* 4 (measures 49–64) the cantus firmus appears in the alto (see example 116); because the bass is absent

Example 116.

Cantus firmus   Measure 50

---
d

during the first phrase, the texture is temporarily reduced to three voices. The parts which accompany the cantus firmus introduce a cambiata figure; otherwise the figuration is little changed.

In the final *diferencia* (measures 65–80) the cantus firmus returns to the tenor voice but actually assumes the role of bass, since the true bass drops out at this point until the closing measures. The only cadential change to be found in the entire composition takes place in measures 71–72, quite probably as the result of the cantus firmus appearing, for the first time, as the lowest part; compare example 117 with measures

Example 117.

7–8 of the theme (example 111). The excerpt quoted reveals that the general construction of the concluding *diferencia* is not unlike the trio style of certain of Bach's chorale preludes.

The continuity shown by this early song variation is not a requirement of the cantus firmus technique, for later writers generally separate the successive variations. Cabezón's figural restraint, too, later gave way to considerable figural diversity. Nevertheless, this set of *diferencias* is typical in many respects of the entire genre of cantus firmus variations. Its reliance upon the nearly literal melodic subject, its transfer of the subject to different voices, its prevailing employment of the contrapuntal style, and its harmonic flexibility and variety—all of these traits distinguish the cantus firmus variation technique throughout the period of the late renaissance and the baroque.

2. HARMONIC TECHNIQUE

J. K. F. Fischer's unpretentious *Chaconne in G*,[3] for harpsichord, appeared originally in *Les Pièces de clavecin*, Op. 2 (Schlackenwerth, 1696), a collection republished two years later at Augsburg under the title *Musicalisches Blumenbuschlein*. In its wealth of ornamentation the chaconne shows, in common with the entire collection, the influence of contemporary French clavecin music; its texture, too, is thinner than that of most seventeenth-century German chaconnes and passacaglias.

The work is divided into three large divisions, the first (variations 1–10) in major, the second (variations 11–20) in the tonic minor, and the last (variations 21–36) again in the major. Within these large groupings come smaller ones based upon similar figuration and general style; these, in turn, may be broken down into variation pairs and, ultimately, into single variations.

The ostinato bass upon which the piece is built is the customary stock theme of the seventeenth century, a four-measure descending line from tonic to dominant. The opening statement of the theme is rigorously diatonic (example 118).

Example 118.

The first main division (variations 1–10) consists of three sections; the first of these (variations 1–4) is moderately contrapuntal, the second (variations 5 and 6) uses broken chord figures, and the last (variations 7–10) exploits scale lines. Variation 2 is formed from variation 1, and variation 6 from variation 5, through the free inversion of the upper two voices, a unifying means which, although fairly common among basso ostinato variations in general, Fischer uses here with reserve. Only one other pair in the entire chaconne is dependent upon it, variations 13 and 14, and that only partly. The original bass serves as the foundation of the first eight variations with slight change, but it assumes a figured form in variations 9 and 10. Of these, variation 9 reveals the freest usage, inasmuch as the changed direction of the bass—upward instead of downward—shows that here the harmony of the theme, rather than its melodic contour, constitutes the controlling element (example 119).

Example 119.

This wide departure from the ostinato, the greatest to be found prior to the third division (variation 21), may be accounted for on structural grounds, for upon inspection it will be observed that the bass of variation 9 is virtually the same as the soprano line of variation 7 (see example 121). In thus echoing a previous soprano figuration, the bass of variation 9 serves the structural purpose of creating an 8-measure pairing between variations 7 and 8 on the one hand and variations 9 and 10 on the other. The existence of this super-pairing clarifies a further point: the curious lack of correspondence between variations 7 and 8. In the entire chaconne these two variations are the only ones which lack a unifying bond, all the rest exhibiting a consistent pairing. But since variations 7 and 8 together form part of a still larger pairing, their lack of correspondence does not necessarily contradict the plan of consistent pairing upon which the chaconne as a whole is built.

One of the most interesting of the subtleties in this composition is Fischer's modification of the original harmony in such a way as to create transient implications of new keys. Such modifications are discernible as early as the third variation, where the opening measures produce a temporary impression of E minor, in great part through the introduction of D sharp as part of a secondary dominant (B, D sharp, F sharp, A) in measure 2 (example 120). Again in variation 7, the consistent employment of C sharp creates a feeling of D major (example 121). These alterations are admittedly slight, yet they contribute ma-

Example 120.

Example 121.

terially to the sense of harmonic flexibility which this chaconne imparts. Further harmonic modifications, but of wider scope, will be discussed in connection with the next division.

The second main division (variations 11–20), in the tonic minor, again comprises three principal sections; this time, however, they are organized somewhat in the manner of an ABA design. The first and third groups (variations 11–14 and 17–20) are quietly animated and partly chromatic, and recall the moderately contrapuntal style of the opening variations; the contrasting middle group (variations 15 and 16) employs rapid diatonic scale figuration. Pairs of variations are notable for their strictness, for aside from the cadence measures, the second of a pair presents almost note for note the material of the first. The bass preserves its original form with little change; apart from change of mode and occasional chromaticism its main alterations consist of simple figurations such as the suspensions of variations 13 and 14 and the repeated notes and passing tones of variations 17–20. These modifications are shown in example 122.

Example 122.

Unquestionably the chief interest in this division lies in its increased harmonic departures. These consist in part of new chord qualities incident to the change of mode, as in variation 11 (example 123), where a

Example 123.

darker harmonic color is immediately evident. Even more, the changes are the outgrowth of chromaticism and increased harmonic movement, as in variation 13 (example 124). A third factor making for harmonic

Example 124.

change and complexity is the increased use of dissonant figuration, observable both in the appoggiaturas of example 123 and the suspensions of example 124. Still another element is the presence of secondary dominants, implying, as in the foregoing division, transient excursions to new keys, and contributing greatly thereby to the avoidance of harmonic rigidity. Note, in example 124, the passing reference to D minor brought about by the secondary dominant in measure 2 (A, C sharp, E, G) as well as by the secondary Neapolitan-chord effect of measure 1 (E flat, G, B flat). Another example of this temporary renunciation of the original tonic appears in variations 15 and 16, where measure 2 implies a feeling of F major.

But the widest departure from the harmony of the theme is reserved for variations 17 and 18, in which all the ingredients mentioned above find a place: chord qualities indigenous to the minor mode, increased rate of chord change (three chords per measure instead of one), chromaticism, dissonance within the figuration, and the implication of new keys (see example 125). In respect to the last, the plan is both symmet-

Example 125.

Var. 17 (measure 65)

rical and striking, for the sequential construction dictates a series of key impressions corresponding to the tones of the ostinato itself: G, F, E flat, and D.

It was shown in chapter iii that baroque composers sometimes used fairly extensive harmonic changes in their basso ostinato variations. The entire middle section of the chaconne is a striking confirmation of this point, for it appears that the composer sought to impart the maximum of harmonic variety compatible with the almost literally recurring bass line. Sections such as this may be said to represent the fusion of basso ostinato and cantus firmus practices.

The last of the three main divisions is once more in major. It contains two sections. In the first (variations 21–32) Fischer audaciously uses a shortened form of the theme, cutting its length from four measures to two (see example 126). At the same time he tempers the adventuresome

Example 126.

Var. 21 (measure 81)

harmony of the minor division by renouncing chromaticism and by confining the harmony largely to tonic and dominant. The resulting variations are delightful in their directness and open-air freshness.

It is apparent from this quotation that the new ostinato theme is not a strictly diminished form of the original but a freely embellished one which, although true to the initial cadence design and downward direction, has a distinct individuality of its own. A strictly applied diminution, it may be noted, would have resulted in a persistent cross rhythm; furthermore, it seems that Fischer needed at this point the increased movement which an embellished, flowing bass provides, for the chief intent of the section is one of climax and rhythmic intensification. Up to this time the increase in animation which one expects in a typical basso ostinato variation has been slight. It is true that in the first division a faster movement was initiated at variation 5, but this subsided somewhat at the beginning of the second division (variation 11). Again at variation 15 occurred another and greater increase, but this, likewise, gave way to quieter movement at variation 17.

The climactic purpose of the section under discussion is clearly shown by variation 23, in which the flowing bass, inaugurated two variations before, is joined by rapid figuration of the soprano voice (example 127). At variation 25 this more florid figuration is taken over by the bass. The result (example 128) is a new form of the shortened

Example 127.

Example 128.

ostinato (compare with variation 21, example 126). At variation 27 the rapid figuration returns to the soprano,[4] while the bass presents the ostinato in a new, simplified way (example 129).

Example 129.

Example 130.

In variation 28 (example 130), the initial form of the shortened ostinato returns; in this and the ensuing three variations, the upper parts resume the fragmentary figuration of variation 21 (see example 126). Because of these recurrences, the entire section resembles a miniature

ABA design, similar to that found in the minor division. Here, however, the three-part likeness is more precise, for variation 31 shows an appreciable thematic correspondence to variation 21.

The final section within the third division begins with variation 33; it consists of four variations. In their general style and treatment these concluding variations resemble those at the very opening, for not only does the original form of the ostinato return at this point, but variations 33 and 34 follow closely the melodic line and harmony of variations 3 and 4. Thus the final section has somewhat the effect of a da capo, a device uncommon in basso ostinato variations as a whole. In the two final variations, the insertion of F natural into the bass (creating the secondary dominant seventh chord G, B, D, F) throws emphasis upon subdominant harmony and cleverly reinforces the closing effect of the final cadence (example 131).

Example 131.

Var. 35 (measure 113)

Although this chaconne lacks the powerful vigor of Bach's organ *Passacaglia* and the diversity of Buxtehude's basso ostinato pieces, it has merits of another kind, attracting primarily by its graceful movement and its mood of quiet melancholy. A review of its main technical aspects shows that in spite of its singularly firm attachment to the given bass, it skilfully avoids monotony by means of its ingenious figurations and, even more, through its novel harmonic departures and implications of new keys. The reduction in the length of the ostinato, in the third division, is both unusual and effective, and the virtually complete adherence to the plan of variation pairs, although extreme, is appropriate to the style employed. Finally, although the work lacks features occasionally seen in other baroque ostinato pieces, such as true modulation and the prominent use of the ostinato theme in contrary motion, it contains most of the typical devices. On the whole, therefore, the cross section which this work gives of baroque ostinato treatment is not only clear but reasonably complete.

3. Melodico-Harmonic Technique

J. S. Bach's chorale variations on *Sei gegrüsset, Jesu gütig*[5] was begun at Lüneburg and completed at Cöthen or Weimar.[6] Built prevailingly on the melodico-harmonic plan (certain of the separate variations exemplify cantus firmus technique), it contains many ingenious subtleties.

In conformity with his usual procedure, Bach begins the piece with the chorale itself (example 132). His straightforward harmonization of

Example 132.

the chorale melody, in the customary four parts, takes full advantage of the opportunities for cadential variety; of the six phrases all but the first and last end with implications of related tonalities.

The first variation has but two parts, a *basso quasi ostinato* together with an embellished version of the chorale melody that is extended from time to time by means of *l'amplification thématique* (see pp. 62 ff.). The bass part begins alone, somewhat in the manner of a concerto grosso theme, with a well-defined theme head (modeled in this case after the initial notes of the chorale melody) followed by sequential figuration (see example 133). This line is joined in the fourth measure by the orna-

Example 133.
Var.1.

Circled notes are from theme

mented chorale melody, and from this point the two voices engage in a dialogue. At each entrance of the chorale the bass drops temporarily into the background, only to emerge conspicuously with the theme head at the conclusion of the chorale fragment. In this way the bass serves to connect the several portions of the chorale, not by means of a superficial filler part but through a line that is coördinate in interest and importance with the chorale itself. The shifting of the interest alternately from bass to chorale melody is apparent in the opening phrase, quoted in example 134. As this quotation shows, the appearances of the bass

Example 134.
Var 1, measure 4

theme are not always complete. Often, as in measures 4 and 5, the sequential spinning-out is abbreviated; less frequently, as in measures 9 and 10, it is the theme head which is omitted (see example 135). Despite

Example 135.

such modifications, the unifying function of the bass theme is unmistakable. At times, moreover, it exerts a controlling influence upon the course of the chorale melody. This is true in the second phrase, where the thematic amplification of measures 10 and 11 is fashioned with respect to the bass figuration (example 135).

In the second variation a graceful, imitative figuration runs through all the parts, affecting the chorale melody somewhat less than the supporting voices (see example 136). Bach's technical facility shows itself

Example 136.

in his easy alternation of the normal and inverted forms of the chosen figures, and in his simultaneous presentation of the figure in different voices, for climactic effect, at the approach to the final cadence (measures 10–13, not quoted). Throughout the variation the given harmony undergoes slight but fairly persistent alteration, chiefly by means of changes in chord position and the occasional substitution of new roots; original cadence objectives, however, are preserved intact. The opening measures are typical of the straightforward procedure employed.

The third variation, like the first, is in two parts (see example 137). Bach dissolves the chorale melody into a remarkable running figuration which, although prevailingly true to the given melodic outline, is marvelously free in effect. The freedom is due in large part to Bach's method of implying two voices by a single line, a characteristic common to much of his melodic writing in general. Even more, the feeling of independence is the result of Bach's introduction of new points of climax. (The chorale theme, it should be noted, is deficient in true climax, since the same high point, E flat, is attained three different times; because of

Example 137.

this fact, Bach's changes within the variation are especially instructive.)
After a quick preliminary rise to A and B flat in the second and third
measures (marked by asterisks in example 137), the melody drops back
in preparation for a second ascent. The new rise is accomplished in
waves, the successive high points being E flat and F in measure 4, G
in measure 6, and A flat in measure 8 (these later measures are not
quoted). Then comes a decline to the low register and quasi da capo
effect of measure 10, after which the line builds to a climactic high C
in measure 12. The melody thus constructed is no servile follower of the
chorale theme but, rather, a line of remarkable individuality, the varied
contour of which is largely responsible for the musical interest in the
variation.

Both of the aspects referred to above, the outlining of two voices by
the figured melody and the attainment of new climax points, appear in
example 137. Important changes such as these become possible only
when a composer follows a theme imaginatively, and it will be observed that Bach does not hesitate to alter the rhythmic position of
the skeletal tones nor to alter their register by means of octave transpositions. Moreover, he sometimes omits the skeletal tones entirely, a
practice not apparent in the example above but which operates to
secure the final climax in measure 10.

Variation 4 resembles variation 2 in general procedure but lacks its
graceful interplay of figuration. The chorale appears almost unchanged
in the soprano voice; in the lower parts flowing scale lines alternate with
short circumscribing figures.The total effect, although displaying Bach's
unfailing craftsmanship, is deficient in poetic feeling compared with the
earlier variations.

The use of the nearly literal chorale melody in the upper voice also
characterizes the fifth variation, but this time the chief figural interest
is concentrated in the bass instead of being apportioned evenly among
the supporting parts (see example 138). Such an assumption by the bass
of the main figural role, while the soprano reverts to its original form,
occurs during the course of many variations built upon the melodico-

Example 138.
Var.5, measure 5

harmonic plan, as we have already seen. The bass figuration, compounded of a peculiar, jerking motive of which Bach was evidently fond (for it appears frequently in his clavier works), proceeds relentlessly throughout the variation. Above it the upper voices engage in smoothly flowing chords and rich suspensions which produce a slight but effective involvement of the given harmony. The third phrase, quoted in example 138, displays this contrast between bass and upper parts with especial force.

Example 139.
Var.6

Cantus firmus

Variation 6 (see example 139) is the first of three cantus firmus variations which, because of their tendency toward progressively greater contrapuntal intricacy, lend cumulative interest to the conclusion of the series. The procedure in variation 6, where the sober chorale melody appears in the bass, accompanied by two ornately figured upper voices, is thoroughly orthodox and calls for no particular discussion. Attention should be directed, however, to the expressiveness and flexibility of the added voices, qualities which derive from Bach's effective exploitation of descending leaps, especially of sevenths, and from his free handling of ornamentally treated suspensions. The variation, like so many others Bach wrote, shows his power to create the impression of great freedom while remaining close to the given thematic outline. The appropriateness of its idiomatic trio style, the melodic depth of the voices superimposed upon the cantus, and the effect of fantasy which these voices create, combine to make it a cantus firmus variation of the highest type.

The seventh variation reverts to the melodico-harmonic technique. It brings the chorale melody once more to the soprano voice and, as a decorative device, threads a syncopated figure through the melody and the supporting parts (see example 140). This variation is more straight-

Example 140.

Var.7, measure 5

forward than the expressive sixth variation, and its development more obvious, despite the delightful seriousness and richness of its harmony. The quoted phrase is characteristic of the style employed.

The eighth variation follows a procedure not unlike that of variation 7 by keeping the chorale melody in the uppermost part and weaving a figure through the different voices, yet its general effect is one of greater lightness and transparency (see example 141). The rapidity of the figur-

Example 141.

Var.8

ation makes impracticable its assignment to the pedals; Bach confines it altogether to the middle and upper parts. The chorale melody appears unchanged, for the most part, and only occasionally takes over the figuration; in the fifth phrase it temporarily enters the alto voice. The entire conception is instrumentally impressive, and its freshness and originality of treatment give further proof of Bach's superlative skill in creating diverse styles and moods within the bounds of the structural variation plans. The initial measures show the imitative, dialogue-like figuration typical of the entire variation.

Variation 9, like variation 6, is a three-part cantus firmus variation that recalls the style of Bach's trio sonatas for organ (see example 142).

Example 142.

Var.9

Cantus firmus

The cantus, although played on the pedal keyboard, is the middle voice; the two surrounding parts, elaborately figured, imitate each other throughout much of the variation. The change from the quadruple meter of the theme to triple meter in the variation is a modification of importance; altering as it does the basic rhythm of the cantus firmus, the change produces a modification akin to the theme transformations of the late nineteenth-century free variation.

Variation 10, the last and most intricate of the three cantus firmus variations, continues the three-beat measure of the preceding variation (see example 143). Here the chorale melody, as cantus firmus, is pre-

Example 143.

sented in the soprano voices in tripled note values, while the three remaining parts offer a quiet contrapuntal support. The variation is much the longest of any in the entire composition, a fact which results in part from the augmented cantus, in part from the lengthy connecting interludes, the opening prelude, and the concluding postlude. Because of the greater scale of this variation, wherein four measures are used to represent one of the theme, a considerable degree of harmonic deviation is to be expected. In point of fact, passing chords, substitutions, secondary dominant embellishments, and even new cadential objectives appear in such profusion as to create at times virtually a complete reharmonization of the chorale. The extent of this recasting may be judged from the excerpt in example 143, taken from the fourth phrase (compare with measures 8 and 9 of the theme).

In the final variation Bach returns to the melodico-harmonic technique but employs it in a unique way (see example 144). Instead of

Example 144.

applying the figuration to one of the extreme parts, in accordance with customary procedure, he embellishes the middle voices and leaves the chorale melody practically unchanged. Since the simplification of the outer parts brings the theme prominently to the fore, it seems probable that the composer's intention was to restate the theme in quasi da capo fashion; the fact that he later used an outright da capo restatement of the theme at the close of the *Goldberg Variations* lends added weight to this conjecture. The quiet character of the concluding variation shows itself at once in the opening measures.

The over-all impression received from this set is of great technical skill coupled with strikingly diverse moods and styles. Most of the variations are markedly different from the others: the freely unfolding first variation, with its melismatic, colored melody, the transparent and gracefully figured second variation, the supple yet vigorous third, the sixth, with its depth of expression, the contrapuntally animated ninth—these are typical of the opposing styles exhibited. It is true that such contrasts are less sharp than those which one finds in an outright character variation like the *Goldberg Variations;* nevertheless, they presage the more dramatic manner which Bach employed in the later work.

On the technical side one is immediately conscious of Bach's wealth of figural ideas. Of especial significance is the way in which these ideas tend to assume, at times, the molding and directing influence normally wielded by the theme. Unquestionably it is the theme which, for the most part, directs and controls the unfolding of the figuration, yet it is also true that the theme, in turn, is occasionally molded and changed by the inner necessities of the figuration. The molding influence of the figuration has already been noted in connection with the *basso quasi ostinato* of variation 1 and is clearly apparent as well in variation 3, where the dynamically figured chorale melody leads to a radically new melodic contour; it also appears, but with less force, in variations 7 and 8. The ability of a composer thus to originate figural ideas which, although serving primarily a decorative purpose, are so individual as to be able to contend with the theme for supremacy, is a mark of true variation mastery. Bach possessed this ability to a high degree, and used it in *Sei gegrüsset, Jesu gütig* with effective result.

4. FREE TECHNIQUE

Franck's *Variations symphoniques* (1885)[7] is not only a typical example of the free variation but is also one of the composer's most important works. It combines melodic fluency with strikingly original harmony, and expresses both most happily by means of an idiomatic and sensitive piano style, and through an intimate welding of the piano with the orchestra. Based upon two themes instead of the customary single theme, the variations are joined without pause.

The work as a whole is in four large divisions, of which the first (measures 1–99) is introductory and improvisatory, the second (measures 100–249) is lyrical and more continuous, the third (measures 249–285) is in the nature of a quiet interlude, and the fourth (measures 285–end) is a brilliant *allegro*.

The opening division is concerned chiefly with stating the first theme, although it suggests the second at two points. Following a restless orchestral phrase in F-sharp minor (example 145), the piano responds with a quiet and somber answering phrase (example 146). The dialogue

Example 145.

Example 146.

between the orchestra and the piano continues, with modulations to A (measure 13) and C sharp (measure 21). At this point a third phrase is presented by the piano (example 147). These three ideas constitute the

Example 147.

material of the first theme. Of the three, the second (example 146) is much the most important and may of itself be considered the first theme; but since the other two are also utilized in the developments which follow, it is convenient to assume that the theme is made up of all three.

The precise limits of the first theme are hard to define because of its fragmentary, improvisatory nature, but shortly after *l'istesso tempo* it definitely gives way to an intimation of the coming second theme, in the key of A, beginning (measure 35) as in example 148. This foreshadowing of the second theme is followed, at *poco più lento*, by an extended statement of the somber first-theme idea quoted in example 146. Again the

Example 148.

theme is given out by the piano alone, but now it begins in C-sharp minor, and is made more agitated by means of a surging accompanimental figure (example 149).

Example 149.

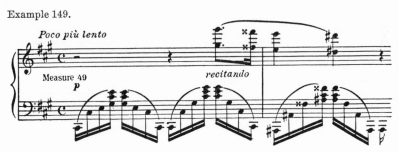

In the ensuing *allegro* section (beginning in measure 65), the alternations between the orchestra and the piano are resumed. The orchestral part is built from the figures of example 145; the piano responds with the idea in example 147, later with that in example 146. Shortly after the *allegretto* (measure 92) we hear once more an anticipatory allusion to the second theme similar to that quoted in example 148, but in a more tentative and indirect way. The first main division closes with this reference to the second theme.

The second main division begins with the announcement of the second theme in its entirety, given out by the piano alone (see example 150). This theme, like the first, is in the key of F-sharp minor, but is more

Example 150.

lyrical and questioning. It contrasts with the main idea of the first
theme (example 146) through its faster tempo and its triple meter, as
well as through the symmetry and completeness of its design.

The remainder of the division consists of five variations built upon
this theme. Of these, the first three and the last revert to the traditional
structural techniques. Variation 1 (measures 117–135) is a melodico-
harmonic treatment in which the orchestra and the piano alternately
decorate the melody of the theme, the embellishment becoming more
free and ingenious as the variation proceeds (example 151).

Example 151.

Variation 2 (measures 135–153) is a cantus firmus treatment. The
melody of the theme (at first in the cellos and later in the violins) is
heard against a rich background of harmony, transient countermelodies,
and broken-chord figuration (example 152).

Example 152.

Variation 3 (measures 153–171) exemplifies the harmonic technique;
the original structure and harmony of the theme are preserved but the
melody is completely abandoned (example 153).

Example 153.

A vigorous crescendo in the last part of the third variation ushers in the strongly contrasting fourth (measures 171–230). The key changes to D, the mode changes from minor to major, and the quiet dynamics of the preceding variations are intensified into a powerful *fortissimo* (see example 154). These modifications, together with a new rhythm taken

Example 154.

from the first theme, produce a marked character change and at the same time give rise to a radical transformation of the melody.

The design of this free variation is instructive, for it consists essentially of a rearrangement of entire phrases of the theme rather than a development of thematic motives. The plan of the theme is binary (see example 150):

Part 1: ab (4 + 4), F-sharp minor modulating to A
Part 2: cd (4 + 6), A major modulating to F-sharp minor

In the variation this binary structure is replaced by a ternary one, much expanded:

Part 1: ab (4 + 4), D modulating to B
      ab (4 + 4), B modulating to G sharp (sequence of preceding)
Part 2: d (4) in G-sharp minor
      d (4) in E minor (sequence of preceding)
      a, a, extension (4 + 4 + 6), leading back to D
Part 3: ab (4 + 4) in D
      a, extension (4 + 9) in F-sharp minor, changing to F-sharp major at
      elision with next variation.

In all, the eighteen-measure theme is expanded into a fifty-nine measure variation, chiefly by the use of sequential restatements in new keys and the recombination of the original phrases in such a way as to secure the effect of contrast and reprise.

The fifth variation (beginning at *molto più lento*, measure 230) again conforms to the exact structure of the theme (see example 155). Essentially it is another cantus firmus treatment, like variation 2 but more subdued and expressive. With this variation the second division comes to a close.

The third division (measures 247–285) is relatively short, and consists of a free development of the main idea of theme 1 (quoted in example

Example 155.

146). At first glance, the procedure is much the same as in the foregoing cantus firmus variation, where the low-pitched melody in the cellos acted primarily as a support for the shimmering figuration of the piano; but actually the method is quite different, for here the cello melody claims the chief attention and the piano figuration assumes a background role (example 156). Another difference from the preceding varia-

Example 156.

tion is that here the melodic line is transformed and extended instead of being taken literally from the theme (example 157).

Following a deceptive cadence leading to A minor, the entire melody quoted in example 157, *b*, is sequenced beginning in this new key (meas-

Example 157.

ures 261–273), but the ending is so changed as to lead to C-sharp major, the dominant of the final division. The rest of the third division is primarily an intensification of this dominant, built upon fragments of the transformed theme. Franck's lyrical development of these motives is admirable (example 158).

Example 158.

The final division (beginning at *allegro non troppo*, measure 285) consists of a series of transformations and developments of both themes. At the outset of the *allegro*, the somber first subject (see example 157, *a*) is presented in a gay and dancelike manner (example 159). Later it assumes the decorated form shown in example 160, *a*, and the more meditative aspect of example 160, *b*. The second theme is transformed in an equally striking way (example 161).

Example 159.

Example 160.

Example 161.

The structural organization of the final division shows the influence of sonata form. A lengthy opening section (measures 288–333), based upon the transformed first theme (example 159), corresponds to the principal group; a transitional phrase (measures 333–337), beginning as in example 162, leads to a section in the key of D based upon the

Example 162.

transformed second theme (see example 161). This section (extending from measures 337–355) corresponds to the subordinate group and concludes the "exposition."

The "development" (measures 355–393) begins with a sequential treatment of the first-theme idea quoted in example 159, and proceeds, through D minor and F major, to the transformation quoted in example 160, *b* (measure 367). This phrase, in E flat, is sequenced in G flat (measure 375); it then develops into a modulatory passage which leads back to E flat and the original form of the "principal theme" shown in example 163 (measure 385). A restatement of this melody in E-flat

Example 163.

minor (measure 389) is followed by its sequential appearance in F-sharp major (measure 393).

The "recapitulation" (measures 393–442) begins with this F-sharp major entry. It closely parallels the plan of the "exposition," except that both themes are now stated in the tonic key of F sharp (measures 393 and 423); also, the transitional phrase (see example 161) is now omitted. A coda (measures 442–end) built upon the opening figure of example 159 concludes the division and the entire composition.

It is plain that this work is a mixture of the free technique with the older and more conventional structural techniques. Franck's method is predominantly that of unrestricted development, yet his fairly consistent use of the structural treatments in the second division shows a partial reliance upon past devices. The use of two themes is unusual, as is the introduction of sonata-form relationships into the finale. On the other hand, the transformation of motives and phrases taken from the themes, and the use of the transformed material in a free development, are highly characteristic. The *Variations symphoniques*, by virtue of its unique form, its harmonic and modulatory flexibility, its manifold moods, and its innate expressiveness, clearly suggests the infinite scope of the free variation.

NOTES

ABBREVIATIONS

In each chapter, listings of a reference subsequent to the first are generally abbreviated to the name of the author, editor, or composer; or, where this would be ambiguous, to a name followed by a shortened form of the title (*i.e.*, Straube, *Alte Meister*).

The following special abbreviations are also employed:

D. d. T.   *Denkmäler deutscher Tonkunst*
D. T. Ö.   *Denkmäler der Tonkunst in Österreich*
F. V. B.   *The Fitzwilliam Virginial Book*

In references to the *D.T.Ö.* and similar collections, Roman numerals indicate the bibliographic a volume (*Jahrgang*); superscript Arabic numerals, its subdivisons (*Band* or *Teil*). Thus Pachelbel, *D.d.T.*, 2d series, II[1].

Notes

INTRODUCTION

(Pages 1–2)

[1] See Victor Luithlen, "Studie zu Johannes Brahms' Werken in Variationenform," Denkmäler der Tonkunst in Österreich, *Studien zur Musikwissenschaft*, XIV (1927), 286–320.

[2] Adolf Bernhard Marx, *Die Lehre von der musikalischen Komposition*, 4th ed., 4 vols. (Leipzig, 1868), III, 53.

[3] Charles V. Stanford, *Musical Composition* (London, 1911), p. 51.

[4] For the variations of the English virginalists see Lucia Neudenberger, *Die Variationstechnik der Virginalisten im Fitzwilliam Virginal Book* (Berlin, n.d.), and Charles van den Borren, *The Sources of Keyboard Music in England*, Eng. trans. J. E. Matthew (London, n.d.). For the pre-Bach clavier variations in general see Richard Gress, *Die Entwicklung der Klaviervariation von Andrea Gabrieli bis zu Johann Sebastian Bach*, dissertation, Tübingen (Stuttgart, 1929), and Tomac̆-Wukadinovic, *Die Veränderungs* (sic) *bei den Hauptmeistern der Klavier-Musik vor Bach*, unpublished dissertation (Prague, 1928), not available for this study. For variations of the romantic period see Martin Friedland, *Zeitstil und Persönlichkeitsstil in den Variationenwerken der musikalischen Romantik* (Lepizig, 1930;) Henry Swoboda, *Die nachbeethoven'sche Variationenform*, unpublished dissertation (Prague, 1922), not available for this study.

The variations of individual composers have been studied by Ernst Reichert, *Die Variationenarbeit bei Haydn*, unpublished dissertation (Vienna, 1926), not available for this study; Paul Mies, "W. A. Mozarts Variationenwerke und ihre Formungen," *Archiv für Musikforschung*, II (1937), 466–495; Herbert Viecenz, "Über die allgemeinen Grundlagen der Variationskunst, mit besonderer Berücksichtigung Mozarts," *Mozart Jahrbuch*, II (1924), 185–232; Otto Klauwell, "Ludwig van Beethoven und die Variationenform," *Studien und Erinnerungen* (Langensalza, 1906), pp. 56–80; J. M. Müller-Blattau, "Beethoven und die Variation," Internationaler Musikhistorischer Kongress, *Beethoven Zentenarfeier* (Vienna, 1927), pp. 55–57; Werner Schwarz, *Robert Schumann und die Variation, mit besonderer Berücksichtigung der Klavierwerke*, XVI Band der Königsberger Studien zur Musikwissenschaft (Kassel, 1932); Victor Luithlen, "Studie zu Johannes Brahms' Werken in Variationenform," *Studien zur Musikwissenschaft*, XIV (1927), 286–320; and Gaston R. Dejmek, *Der Variationszyklus bei Max Reger*, dissertation, Rheinischen Friederich-Wilhelms Universität, Bonn (Essen, 1930).

Discussions of separate variation types include Andreas Moser, "Zur Genesis der Folies d'Espagne," *Archiv für Musikwissenschaft*, I (1919), 358–371; Paul Nettl, "Die Bergamaska," *Zeitschrift für Musikwissenschaft*, V (1922–23), 291–295; Lili Propper, *Der Basso ostinato als technisches und formbildendes Prinzip*, inaugural-dissertation, Friedrich-Wilhelms-Universität, Berlin (Hildburghausen, n.d.); and Richard Litterscheid, *Zur Geschichte des Basso ostinato*, dissertation, Marburg (Dortmund, 1928).

Chapters on the variation can be found in many books on composition and form, among them Karl Blessinger, *Grundzüge der musikalischen Formenlehre* (Stuttgart, n.d.); Percy Goetschius, *The Larger Forms of Musical Composition*, 2d ed. (New York, 1915); Vincent d'Indy, *Cours de composition musicale*, 2 vols. (Paris, 1909); Stephan Krehl, *Musikalische Formenlehre*, I Teil: Die reine Formenlehre (Leipzig, 1902); Hugo Leichtentritt, *Musikalische Formenlehre*, 3d ed. (Leipzig, 1927); Adolf Bernhard Marx, *Die Lehre von der musikalischen Komposition*, 4th ed., 4 vols. (Leipzig, 1868); Ebenezer Prout, *Applied Forms*, 3d ed. (London, 1895); Charles Villiers Stanford, *Musical Composition* (London, 1911); and Richard Stöhr, *Musickalische Formenlehre*, 4th ed. (Leipzig, 1921).

[5] Leichtentritt, p. 99.

CHAPTER I
(Pages 3–27)

[1] Hugo Leichtentritt, *Musikalische Formenlehre*, 3d ed. (Leipzig, 1927), p. 100.

[2] Under the influence of the current musical style still further types have developed during the past twenty-five years. Although the consideration of these newest types is beyond the scope of this study, it may be pointed out that the passacaglias of Paul Hindemith exemplify the contemporary basso ostinato variation, that most of Arnold Schönberg's variations may be regarded as contemporary character variations, and that a contemporary free type finds expression in pieces such as the *Quattro variazioni* movement of Igor Stravinsky's *Concerto per due pianoforti soli* (Mainz, 1936).

[3] Vincent d'Indy, *Cours de composition musicale*, 2 vols. (Paris, 1909), II, 448–487. With d'Indy, the division into two opposing categories is not absolute, for some of his examples of *la variation amplificatrice* retain the structure of the theme.

[4] Leichtentritt, pp. 98–114 and pp. 332–335.

[5] Percy Goetschius, *The Larger Forms of Musical Composition*, 2d ed. (New York, 1915), p. 72; see also the entire section, pp. 58–82. Goetschius is here using the word *design* as synonymous with *structure*.

[6] *Ibid.*, p. 83; see also the entire section, pp. 82–92.

[7] See Gustave Reese, *Music in the Middle Ages* (New York, 1940), chaps. ix, xi, and xii.

[8] See Willi Apel, "Early German Keyboard Music," *The Musical Quarterly*, XXIII (1937), 210–237.

[9] See Richard Gress, *Die Entwicklung der Klaviervariation von Andrea Gabrieli bis zu Johann Sebastian Bach*, Tübingen dissertation (Stuttgart, 1929), p. 25.

[10] Herbert Viecenz, "Über die allgemeinen Grundlagen der Variationskunst, mit besonderer Berücksichtigung Mozarts," *Mozart Jahrbuch*, II (1924), 185–232; Charles van den Borren, *The Sources of Keyboard Music in England*, English trans. J. E. Matthew (London, n.d.), p. 206, pp. 211–222.

[11] Leichtentritt, pp. 100 f.; d'Indy, II, 457–465.

[12] Van den Borren, p. 206.

[13] *Ibid.*, pp. 212 f.

[14] Viecenz, pp. 199 f.

[15] *Ibid.*, p. 200.

[16] Leichtentritt, p. 100.

[17] D'Indy, *Cours*, II, 468.

[18] *Ibid.*, pp. 440 f.

[19] See Wilhelm Fischer, "Instrumentalmusik von 1450–1600," *Handbuch der Musikgeschichte*, ed. G. Adler, 2d ed. (Berlin, 1930), I, 382–397; van den Borren, pp. 253 f., 259–264.

[20] See, for example, Mudarra's *O guárdame las vacas* in *Les luthistes espagnols du 16e Siècle*, ed. G. Morphy, 2 vols. (Leipzig, 1902), II, 98 f.; and Cabezón's *Diferencias sobre la gallarda milanesa* in *Hispaniae Schola Musica Sacra*, ed. P. Pedrell, 8 vols. (Leipzig, 1898), VIII, 1 ff.

[21] Van den Borren, p. 232.

[22] Leichtentritt, p. 100; d'Indy, *Cours*, II, 459–462; van den Borren, pp. 207–209 and pp. 232–248.

[23] Karl Blessinger, *Grundzüge der musikalischen Formenlehre* (Stuttgart, n.d.), pp. 137–142; Viecenz, pp. 200–204.

[24] Van den Borren, pp. 208 f.

[25] Leichtentritt, p. 100.

[26] D'Indy, *Cours*, II, 461.

[27] Leichtentritt, p. 100.

[28] D'Indy, *Cours*, II, 464 f.

[29] See, for example, Byrd's virginal variations on the song *O Mistris Myne* (*F. V. B.*, I, 258 ff.), Bach's chorale variations on *Sei gegrüsset, Jesu gütig* (analyzed in detail in the Appendix, p. 140), and the variation movement from Mozart's *C-minor Piano Concerto* (K. 491).

[30] Lili Propper, *Der Basso ostinato als technisches und formbildendes Prinzip* (Hildburghausen, n.d.), pp. 8–24.

[31] *Ibid.*, p. 25. The *Tratado* has been reprinted in German, trans. M. Schneider (Berlin, 1913).

[32] Blessinger, pp. 142–148; van den Borren, p. 207, pp. 227–232; Goetschius, pp. 18–58; Viecenz, p. 199; Victor Luithlen, "Studie zu Johannes Brahms' Werken in Variationenform," Denkmäler der Tonkunst in Österreich, *Studien zur Musikwissenschaft,* XIV (1927), 286–320; Richard Stöhr, *Musikalische Formenlehre,* 4th ed. (Leipzig, 1921), p. 189.

[33] Viecenz, p. 199.

[34] *Ibid.*

[35] *Ibid.*, p. 200.

[36] Van den Borren, p. 207.

[37] *Ibid.*, pp. 230 f. Obviously the reference to C major is a misprint, since the key is definitely that of G.

[38] *Ibid.*, p. 231.

[39] A case in point is the *Allegro energico* from Brahms' *Fourth Symphony* (see chap. v).

[40] For the Valderrábano *diferencias* see Morphy, II, 141; for those of Cabezón see Pedrell, VIII, 13.

[41] Grieg's Op. 24, the *Ballade* for pianoforte, is especially close to the free type, inasmuch as variations 3, 4, 5, 9, and 10 differ noticeably from the outlines of the theme.

[42] D'Indy, *Cours,* II, 466–487; Stöhr, p. 192; Luithlen, p. 308; Gaston R. Dejmek, *Der Variationszyklus bei Max Reger* (Essen, 1930), p. 25; Goetschius, pp. 82–92; Leichtentritt, pp. 332–335; H. C. Colles, additions to C. H. H. Parry's article "Variations," *Grove's Dictionary of Music and Musicians,* 4th ed., ed. H. C. Colles, 6 vols. (London, 1940).

[43] Ebenezer Prout, *Applied Forms,* 3d ed. (London, 1895), p. 92.

[44] Hans Joachim Moser, *Musiklexikon* (Berlin, 1935), article "Variationen."

[45] Stöhr, p. 192.

[46] Luithlen, p. 308.

[47] Goetschius, p. 83.

[48] Leichtentritt, p. 332.

[49] *Ibid.*, p. 333.

[50] *Ibid.*, p. 334.

[51] Colles, "Variations," *Grove's Dictionary.* The reference to Mozart's method of melodic variation is apparently to Mozart's retention of the clear outlines of the melodic subject in his variations.

[52] D'Indy, p. 486.

[53] Goetschius, p. 90.

[54] For example, the tendency to create new treatments is apparent in Aaron Copland's *Piano Variations* (New York, 1932), in which the old idea of a cantus firmus is modified by having the tones of the cantus appear in octave transpositions. Thus, whereas the theme begins as in *a,* below, the second variation begins as in *b.* The method suggests the possible influence of Schönberg's twelve-tone row upon the variation form.

CHAPTER II
(Pages 28–54)

[1] The variation suite is a cycle of dance pieces built upon a common theme. An outgrowth of the dance pair, it was cultivated with particular vigor during the early seventeenth century. Among its earliest exponents were Paul Peurl, in his *Neue Paduanen* (1611) and *Ganz neue Paduanen* (1625), and Johann Hermann Schein (1586–1630), in his *Banchetto musicale* (1617). The method of Peurl and Schein is to take the melodic figures of one dance and rearrange them in another, somewhat in the manner of a very free theme transformation. Not all the suites of these men use the variation principle, and even in those which do apply it, there are generally individual dances written independently. Both Peurl and Schein wrote their suites for orchestra; later composers of the orchestral variation suite include Isaak Posch (early seventeenth century) and Andreas Hammerschmidt (1612–1675). See Wilhelm Fischer, "Instrumentalmusik von 1600–1750," *Handbuch der Musikgeschichte*, 2d ed., ed. G. Adler, 2 vols. (Berlin, 1930), I, 540–573.

After 1650 the idea of the variation suite was carried on in the keyboard suite, though with much less force. Here the variation element is limited to the *allemande* and the *courante*, as a rule, and the correspondence is frequently reduced to brief melodic likenesses, especially at the beginnings of the two dances. Composers of this kind of keyboard suite include J. J. Froberger (1616–1667), Alessandro Poglietti (latter seventeenth century), Johann Pachelbel (1653–1706), Johann Kuhnau (1660–1722), J. S. Bach (1685–1750), and G. F. Handel (1685–1759). Occasionally the resemblance between the *allemande* and the *courante* is more complete, as in certain suites of Froberger and Poglietti where the melodico-harmonic plan of the variation form is followed. See Richard Gress, *Die Entwicklung der Klaviervariation von Andrea Gabrieli bis zu Johann Sebastian Bach* (Stuttgart, 1929), p. 98.

The term *variation ricercar* refers to any of the variously titled imitative pieces of the late renaissance and baroque periods (the *ricercar* itself, the *fantasia*, *canzona*, *capriccio*, and *fugue*) in which each section after the first is constructed upon a variant of the original theme. Composers of the variation ricercar for clavier include Andrea Gabrieli (*ca.* 1510–1586), J. P. Sweelinck (1562–1621), Samuel Scheidt (1587–1654), Gerolamo Frescobaldi (1583–1644), J. J. Froberger (1616–1667), Matthias Weckmann (1621–1674), J. K. Kerll (1627–1693), Alessandro Poglietti (?–1683), Dietrich Buxtehude (1637–1707), Johann Krieger (1651–1735), Georg Böhm (1661–1733), and J. S. Bach (1685–1750). The masterwork in the field of the variation ricercar is Bach's *Art of the Fugue*, which consists of about twenty fugues and canons based upon one theme.

The techniques used to form thematic variants in the variation ricercar range from augmentation, diminution, and change of meter (these are the devices used by Gabrieli, Sweelinck, and Scheidt) to embellishment, simplification, inversion, and free expansion and reduction (these are the devices favored beginning with Frescobaldi).

An outgrowth of the polyphonic mass and motet, the variation ricercar also possesses a relationship to the cantus firmus variation, inasmuch as its underlying motive or theme may be regarded as a brief cantus firmus which is used again and again in each section or "variation." Since the successive sections lack a structural correspondence, we have here a foreshadowing of the free variation of the late nineteenth and early twentieth centuries. However, the consistency shown in the variation ricercar through its imitative development of a single motive or theme throughout the successive sections is strict, and quite unlike the plan of the later free variation.

[2] Fischer, "Instrumentalmusik," p. 558.

[3] For the historical development of the song variation see Gress; Charles van den Borren, *The Sources of Keyboard Music in England*, English trans. J. E. Matthew (London, n.d.), pp. 201–248; and Lucia Neudenberger, *Die Variationstechnik der Virginalisten im Fitzwilliam Virginal Book* (Berlin, n.d.).

For the scores of representative song variations see *Les Luthistes espagnols*, ed. G. Morphy, 2 vols. (Leipzig, 1902); *Hispaniae Schola Musica Sacra*, ed. P. Pedrell, 8 vols. (Leipzig, 1898), III, VIII; *Musik aus früher Zeit*, ed. W. Apel, 2 vols. (Mainz, 1934); *The Fitzwilliam Virginal*

Book, ed. J. A. Fuller Maitland and W. Barclay Squire, 2 vols. (Leipzig, 1899); *Antologia di musica antica e moderna*, ed. G. Tagliapietra, 18 vols. (Milan, 1931), II–XI; *L'Arte musicale in Italia*, ed. L. Torchi, 7 vols. (Milan, n.d.), III; *Denkmäler deutscher Tonkunst*, 1st series (Leipzig, 1892 ff.), I; *Denkmäler deutscher Tonkunst*, 2d series (Leipzig, 1900 ff.), II, XVIII; *Denkmäler der Tonkunst in Österreich*, XII²; J. P. Sweelinck, *Klavierwerke*, ed. M. Seiffert (Leipzig, 1894); J. S. Bach, *Werke*, 47 vols. in 60 (Leipzig, 1851–1926), III¹; G. F. Handel, *Werke*, ed. F. Chrysander, 96 vols. in 98 (Leipzig, 1859–1901), II.

⁴ For transcriptions of these tablatures see Morphy, I, 76–84; II, 96–99, 137–141. Van den Borren (p. 201) attributes a prior use of the variation to Luis Milan in 1536, but Milan's variations were for voice and lute, and thus lie outside the realm of the strictly instrumental variation.

Occasional examples of instrumental variations are found prior to the Spanish *diferencias*, among them the late fourteenth-century *Molendinum de Paris*, partly quoted in R. Haas, *Aufführungspraxis der Musik* (Wildpark-Potsdam, c1931), p. 104; the early sixteenth-century *Hornepype* of Hugh Aston, found in Apel, II, 5–7, also in *Sing- und Spielmusik aus älterer Zeit*, ed. J. Wolf (Leipzig, 1931), pp. 57 ff.; and the early sixteenth-century *My Lady Carey's Dompe*, found in J. Stafford Smith, *Musica Antiqua* (1812), p. 42, also in *Historical Anthology of Music*, ed. A. T. Davison and W. Apel (Cambridge, Mass., 1946), p. 105. These, however, are relatively isolated pieces, and it remains true that the first consistent use of the instrumental variation came with the Spanish lute and keyboard composers. See, in this general connection, van den Borren, pp. 204 f.

⁵ Reprints of Cabezón's variations appear in Pedrell, vols. III and VIII.

⁶ This set is reprinted in Pedrell, VIII, 25 ff. For an appreciative account of early Spanish instrumental music in general see Willi Apel, "Early Spanish Music for Lute and Keyboard Instruments," *The Musical Quarterly*, XX (1934), 289–301.

⁷ The early English variations have been studied with greater thoroughness than those of any other period. The most authoritative treatment is found in van den Borren's *Sources;* the studies of Gress and Neudenberger owe much to this work. The most important source of the music itself is the *F.V.B.*

Of the dated virginal music listed by van den Borren (chap. iii), the earliest piece which can be called a true variation is William Byrd's *The Woods so Wild*, dated 1590. Since the *F.V.B.*, containing the most significant of the variations, was compiled by 1619 (van den Borren, pp. 33–36), this date marks the end of important variation production by the virginalists.

⁸ See Willi Apel, "Neapolitan Links between Cabezón and Frescobaldi," *The Musical Quarterly*, XXIV (1938), 419–437.

Gress (p. 7) calls Gabrieli's *Pass' e mezzo antico*, published posthumously in *Il terzo libro de ricercari* . . . (Venice, 1596), the first Italian keyboard variation, but Apel's research proves this statement untenable. For reprints of the *Pass' e mezzo antico* see Torchi, vol. III, and Tagliapietra, vol. V.

⁹ According to Luigi Ronga's *Gerolamo Frescobaldi* (Turin, 1930), the variations of Frescobaldi appeared originally in *Toccate e partite d' intavolatura di Cimbalo* (Rome, 1614) and *Il secondo libro di toccato* . . . (Rome, 1627). The reprints I used are in Tagliapietra, vols. IV and V.

¹⁰ Gress, p. 64.

¹¹ *Ibid.*, pp. 64–end.

¹² Perhaps no single variation cycle, save possibly Beethoven's *Diabelli Variations*, has been more highly or more generally praised by critics and historians. Philipp Spitta, in *J. S. Bach* (London, 1899), III, 168–169, considers it the ultimate development of the variation form; Donald Francis Tovey, in *The Goldberg Variations: An Essay in Musical Analysis* (London, n.d.), p. 5, calls it "one of the two greatest sets of variations ever written"; and Ebenezer Prout, in *Applied Forms* (London, 1895), p. 102, says that "The 'Thirty Variations' may be described as an anticipation by a hundred years of the free variations of Beethoven, Schumann, and Brahms." (It was shown on p. 24 that Prout uses the term *free variation* in a different sense from that employed in this study.)

¹³ See, for example, his *Passamezzo*, in *D.d.T.*, 1st series, I, 40 ff., and *Ach du feiner Reiter*, in *ibid.*, I, 59 ff.

¹⁴ That the number of separate units is not large may be seen from the variations of Scheidt (*D.d.T.*, 1st series, I), whose sets written on secular song and dance melodies have 12, 12, 7, 10, 5, 10, and 7 statements respectively. Now and again more extensive series occur, such as Bull's *Walsingham* (*F.V.B.*, I, 1 ff.) and Bach's *Goldberg Variations* (Tagliapietra, XI, 82 ff.), each with 30 statements; and Ebner's *Variazioni sopra un' Aria dell' Imperatore Ferdinando III* (Tagliapietra, VII, 3 ff.) with 36, but these are exceptional.

Occasional deviations from the sectional plan appear among the works of the earlier composers, the variations being joined by figural bridging; note, for example, the uninterrupted flow of Cabezón's *Diferencias sobre la pavana italiana* (Pedrell, VIII, 6 ff.). Such continuity is rare in comparison with the practice of cadencing at the ends of the separate variations.

¹⁵ For a set which, exceptionally, shows a systematic grouping see Frescobaldi's *Partite sopra l'aria della Romanesca* (Tagliapietra, IV, 20 ff.). *Partite* 1–4 show a gradual increase in figural complexity; *partita* 5 is smoothly flowing; *partite* 6 and 7 are ornately figured; *partite* 8 and 9 are prevailingly harmonic; *partite* 10–12 are, like 6 and 7, ornately figured; and the concluding *partite*, 13–15, are graceful and quiet.

See also Ebner, *36 Variations on an Air of Emperor Ferdinand III* (Tagliapietra, VII, 3 ff.), a work whose unusual plan is the result of suite influence. After twelve variations on the original aria theme come twelve subtitled *courante* and finally twelve subtitled *sarabanda*. All, however, are built upon the initial aria theme.

¹⁶ Performers of today often use considerable dynamic contrast in playing these variations; see, for example, Carl Weinrich's recording of Cabezón's *Diferencias sobre el canto de La Dama le demanda* (Musicraft) and Wanda Landowska's performance of Bach's *Goldberg Variations* (His Master's Voice).

¹⁷ See van den Borren's description of songs which serve as the basis for the virginal variations (*Sources*, pp. 215–247, footnotes); compare, for example, the melody of the humorous *John come kisse me now* (*F.V.B.*, I 47 ff.) with that of the melancholy *Quodling's Delight* (*ibid.*, II, 19 ff.). For fuller information concerning the songs see W. Chappell, *Popular Music of the Olden Time*, 2 vols. (London, n.d.).

¹⁸ Spitta, III, 170 f.

¹⁹ For typical examples of dance themes see Bull, *Spanish Pavan*, in *Geschichte der Musik in Beispielen*, ed. A. Schering (Leipzig, 1931), pp. 146–148; A. Gabrieli, *Pass' e mezzo antico* (Torchi, III, 71 ff.); and Handel, *Sarabande* from the *Fourth Suite* (*Werke*, II, 82 f.).

²⁰ Willi Apel, "Neapolitan Links between Cabezón and Frescobaldi," *The Musical Quarterly*, XXIV (1938), 419–437.

²¹ Van den Borren, pp. 239–241.

²² Paul Nettl, "Zwei spanische Ostinatothemen," *Zeitschrift für Musikwissenschaft*, I (1918–1919), 694–698.

²³ A peculiarity of the renaissance and baroque variation is that many sets omit the theme entirely and begin with the first variation. For practical purposes the initial variation may, in such sets, be considered as the "theme."

²⁴ For these variations see Morphy, I, 92 f. (Navaréz); *F.V.B.*, I, 47 ff. (Byrd); and Tagliapietra, V, 37 ff. (Frescobaldi). Occasionally one finds themes which are relatively continuous, lacking marked phrase division, or those which are asymmetric; both of these exceptional types can be seen in Scheidt (*D.d.T.*, 1st series, I).

²⁵ *F.V.B.*, I, 258 ff.

²⁶ Tagliapietra, XI, 82 ff.

²⁷ The date 1625 is a convenient approximation inasmuch as Scheidt's *Tabulatura Nova*, containing the last significant examples of cantus firmus song variations, was published during the preceding year.

The following cantus firmus song variations were examined: Cabezón, *Diferencias sobre el canto del Caballero* (Pedrell, VIII, 3 f.); Cabezón, *Otras diferencias de Vacas* (*ibid.*, VIII, 25 f.); Inglott, *The Leaves bee Greene* (*F.V.B.*, II, 381 ff.); Byrd, *The Woods so Wild* (*ibid.*, I, 263 ff.); Byrd, *Walsingham* (*ibid.*, I, 267 ff.); Byrd, *The Mayden's Song* (*ibid.*, II, 67 ff.); Byrd, *John come kisse me now* (*ibid.*, I, 47 ff.); Byrd, *The Carman's Whistle* (*ibid.*, I, 214 ff.); Gibbons, *The Woods so Wilde* (*ibid.*, I, 144 ff.); G. Farnaby, *Grounde* (*ibid.*, II, 353 ff.); Sweelinck, *Ich fuhr mich über Rhein* (*Klavierwerke*, I, 111 ff.); Scheidt, *Französisches Lied, Est-ce Mars* (*D.d.T.*, 1st series, I, 65 ff.); Scheidt, *Niederländisches Lied,Wehe,Windgen, wehe* (*ibid.*, I, 51 ff.); Scheidt *Allemande, Soll es sein* (*ibid.*, I, 135 ff.); Scheidt, *Allemande, Also geht's, also steht's* (*ibid.*, I, 142 ff.). In the Sweelinck and Scheidt variations strong melodico-harmonic intermixture will be found.

28 *D.d.T.*, 1st series, I, 51 ff.

29 *F.V.B.*, I, 267 ff. Note the incidental figuration of the cantus firmus in measures 1 and 7.

30 *D.d.T.*, 1st series, I, 65 ff. For a discussion of double variation see chap. iv.

31 *F.V.B.*, I, 47 ff. For other examples of stretto overlapping and quasi-canon see Gibbons, *The Woods so Wilde* (*ibid.*, I, 144 ff.), var. 1; Byrd, *Walsingham* (*ibid.*, I, 267 ff.), var. 13; Byrd, *The Carman's Whistle* (*ibid.*, I, 214 ff.), var. 7; Tomkins, *A Grounde* (*ibid.*, II, 87 ff.), vars. 2, 15–18.

32 *F.V.B.*, I, 267 ff. The cantus firmus variations of Byrd are especially rich in derived motives, and his imitative treatment evokes the highest admiration for its skill. All Byrd's cantus firmus variations are deserving of careful study; note especially the ingenious imitations and derivations in *The Mayden's Song* (*ibid.*, II, 67 ff.), vars. 3, 7.

33 It is obvious that new figures are least disturbing to the unity of a variation when they are inaugurated at the beginnings of phrases or parts, whereas their haphazard introduction endangers structural clarity. A case in point is Scheidt, whose variations often suffer from an amorphous structural feeling, owing to his freedom in introducing new figures.

34 *D.d.T.*, 1st series, I, 135 ff.

35 Another factor which may have prompted the writers of cantus firmus variations to introduce new figures progressively was the influence of other cantus firmus compositions, especially cantus firmus masses, since in these pieces succeeding sections are sometimes formed imitatively on successive fragments of the cantus. Note also the appearance of the practice in the cantus firmus chorale prelude, of which Pachelbel's expressive *Vater unser im Himmelreich* (in Karl Straube, ed., *Alte Meister [des Orgelspiels]*, Leipzig, 1904, pp. 76 ff.) is a good example.

36 *D.d.T.*, 1st series, I, 65 ff.

37 *F.V.B.*, I, 263 ff.

38 *D.d.T.*, 1st series, I, 65 ff.

39 Tagliapietra, III, 1 ff.

40 One difficulty in investigating this problem lies in the fact that the harmonic changes do not often call attention to themselves in a conspicuous way; being the result, ordinarily, of the contrapuntal movements of voices, they tend to assume a wholly secondary position to the voices which create them.

41 *F.V.B.*, II, 381 ff.

42 *Ibid.*, I, 267 ff.

43 *Ibid.*, I, 47 ff.

44 The following variations of this type were examined: Navaréz, *O guárdame las vacas* (Morphy, I, 92 f.); Mudarra, *O guárdame las vacas* (*ibid.*, II, 98 f.); Cabezón, *Diferencias sobre la Gallarda milanesa* (Pedrell, VIII, 1 f.); Cabezón, *Diferencias sobre el canto de La Dama le demanda* (*ibid.*, VIII, 10 ff.); Cabezón, *Fabordones* (*ibid.*, III, 32–47).

By G. Farnaby: *Quodling's Delight* (*F.V.B.*, II, 19 ff.); *Up T(ails) All* (*ibid.*, II, 360 ff.); *Bony sweet Robin* (*ibid.*, II, 77 ff.); *Daphne* (*ibid.*, II, 12 ff.); *Pawles Wharfe* (*ibid.*, II, 17 f.); *Putt up thy Dagger,*̧*Jemy* (*ibid.*, II, 72 ff.); *Wooddy-Cock* (*ibid.*, II, 138 ff.); *Rosasolis* (*ibid.*, II, 148 ff.); *Loth to depart* (*ibid.*, II, 317 ff.); *Tell mee, Daphne* (*ibid.*, II, 446).

By Byrd: *All in a Garden Greene* (*F.V.B.*, I, 411 ff.); *Sellinger's Round* (*ibid.*, I, 248 ff.); *Gipseis Round* (*ibid.*, II, 292 ff.); *Fortune* (*ibid.*, I, 254 ff.); *O Mistris Myne* (*ibid.*, I, 258 ff.); *Callino Casturame* (*ibid.*, II, 186 ff.).

Morley, *Goe from my Window* (*F.V.B.*, I, 42 ff.); Morley, *Nancie* (*ibid.*, I, 57 ff.); Bull, *The Spanish Paven* (*ibid.*, II, 131 ff.); Bull, *Walsingham* (*ibid.*, I, 1 ff.); Tomkins, *Barafostus Dreame* (*ibid.*, II, 94 ff.); Anonymous, *Barafostus Dreame* (*ibid.*, I, 72 f.).

Frescobaldi, *Aria detta Balletto* (Tagliapietra, V, 37 ff.); Sweelinck, *Mein junges Leben hat ein End* (*Klavierwerke*, I, 99 ff.); Sweelinck, *Unter der Linden grüne* (*ibid.*, I, 103 ff.); Scheidt, *Niederländisches Lied, Ach du feiner Reiter* (*D.d.T.*, 1st series, I, 59 ff.); Scheidt, *Cantilena Anglica Fortuna* (*ibid.*, I, 126 ff.).

Poglietti, *Aria allemagna con alcune variazioni sopra l' età della Maestà vostra* (Tagliapietra, VIII, 1 ff.); Ebner, *36 Variazioni sopra un' aria dell' Imperatore Ferdinando III* (*ibid.*, VII, 3 ff.); Reincken, *18 Partite diverse sulla "Meyerin"* (*ibid.*, VII, 54 ff.); J. P. Krieger, *Aria D.d.T.*, 2d series, XVIII, 183 ff.).

By Pachelbel (all in *D.d.T.*, 2d series, II^1); *Aria prima* (pp. 3 f.); *Aria secunda* (pp. 5 ff.); *Aria tertia* (pp. 8 f.); *Aria quarta* (pp. 10 ff.); *Aria quinta* (pp. 13 f.); *Aria sebaldina* (pp. 15 ff.); *Aria* (pp. 18 ff.); *Arietta* (pp. 21 ff.); *Aria* (p. 24); *Aria* (p. 25).

Biber, *Sonata I, Variatio* (*D.T.Ö.*, XII^2, 5 f.); *Sonata X, Aria* (*ibid.*, XII^2, 45 f.). J. C. Bach, *Sarabanda con 12 Variazioni* (Tagliapietra, IX, 1 ff.). Murschhauser, *Variationes super Cant. Last uns dass Kindelein wiegen, per imitationem Cuculi* (*D.d.T.*, 2d series, XVIII, 104 f.); Murschhauser, *Aria Pastoralis variata* (*ibid.*, 2d series, XVIII, 106 ff.); Murschhauser, *Variationes super Cantilenam Gegruest seyest du O Jesulein* (*ibid.*, 2d series, XVIII, 110 f.); Murschhauser, *Aria Pastoralis variata* (*ibid.*, 2d series, XVIII, 112 ff.).

By Handel (all in *Werke*, II); *Third Suite, Air* (pp. 17 ff.); *Fifth Suite, Air* (pp. 36 ff.); 2d Collection, *First Suite, Air*, (pp. 66 ff.); 2d collection, *Third Suite, Menuetto* (pp. 79 ff.); 2d Collection, *Fourth Suite, Saraband* (pp. 82 ff.); 2d Collection, *Eighth Suite, Gavotta* (pp. 106 ff.).

[45] Schering, pp. 146 ff.; also in *F.V.B.*, II, 131 ff. Note that, in distinction from example 10, where alternate soprano-bass figurations appear in a cantus firmus context, the melodic subject itself here undergoes figuration.

[46] *F.V.B.*, II, 186 f. This effect comes under the heading of double variation. Already alluded to in connection with the cantus firmus song variation (see p. 36), double variation plays a part in the other treatments of the song variation as well.

[47] G. F. Handel, *Werke*, II, 106 ff.

[48] *F.V.B.*, I, 66 f.

[49] *Ibid.*, II, 17 f.

[50] Tagliapietra, VII, 3 ff.

[51] *Ibid.*, VII, 54 ff. . .

[52] *Ibid.*, VII, 3 ff.

[53] *Ibid.*, VII, 54 ff.

[54] *F.V.B.*, II, 360 ff.

[55] Tagliapietra, VIII, 1 ff.

[56] *Ibid.*, V, 37 ff.

[57] *F.V.B..* II, 360 ff. Derived figures, such as the one in example 27, are infrequent in the melodico-harmonic variation.

[58] *D.d.T.*, 2d series, II^1, 15 ff. A special kind of imitative procedure occasionally observed is that wherein a variation begins with a series of imitative entrances, after the manner of a fugue. Example 23, from Ebner's *36 Variations on an Air*, has already shown this method, and it may be seen even more conspicuously in the eleventh and twelfth variations of the *Courante* in the same set, as well as in the fourth variation of Pachelbel's *Aria sebaldina* (*D.d.T.*, 2d series, II^1, 15). Imitative beginnings are not, however, a peculiarity of the melodico-harmonic variation, for they also occur in the other two structural plans; Byrd's *The Carman's Whistle*, variation 4, shows its employment in the cantus firmus treatment, and variations 7 and 8 of Frescobaldi's *Partite sopra la Monicha* prove that it may appear with equal effectiveness in the harmonic treatment.

[59] *F.V.B.*, II, 94 ff.

[60] The following variations of this type were examined: Byrd, *Pescodd Time* (*F.V.B.*, II, 430 ff.); Byrd, *Treg. Ground* (*ibid.*, I, 226 ff.); Byrd's *Malt's come downe* (*ibid.*, II, 166 ff.); Inglott, *A Galliard Ground* (*ibid.*, II, 375 ff.); R. Farnaby, *Fayne would I wedd* (*ibid.*, II, 263); A. Gabrieli, *Pass' e mezzo antico* (Torchi, III, 71 ff.); G. Picchi, *Pass' e mezzo antico* (Tagliapietra, V, 80 ff.).

By Frescobaldi (all in Tagliapietra): *Partite sopra l' aria della Romanesca* (IV, 20 ff.); *Partite sopra la Monicha* (IV, 31 ff.); *Partite sopra Ruggiero* (IV, 38 ff.); *Partite sopra la follia* (IV, 45 ff.); *Aria detta "La Frescobalda"* (V, 47 ff.).

Scheidt, *Passamezzo* (*D.d.T.*, 1st series, I, 40 ff.); Biber, *Sonata XV, Aria* (*D.T.Ö.*, XII^2, 76 ff.); J. S. Bach, *Aria with 30 Variations*, commonly called the *Goldberg Variations* (Tagliapietra, XI, 82 ff.).

[61] Such casual correspondence may be seen in certain of the Frescobaldi sets, particularly the *Partite sopra l'aria della Romanesca* (Tagliapietra, IV, 20 ff.).

[62] Note that example 27 (a melodico-harmonic variation in which the imitating figures pervade the entire texture) is extremely rare.

[63] Tagliapietra, IV, 20 ff.

[64] *Ibid.*, IV, 38 ff.

[65] See Weber's *Zigeunerlied Variations*, Op. 55, var. 4; Schumann's *Symphonic Etudes*, Op. 13, étude 4; and Brahms' *Handel Variations*, Op. 24, var. 6.

[66] An example is the twenty-fourth of the *Diabelli Variations*.

[67] Tagliapietra, XI, 82 ff.

[68] An interesting exception is var. 18, in which the four-measure phrase plan is followed with surprising exactness.

[69] Tagliapietra, V, 80 ff.

[70] This alternation is not unlike the imitation of long figures described earlier (see example 31).

[71] The sequences and canons of the *Goldberg Variations* are not mere accessory, decorative elements, but significant structural factors which give independent life to the variations. It is of course true that most baroque figuration, as opposed to the earlier and more haphazard diminution, has a structurally unifying action. The point emphasized here is that canon and strictly applied sequence, being unusually systematic forms of figuration, possess this unifying action to a high degree.

CHAPTER III
(Pages 55–78)

[1] For modern reprints of these variations see *Alte Meister [des Orgelspiels]*, ed. K. Straube (Leipzig, 1904); *Choralvorspiele alter Meister*, ed. K. Straube (Leipzig, 1907); *Alte Meister des Orgelspiels*, ed. K. Straube, neue Folge, II Teile (Leipzig, 1929); *Antologia di musica antica e moderna*, ed. G. Tagliapietra, 18 vols. (Milan, 1931), IX; *Denkmäler deutscher Tonkunst*, 1st series (Leipzig, 1892 ff.), I, XXVI–XXVII; *Denkmäler deutscher Tonkunst*, 2d series (Leipzig, 1900 ff.), II¹, IV¹, XVIII; *The Fitzwilliam Virginal Book*, ed. J. A. Fuller Maitland and W. Barclay Squire, 2 vols. (Leipzig, 1899); J. P. Sweelinck, *Klavierwerke*, ed. M. Seiffert (Leipzig, 1894); Dietrich Buxtehude, *Orgelcompositionen*, ed. P. Spitta, 2 vols. (Leipzig, n.d.); Georg Böhm, *Sämtliche Werke*, ed. J. Wolgast, 2 vols. (Leipzig, 1927); J. S. Bach, *Orgelwerke*, ed. K. C. Griepenkerl and F. Roitzsch, 9 vols. (Leipzig, 1928), V.

[2] Arnold Schering, "Evangelische Kirchenmusik," *Handbuch der Musikgeschichte*, ed. G. Adler, 2d ed., 2 vols. (Berlin, 1930), I, 446–481. See also scattered references to the performance of the chorales in Friedrich Blume, *Die evangelische Kirchenmusik* (Potsdam, 1931).

[3] Charles van den Borren, *Sources of Keyboard Music in England*, English trans. J. E. Matthew (London, n.d.), p. 172.

[4] Wilhelm Fischer, "Instrumentalmusik von 1600–1750," *Handbuch der Musikgeschichte*, ed. G. Adler, 2d ed., 2 vols. (Berlin, 1930), I, 540–573. Here Fischer is using the term chorale variation in a generic sense to include both plain-song and chorale variations.

[5] For these scores see, respectively, Tagliapietra, IX, 53 ff.; and Straube, *Choralvorspiele*, pp. 142 ff.

[6] See, respectively, Bach, *Orgelwerke*, V, 68 ff.; and Straube, *Alte Meister*, pp. 8 ff.

[7] This set is in Straube, *Choralvorspiele*, pp. 33 ff.

[8] *D.d.T.*, 1st series, XXVI–XXVII, foreword. Three of these variations appear in *D.d.T.*, 2d series, II¹.

[9] The Buxtehude set (*Orgelcompositionen*, II, 124 ff.) shows suite influence, var. 2 being subtitled *Sarabande*, var. 3 *Courante*, and var. 4 *Gigue*.

[10] Van den Borren, p. 161.

[11] The chorale *partite* of J. S. Bach, consisting of 6, 8, 11, and 5 variations respectively, are of typical length. Exceptionally, as in the plain-song variations of Sweelinck, the members are arranged continuously.

[12] See Albert Schweitzer, *J. S. Bach*, English trans. Ernest Newman, 2 vols (London, 1935), I. 35, 282–283.

[13] See vars. 3–6. The score is in Bach, *Orgelwerke*, V, 68 ff.

[14] Bach's *Sei gegrüsset, Jesu gütig* (*ibid.*, V, 76 ff.) is especially rich in meter change, var. 7 being in 12/8, var. 8 in 24/16, and vars. 9 and 10 in 3/4. The theme, as usual, is in 4/4.

[15] *D.d.T.*, 1st series, I, 33 ff.

[16] *Orgelwerke*, V, 76 ff. This set is analyzed in detail in the *Appendix*, pp. 140 ff.

[17] The following cantus firmus variations were examined: Bull, *Salvator Mundi* (*F.V.B.*, I, 163 ff.); *Miserere* (*ibid.*, II, 442 ff.). Sweelinck, *Da Pacem, Domine* (*Klavierwerke*, I, 91 ff.); *Psalm 140* (*ibid.*, I, 95 ff.). Scheidt, in *D.d.T.*, 1st series, I, nos. 1, 3, 5, 12 of Part I; nos. 4, 5, 7, 9 of Part II; nos. 11–16, 18 of Part III. F. Tunder, *Jesus Christus, unser Heiland* (Straube, *Choralvorspiele*, pp. 130 ff.). M. Weckmann, *Ach wir armen Sünder* (*ibid.*, pp. 161 ff.). Walther, in *D.d.T.*, 1st series, XXVI–XXVII, nos. 3, 7, 8, 11, 27, 63. Bach, *Vom Himmel hoch da komm' ich her* (*Orgelwerke*, V, 92 ff.).

[18] Schweitzer, I, 42–47. It is apparent that even chorale preludes may be regarded as single variations of a theme not stated. Because of the limitations placed upon the scope of this study (see Introduction), they are not included here.

[19] *D.d.T.*, 1st series, I, 120 ff.

[20] *Ibid.*, XXVI–XXVII, 60 ff.

[21] *Orgelwerke*, V, 92 ff.

[22] *D.d.T.*, 1st series, XXVI–XXVII, 4 ff.

[23] *Ibid.*, 43 ff.

[24] The following melodico-harmonic variations were examined: Pachelbel, *Ach was soll ich Sünder machen* (*D.d.T.*, 2d series, II[1], 26 ff.); *Werde munter mein Gemüthe* (*ibid.*, pp. 30 f.); *Alle Menschen müssen sterben* (*ibid.*, pp. 32 ff.). Böhm, *Jesu, du bist allzu schöne* (*Werke*, I, 69 ff.); *Ach wie nichtig, ach wie flüchtig* (*ibid.*, I, 74 ff.); *Freu dich sehr o meine Seele* (*ibid.*, I, 106 ff.); *Gelobet seiest du, Jesu Christ* (*ibid.*, I, 115 ff.); *Wer nur den lieben Gott lässt walten* (*ibid.*, I, 143 ff.). W. B. Bach, *Du Friedenfürst, Herr Jesu Christ* (Straube, *Choralvorspiele*, pp. 12 ff.). Walther, in *D.d.T.*, 1st series, XXVI–XXVII, nos. 54 and 68. J. S. Bach, *Christ, der du bist der helle Tag* (*Orgelwerke*, V, 60 ff.); *O Gott du frommer Gott* (*ibid.*, V, 68 ff.); *Sei gegrüsset, Jesu gütig* (*ibid.*, V, 76 ff.).

[25] Many sets present the chorale melody in a lower part, generally the bass, toward the close of the series. This usage, an intermixture of cantus firmus treatment, shows itself in Pachelbel, *Ach was soll ich Sünder machen* (Tagliapietra, IX, 53 ff.), var. 6.

[26] See, for example, J. G. Walther, *Partite sopra: Jesu, meine Freude* (Straube, *Choralvorspiele*, pp. 142 ff.), var. 4.

[27] Vincent d'Indy, *Cours de composition musicale*, 2 vols. (Paris, 1909), II, 468–470.

[28] Philipp Spitta, *Johann Sebastian Bach*, English trans. Clara Bell and J. A. Fuller-Maitland, 3 vols. (London, 1899), I, 212.

[29] *Ibid.*, I, 206.

[30] *Orgelwerke*, V, 68 ff.

[31] *Ibid.*, V, 60 ff. See also G. Böhm, *Partite sopra: Herr, wie du willst, so schick's mit mir* (Straube, *Choralvorspiele*, pp. 42 ff.).

[32] *Orgelwerke*, V, 60 ff.

[33] Spitta, I, 208; Hugo Riemann, "Basso ostinato und Basso quasi ostinato," *Liliencron Festschrift* (Leipzig, 1910), pp. 193–202.

[34] Spitta, I, 208.

[35] *Ibid.*, I, 212.

[36] *Orgelwerke*, V, 68 ff.

[37] For the history of the basso ostinato variation see Lily Propper, *Der Basso ostinato als technisches und formbildendes Prinzip* (Berlin, n.d.) and Richard Litterscheid, *Zur Geschichte des Basso ostinato* (Dortmund, 1928).

Representative scores appear in *D.d.T.*, 1st series, IV, X, XI; *D.d.T.*, 2d series, I, II[1], II[2], IX[1], XVIII, XXVII–XXVIII; *Denkmäler der Tonkunst in Österreich*, I[2], II[2], III[3], V[2], XI[2], XII[2], XXIII[2], XXV[2]; Tagliapietra, IV, V, VII–XI; Straube, *Alte Meister*; Straube, *Alte Meister*, 2d series, I; J. S. Bach, *Orgelwerke*, I; J. S. Bach, *Sonaten und Partiten für Violine solo*, ed. J. Hellmesberger (Leipzig, n.d.); *L'Arte musicale in Italia*, ed. L. Torchi, 7 vols. (Milan, n.d.), III, VII; Arcangelo Corelli, *Œuvres*, ed. J. Joachim and F. Chrysander, 5 vols. (London, n.d.), I, III; Henry Purcell, *Original Works for Harpsichord*, ed. W. Barclay Squire, 4 vols. (London, 1918), II–IV; *Old English Composers for the Virginal and Harpsichord*, ed. E. Pauer, 6 vols. (London, n.d.), IV; François Couperin, *Pièces de claveçin*, ed. J. Brahms and F. Chrysander, 4 vols. (London, n.d.), II; G. F. Handel, *Werke*, ed. F. Chrysander, 96 vols. in 98 (Leipzig, 1859–1901), II, XLVIII; Fischer, J. K. F., *Sämtliche Werke für Klavier und Orgel*, ed. E. v. Werra (Leipzig, n.d.).

[38] Rondo influence can be observed not only in chaconnes for instruments but also in those employed in the closing ballet of the eighteenth-century French opera. See Karl Blessinger, *Grundzüge der musikalischen Formenlehre* (Stuttgart, n.d.), p. 245; Spitta, II, 95.

[39] In both Italy and England the basso ostinato idea found further application in vocal music; and the English treatise of Christopher Simpson, *The Division-Violist* (London, 1659), shows that the art of improvising upon ostinato basses practiced a century earlier by Diego Ortiz and his contemporaries was still alive. See Litterscheid, pp. 20 f. and van den Borren, pp. 218–220.

[40] For the distinction between basso ostinato variations built upon dance basses and dance variations which use the harmonic technique see pp. 33 f.

[41] Van den Borren, pp. 217–222.

[42] See *ibid.*, pp. 217–222; H. W. Shaw, "Blow's Use of the Ground Bass," *The Musical Quarterly*, XXIV (1938), 31–38; and H. C. Colles, "Purcell," *Grove's Dictionary*, 4th ed., ed. H. C. Colles, 6 vols. (London, 1940).

[43] Purcell, *Harpsichord Works*, III, 6 ff.

[44] J. B. Trend, "Folia," *Grove's Dictionary*. Paul Nettl, in his article "Zwei spanische Ostinato-themen," *Zeitschrift für Musikwissenschaft*, I (1918–1919), 694–698, shows the appearance of the folia theme still earlier in the lute books of the middle 16th century; these themes were not specifically named folia, however.

See also A. Moser, "Zur Genesis der Folies d'Espagne," *Archiv für Musikwissenschaft*, I (1919), 358–371.

[45] Tagliapietra, IX, 112 ff.

[46] *Œuvres*, III, 96 ff.

In the nineteenth century Franz Liszt made a novel use of the folia theme in his *Spanish Rhapsody* for piano and orchestra. After a brief introduction the folia theme appears in the form used by Corelli, but with this peculiarity: only the melody of the theme is stated. Later (measure 17) the orchestra states the complete melodic and harmonic form of the folia theme, and a free development of this theme ensues. The concluding section of the work consists of an even freer treatment of another Spanish theme, the *Jota Aragonesa;* hence the entire composition is not a true variation cycle, unless it may be said to belong to the free-variation category.

[47] Paul Nettl, "Die Bergamaska," *Zeitschrift für Musikwissenschaft*, V (1922–1923), 291–295.

[48] Litterscheid, pp. 14 f.

[49] Propper, p. 27, cites a passacaglia and a ciaconna from the guitar tablature of Foriano Pico to show their essential sameness as early as 1628.

[50] Litterscheid, p. 18.

[51] Tagliapietra, X, 60 ff.; Fischer, *Werke*, pp. 30–32.

[52] Straube, *Alte Meister*, pp. 79 ff.

[53] Torchi, VII, 159 ff.

[54] *D.T.Ö.*, V^2, 50–53.

[55] See the discussion of type basses in W. Fischer, "Instrumentalmusik."

[56] Tagliapietra, XI, 63 ff.

[57] Straube, *Alte Meister*, 62 ff.

[58] *Orgelwerke*, I, 76 ff.

[59] The six chaconnes of Johann Pachelbel (*D.d.T.*, 2d series, II^1), having respectively 25, 16, 13, 16, 33, and 22 statements of the theme, are typical.

[60] For these variations see Tagliapietra, VIII, 35 ff. (Couperin); *D.d.T.*, 2d series, XVIII, 175 ff. (Krieger); and Torchi, VII, 159 ff. (Vitali).

[61] The Frescobaldi *Partite* are in Tagliapietra, IV, 45 ff.; those of Pasquini are in *ibid.*, VIII, 117 ff.

[62] Bach, *Orgelwerke*, I, 76 ff.

[63] Found in Straube, *Alte Meister*, pp. 35 ff. See also Kerll, *Passacaglia* (*ibid.*, pp. 42 ff.); Georg Muffat, *Passacaglia* (*ibid.*, pp. 62 ff.); Buxtehude, *Ciaconna in C Minor* (Straube, *Alte Meister*, 2d series, I, 34 ff.); Pachelbel, *Ciaconna in D Minor* (Straube, *Alte Meister*, pp. 79 ff.); etc.

[64] See, for example, Falconiero, *Ciaconna* (Torchi, VII, 122 ff.); B. Marini, *Passacalio* (*ibid.*, VII, 86 ff.); G. B. Vitali, *Passagallo* (*ibid.*, VII, 159 ff.); L. Couperin, *Passacaglia* (Tagliapietra, VIII, 35 ff.).

[65] Tagliapietra, IX, 112 ff. The passacaglias and chaconnes of Pachelbel and Handel also contain many such groupings.

[66] Tagliapietra, VIII, 35 ff.

[67] Straube, *Alte Meister*, pp. 20 ff.

[68] Bach, *Sonaten und Partiten*, pp. 30 ff. See also statements 23, 24; 25, 26; 27, 28; 29, 30; 51, 52; and 58–60.

It is difficult to decide upon the length of the theme in this chaconne. Spitta (*J. S. Bach*, II, 95–97) quotes it as being eight measures long, a view supported by the fact that the cadence in measure 4 is less strong than that in measure 8. On the other hand, to assume an eight-measure theme is to assume that Bach used the theme fractionally—16½ times in the first large division in D minor, and 9½ times in the second large division in D major. Such a fractional usage is completely absent from the basso ostinato practice of Bach's day; hence the 4-measure analysis is adopted here.

[69] Straube, *Alte Meister*, pp. 20 ff.

[70] Torchi, VII, 122 ff. This composition, in the key of G, has a contrasting section in C (beginning with the seventh statement), a digression to A minor (statement 16), and returns to C (statement 17) and G (statement 18). The last nine measures form a coda.

[71] *Ibid.*, VII, 159 ff.

[72] Tagliapietra, X, 60 ff.; Fischer, *Werke*, pp. 30–32.

[73] Straube, *Alte Meister*, pp. 79 ff. Other compositions using the literal theme throughout include Buxtehude, *Passacaglia in D Minor* (*ibid.*, pp. 20 ff.) and von Biber, *Ciacona* from *Sonata IV* (*D.T.Ö.*, V², 50–53).

[74] Straube, *Alte Meister*, pp. 42 ff.

[75] *Ibid.*, pp. 35 ff. The basic tones of the *ostinato* (E, D, C, B) can, of course, be discovered on successive strong beats, but since they appear in three different octaves they do not in any way delineate the original contour.

[76] Fischer, *Werke*, p. 44.

[77] *D.d.T.*, 2d series, XXVII–XXVIII, 59–73.

[78] Tagliapietra, VIII, 35 ff.

[79] Spitta, I, 588.

[80] Straube, *Alte Meister*, pp. 20 ff.

[81] *Ibid.*, pp. 79 ff.

[82] Tagliapietra, X, 60 ff. The entire chaconne is analyzed in detail in the *Appendix*, pp. 134 ff.

[83] Spitta, II, 95.

[84] Tagliapietra, VIII, 60 ff.

[85] Willi Apel proposes to call variations like the Muffat *Passacaglia* quoted in example 69, which lack a consistent use of a basso ostinato, by the name *chaconne*, in distinction to variations built upon the strict basso ostinato principle, for which he would reserve the name *passacaglia*; see his article "Chaconne," *Harvard Dictionary of Music* (Cambridge, Mass., 1944). Apel's proposal is similar to those of Goetschius and Luithlen mentioned in chap. i (see p. 20), and although it is valuable for calling attention to the occasional need for a distinction in techniques, it tends, unfortunately, to perpetuate the age-old controversy as to the difference between a passacaglia and a chaconne, about which no general agreement has ever been reached. If a distinction in techniques is to be made, it would seem better to continue to use the term *basso ostinato variation* for pieces built upon a clearly distinguishable ostinato bass, and to oppose this term by one like *harmonic ostinato variation* to denote the occasional pieces in which the ostinato element is primarily a series of chords.

[86] Straube, *Alte Meister*, pp. 20 ff.

[87] *Orgelwerke*, I, 76 ff.

[88] Bach, *Sonaten und Partiten*, pp. 30 ff.

CHAPTER IV
(Pages 79–89)

¹ The *noëls*, written upon popular Christmas songs, have little technical interest but possess an artless charm. Representative examples can be seen in *Archives des maîtres de l'orgue*, ed. A. Guilmant and A. Pirro, 10 vols. (Paris, 1898 ff.), III, IX; and *Les Maîtres français de l'orgue*, ed. F. Raugel, 2 vols. (Paris, Edition de la Scola Cantorum, n.d.). See also André Pirro's article "L'Art des organists," *Encyclopédie de la musique et dictionnaire du conservatoire*, ed. Albert Lavignac, 11 vols. (Paris, 1926), 2d part, II, 1181–1374.

² For examples of late baroque song variations see the compositions of Johann Pachelbel in *Denkmäler deutscher Tonkunst*, 2d series (Leipzig, 1900 ff.), II; F. X. Z. Murschhauser in *ibid.*, XVIII; G. F. Handel, *Werke*, ed. F. Chrysander, 96 vols. (Leipzig, 1859–1901), II; J. C. Bach in *Antologia di musica antica e moderna*, ed. G. Tagliapietra, 18 vols. (Milan, 1931), IX; and Johann Mattheson in *ibid.*, X. These and similar pieces join the true baroque song variation with the variation of the 18th century.

³ Because of an extensive literature of scores, much of which has been analyzed and discussed, there is no dearth of material regarding the ornamental variation. Special works or articles dealing with the music include Ernst Reichert, *Die Variationenarbeit bei Haydn*, unpublished dissertation (Vienna, 1926); Paul Mies, "W. A. Mozarts Variationenwerke und ihre Formungen," *Archiv für Musikforschung*, II (1937), 466–495; and Herbert Viecenz, "Über die allgemeinen Grundlagen der Variationskunst, mit besonderer Berücksichtigung Mozarts," *Mozart Jahrbuch*, II (1924), 185–232. Valuable incidental references can be had in C. F. Pohl and H. Botstiber, *Joseph Haydn*, 3 vols. (Leipzig, 1878–1927); Otto Jahn, *W. A. Mozart*, ed. H. Abert, 2 vols. (Leipzig, 1923–1924); Theodore de Wyzewa and G. de Saint-Foix, *Wolfgang Amédée Mozart*, 3 vols. (Paris, 1936); A. W. Thayer, *The Life of Ludwig van Beethoven*, Eng. trans. H. E. Krehbiel, 3 vols. (New York, 1921); Otto Klauwell, *Studien und Erinnerungen* (Langensalza, 1906); Hugo Leichtentritt, *Musicalische Formenlehre*, 3rd ed. (Leipzig, 1927); Martin Friedland, *Zeitstil und Persönlichkeitsstil in den Variationenwerken der musikalischen Romantik* (Leipzig, 1930); and Victor Luithlen, "Studie zu Johannes Brahms' Werken in Variationenform," *Studien zur Musikwissenschaft*, XIV (1927), 286–320.

The following scores were examined in connection with the present chapter. By Joseph Haydn: *Twenty Piano Compositions by Franz Joseph Haydn*, ed. X. Scharwenka (Boston 1907). *Klavier-sonaten*, ed. H. Zilcher, 4 vols. (Leipzig, Breitkopf und Härtel, n.d.), Nos. 8, 34, and 35. *Sonaten für Pianoforte und Violine*, ed. F. David (Leipzig, n.d.), Nos. 6 and 7. *Symphonies*, miniature score, 4 vols. (Leipzig, Ernst Eulenburg, n.d.), Nos. 85, 94, 95, 97, and 103. *Symphonies*, 4-hand arr. H. Ulrich, 4 vols. (Leipzig, C. F. Peters, n.d.), Nos. 55, 82, and 91. *String Quartets*, miniature score, 3 vols. (Leipzig, Ernst Eulenburg, n.d.), Op. 2, No. 6; Op. 3, No. 2; Op. 9, No. 5; Op. 17, No. 3; Op. 20, No. 4; Op. 50, No. 1; Op. 50, No. 3; Op. 55, No. 2; Op. 55, No. 3; Op. 64, No. 1; Op. 71, No. 3; Op. 74, No. 2; and Op. 76, No. 3.

By W. A. Mozart: *Klavier Variationen* (Leipzig, C. F. Peters, n.d.). *Sonaten für Pianoforte solo*, ed. L. Köhler and R. Schmidt (Leipzig, C. F. Peters, n.d.), K. 284 and 331. *Elf Konzerte für Pianoforte mit Orchester*, miniature score (Leipzig, C. F. Peters, n.d.), K. 453 and 491. *Sonaten für Violine und Klavier*, ed. Flesch and Schnabel (Leipzig, E. Eulenburg, n.d.), K. 305, 377, 379, 481, and 547. *Streich-Quartette*, miniature score (Vienna, Wiener Philharmonischer Verlag, n.d.), K. 421 and 464. *The Chamber Music of Mozart*, ed. A. E. Wier (New York, 1940), K. 233, 268, and 581.

By Ludwig van Beethoven: *Variationen für Pianoforte*, ed. A. Door, 2 vols. (Vienna, Universal Edition, n.d.); in Vol. 1, ornamental variations include Op. 76 and the *Waldmädchen* set; in Vol. 2, all are ornamental variations. *Sonatas for Pianoforte Solo*, ed. H. von Bülow and S. Lebert, 2 vols. (New York, G. Schirmer, n.d.), Op. 14, No. 2; Op. 26; and Op. 57. *Violin Sonatas*, ed. M. Jacobsen (Vienna, Universal Edition, n.d.), Op. 12, No. 1; Op. 30, No. 1; Op. 47; and Op. 96. *String Quartets*, miniature score, 2 vols. (Vienna, Wiener Philharmonischer Verlag, n.d.), Op. 18, No. 5. *Klavier Trios*, ed. R. Fitzner and J. Brandts Buys (Vienna, Universal Edition, n.d.), Op. 1, No. 3; Op. 11; Op. 44; Op. 97; and Op. 121a. *The Chamber Music of Beethoven*, ed. A. E. Wier (New York, 1940), Op. 21.

By Franz Schubert: *Original Kompositionen für Klavier zu Vier Händen*, ed. J. V. Wöss, 3 vols. (Vienna, 1928), Op. 10; Op. 35; Op. 82, No. 1; and Op. 82, No. 2. *Klavierwerke*, ed. by E. Beninger, 5 vols. (Vienna, Universal Edition, n.d.), Op. 42 and Op. 142, No. 3. *Symphony No. 2 in B Flat*, miniature score (Leipzig, Ernst Eulenburg, n.d.). *The Chamber Music of Haydn and Schubert*, ed. A. E. Wier (New York, 1940), Op. 114; Op. 166; and *String Quartet in D Minor*.

By Robert Schumann: *Andante und Variationen für 2 Pianoforte*, Op. 46, ed. C. Kühner (Braunschweig, Henry Litolff's Verlag, n.d.). *Klavierwerke*, ed. E. von Sauer, 5 vols. (Leipzig, C. F. Peters, n.d.), Op. 14 and Op. 118, No. 1. *Sonaten für Pianoforte und Violine*, ed. F. Hermann (Leipzig, C. F. Peters, n.d.), Op. 121. *String Quartets*, miniature score (Vienna, Philharmonischer Verlag, n.d.), Op. 41, No. 2.

By Johannes Brahms: *The Chamber Music of Brahms*, ed. Albert E. Wier (New York, 1940), Op. 18, Op. 67, and Op. 115. *Sonata for Clarinet and Piano*, Op. 120, No. 2 (Berlin, 1895).

Miscellaneous: C. M. von Weber, *Klavierwerke*, ed. L. Köhler and A. Ruthardt, 3 vols. (Leipzig, C. F. Peters, n.d.), Vol. 3. Frederic Chopin, *Complete Work for the Pianoforte*, ed. R. Joseffy (New York, G. Schirmer, n.d.), Vols. 12, 13. *Thirty Compositions by Felix Mendelssohn*, ed. Percy Goetschius (Boston, 1906), Op. 82 and 83. César Franck, 6 *Pièces d'orgue*, Op. 18 (Paris, Durand et Cie, n.d.), No. 3: *Prélude, fugue, et variation*.

The ornamental variations of Mozart, Beethoven, Schubert, Schumann, Brahms, and Mendelssohn are also available in the complete editions of these composers' works (see Bibliography).

[4] Incidental influence of the chorale variation in the 19th century appears in Mendelssohn's *Sixth Organ Sonata*, Op. 65, the opening of which treats *Vater unser im Himmelreich* in a series of variations.

[5] See scattered references to the keyboard variations of Haydn, Mozart, and Beethoven in Pohl, Jahn-Abert, and Thayer, respectively.

[6] Among the more interesting ornamental variations are: Haydn, *Andante con variazioni in F Minor* (clavier); Haydn, *Andante* from *Symphony in C Minor*, No. 95; Haydn, *Adagio* from *String Quartet*, Op. 20, No. 4; Mozart, *Clavier Variations*, K. 455; Mozart, *Andante* from *Clavier Sonata in D*, K. 284; Mozart, *Allegretto* from *Clavier Concerto in C Minor*, K. 491; Mozart, *Andantino cantabile* from *Sonata for Violin and Clavier in G*, K. 379; Mozart, *Andante* from *String Quartet in A*, K. 464; Beethoven, *Waldmädchen* variations for piano; Beethoven, *Andante con variazioni* from *Piano Sonata in A Flat*, Op. 26; Beethoven, *Allegretto* from *Sonata for Violin and Pinao in A*, Op. 30, No. 1; Beethoven, *Andante* from *String Quartet in A*, Op. 18, No. 5; Beethoven, *Andante* from *Piano Trio in B Flat*, Op. 97; Schubert, *Andante* from *Piano Sonata in A Minor*, Op. 42; Schubert, *Andante con moto* from *String Quartet in D Minor* ("Death and the Maiden"); Chopin, *Variations* on *La ci darem*, Op. 2 (piano and orchestra); Schumann, *Andante and Variations for Two Pianos*, Op. 46; Brahms, *Andante* from *String Sextet in B Flat*, Op. 18; Brahms, *Poco allegretto* from *String Quartet in B Flat*, Op. 67; Brahms, *Con moto* from *Clarinet Quintet in B Minor*, Op. 115; and Brahms, *Andante* from *Sonata for Clarinet and Piano*, Op. 120, No. 2.

[7] The conciseness is partly attributable to the use of the variation within multimovement works, where the length of the separate variation movements must naturally be limited. Even in independent cycles, however, the number of statements is not large. Typical are the Mozart *Clavier Variations*, which consist of from 6–12 statements, and the variation movements in Haydn's *String Quartets* which have from 2–5.

[8] The existence of this progressive animation within the frame of the Mozart variations is clearly established by Paul Mies; see the discussion of *Bewegungszug* in his article, "Mozarts Variationenwerke." Otto Klauwell likewise calls attention to progressive animation in the variations of Beethoven, under the name of *Bewegungsmodus;* see his *Studien und Erinnerungen* (Langensalza, 1906), p. 64.

[9] Sometimes, though rarely, the contrasting variation is in a new key; this plan is used effectively in the *Poco allegretto* of Beethoven's Op. 96 (theme in G, var. 6 in E flat). For cycles having two contrasting variations see Beethoven, *12 Variationen über die Menuett à la Vigano*,

and *8 Variationen über das Trio, Tändeln und Scherzen*. Schubert, in his Op. 10, goes so far as to employ four distinct contrasting variations (theme in E minor, var. 3 in C, var. 5 in E, var. 6 in C-sharp minor, var. 8 in E) but this is altogether exceptional. For Mozart's use of the contrasting variations see the discussion of *Einschub*, Mies, "Mozarts Variationenwerke," pp. 490–492.

[10] Out of the 17 cycles which Mozart wrote for the clavier, all but two (K. 54 and K. 398) have *adagio* variations. For examples by other composers see Beethoven's Op. 96 and *Tändeln und Scherzen* variations; also Chopin's Op. 2 and Op. 12. The Chopin usage is unique in that it combines the *adagio* variation with change of mode.

[11] Victor Luithlen, in his "Studie zu Johannes Brahms' Werken in Variationenform," *Studien zur Musikwissenschaft*, XIV (1927), 286–320, likens the *adagio* variation to the slow movement of the sonata. Mies, on the other hand, adopts the stand that the *adagio* variation is an element in the concluding effect (Mies, "Mozarts Variationenwerke," pp. 489–492, discussion of *Finalewirkung*). In view of the length and elaborateness of the *adagio* variation, Luithlen's view seems the more reasonable.

[12] Mies, "Mozarts Variationenwerke," p. 494.

[13] *Twenty Piano Compositions by Franz Joseph Haydn*, pp. 173 ff. The variation movements in the Haydn symphonies also incline toward the use of two themes; see Nos. 82, 90, and 103. See also Ebenezer Prout, *Applied Forms* (London, 1895), pp. 103 f.

[14] Mies, "Mozarts Variationenwerke," p. 467.

[15] Dance themes, consisting principally of minuets, are thinly scattered, but song themes are fairly abundant; among them are French songs and ballads, German, Swiss, Polish, and Gypsy airs, and even patriotic songs and national anthems. French songs occur prominently in Mozart's *Clavier Variations*; they also form the basis for Schubert's Op. 10 and Op. 82, No. 1, and the variation movements in Haydn's *Symphonies*, Nos. 63 and 85. Songs of the other nationalities can be seen in the clavier variations of Beethoven, Chopin, and Weber. Patriotic songs include *God Save the King* and *Rule Britannia*, both used by Beethoven in his clavier variations; and the *Austrian Hymn*, found in Haydn's *Kaiser-Quartett*, Op. 76, No. 3.

[16] A few, like Gretry's *Richard Cœur de Lion* (1784), Paisiello's *La Molinara* (1788), and especially Mozart's *Don Giovanni* (1787), are operas of some importance, but for the most part the themes are from minor works. Many of these are by Gluck, Gretry, Paisiello, Salieri, Sarti, Winter, Süssmayer, and Dittersdorf.

[17] Mozart's clavier variations on *Ein Weib ist das herrlichste Ding*, K. 613, has a 44-measure theme; Beethoven's pianoforte variations on *Kind, willst du ruhig schlafen* uses one of 49 measures.

[18] For additional material see the discussion of Mozart's themes in Mies, "Mozarts Variationenwerke," pp. 468–471.

[19] See Beethoven's Op. 1, No. 3; Op. 30, No. 1; and Op. 96; and Brahms' Op. 18 and Op. 67.

[20] See var. 5, meas. 9 ff. In both, the desire of the composer was evidently to retain the major quality of the tonic and dominant chords.

[21] See his Op. 35, var. 7, and Op. 82, No. 1, var. 6.

[22] A plan favored by Haydn is to supplant the melodic subject, as it moves to the lower part, by a fragmentary counterpoint which has the effect of interposing comments upon the original voice. For a clear example of these fragmentary, "commenting" counterpoints see his *Quartet in B Flat*, Op. 50, No. 1, *Adagio non lento*.

[23] The name *inner variation* is also used (see Mies, "Mozarts Variationenwerke," p. 479). This term is perhaps more exact than *double variation*, inasmuch as the intended meaning of both is that of a variation within a variation. *Double variation*, however, is the more common English term and will be used here.

[24] *Applied Forms*, p. 102.

[25] Mies, "Mozarts Variationenwerke," p. 479.

[26] See Mozart, *Variationen über das Menuet von Duport*, K. 573, var. 7.

[27] See Haydn, *Symphony in C Minor*, No. 95, var. 1.

[28] See his pianoforte variations on *La stessa, la stessissima*, var. 8, where octave shiftings effectually veil the sequencing two-measure groups of the theme; and the *Allegretto* from his *Sonata for*

Violin and Piano, Op. 30, No. 1, var. 4, where octave transpositions are combined with changes in instrumentation.

[29] *W. A. Mozart*, II, 213 f.

[30] The independent cycles show more character change than those forming movements in cyclical works. For examples of conventional styles see Mozart, K. 354, K. 377, and K. 361; Beethoven, pianoforte variations on *Quanto è bello*, *La Stessa, la stessissima*, and *Es war einmal ein alter Mann*; Weber, Op. 5; Chopin, Op. 2 and Op. 12.

CHAPTER V

(Pages 90–111)

[1] There is no treatise devoted entirely to the character variation but many books and articles treat it incidentally or discuss individual composers and their works. Among the most helpful of these are Hugo Leichtentritt, *Musikalische Formenlehre* (Leipzig, 1927); Otto Klauwell, *Studien und Erinnerungen* (Langensalza, 1906); A. W. Thayer, *The Life of Ludwig van Beethoven*, Eng. trans. H. E. Krehbiel, 3 vols. (New York, 1921); George Grove, *Beethoven and his Nine Symphonies* (London, n.d.); Joseph de Marliave, *Beethoven's Quartets* (London, 1928); Martin Friedland, *Zeitstil und Persönlichkeitsstil in den Variationenewerken der musikalischen Romantik* (Leipzig, 1930); Werner Schwarz, *Robert Schumann und die Variation, mit besonderer Berücksichtigung der Klavierwerke* (Kassel, 1932); Victor Luithlen, "Studie zu Johannes Brahms' Werken in Variationenform," Denkmäler der Tonkunst in Österreich, *Studien zur Musikwissenschaft*, XIV (1927), 286–320; Alfred Orel, "Skizzen zu Johannes Brahms' Haydn-Variationen," *Zeitschrift für Musikwissenschaft*, V (1922–1923), 296–315; Edwin Evans, *Handbook to the Chamber and Orchestral Music of Johannes Brahms*, 2 vols. (London, 1933–1935); Gaston R. Dejmek, *Der Variationszyklus bei Max Reger* (Essen, 1930).

Scores of the chief character variations are readily available. The following were consulted here. By Ludwig van Beethoven: *Variationen für Pianoforte*, ed. A. Door, 2 vols. (Vienna, Universal Edition, n.d.); Vol. 1 contains the *Righini* variations, Op. 34, Op. 35, Op. 120. *String Quartets*, miniature score, 2 vols. (Vienna, Wiener Philharmonischer Verlag, n.d.); variation movements in Op. 74, Op. 127, and Op. 131. *Piano Sonatas*, ed. von Bülow and Lebert, 2 vols. (New York, G. Schirmer, n.d.); *Andante molto* from Op. 109 and *Adagio molto* from Op. 111. *Symphonies* (New York, Harcourt, Brace and Co., 1935); *finale* from No. 3.

By Robert Schumann: *Klavier-Werke*, ed. E. von Sauer, 5 vols. (Leipzig, C. F. Peters, n.d.); Vol. 3 contains Op. 1, Op. 5, and Op. 13. *String Quartets*, miniature score (Vienna, Wiener Philharmonischer Verlag, n.d.); *Assai agitato* from Op. 41, No. 3.

By Johannes Brahms: *Klavier-Werke*, ed. E. von Sauer, 2 vols. (Leipzig, C. F. Peters, n.d.); Vol. 1 contains Op. 9; Op. 21, No. 1; Op. 21, No. 2; and Op. 24. *Paganini Variations*, Op. 35 (Leipzig, J. Rieter-Biedermann, n.d.). *The Chamber Music of Brahms*, ed. A. E. Wier (New York, 1940); variation movements in Op. 36 and Op. 87. *Variations on a Theme by Joseph Haydn*, Op. 56a (New York, Books and Music, Inc., 1939).

By Max Reger: *Mozart Variations*, Op. 132, miniature score (Berlin, N. Simrock, n.d.). *Telemann Variations*, Op. 134 (Leipzig, C. F. Peters, n.d.).

Miscellaneous: Camille St. Saëns, *Variations pour deux pianos sur un thème de Beethoven*, Op. 35 (Paris, Durand et Schoenewerk, n.d.). Edvard Grieg, *Ballade*, Op. 24 (Leipzig, C. F. Peters, n.d.). *30 Piano Compositions by Felix Mendelssohn*, ed. P. Goetschius (Boston, 1906); contains the *Variations sérieuses*, Op. 54. Gabriel Fauré, *Thème et variations*, Op. 73 (Paris, J. Hamelle, n.d.).

The character variations of Beethoven, Schumann, Brahms, and Mendelssohn are also available in the complete editions of these composers' works (see Bibliography).

[2] See Klauwell, p. 61. Hugo Leichtentritt says (*Formenlehre*, p. 101) that the *Aria with Variations* of Alessandro Poglietti, written in 1677, is a character variation; the designation might also be applied, with justification, to Bach's *Goldberg Variations*. Because of the isolated position of these earlier works, they have been considered in this study as belonging to the category of baroque song variations.

[3] Despite the long life of the character variation, the total production is small in comparison with that of the ornamental species. It is doubtful, for example, that the number of important pieces exceeds 25, whereas Mozart alone wrote no fewer than 45 sets of ornamental variations. The greater length and complexity of the character variation is no doubt partly responsible for the decrease. In addition, the type was not always appropriate to multimovement works, which, as often as not, utilized the ornamental species in preference.

[4] For isolated appearances of the free technique in the character variation see Beethoven, Op. 55, var. 3 (meas. 117–175) and var. 6 (meas. 258–348); Beethoven, Op. 127, var. 5; Schumann, Op. 1, *Cantabile* and *Finale*; Schumann, Op. 13, études 7 and 9; and Brahms, Op. 9, vars. 5, 11, and 12.

5 *Formenlehre*, p. 102.

6 Klauwell, p. 74.

7 *The Goldberg Variations: An Essay in Musical Analysis* (London, n.d.), p. 5.

8 It was also during the nineteenth century that the orchestra became, for the first time, the vehicle for an independent variation cycle. Separate variation movements had appeared in symphonies as early as Haydn, but the earliest complete cycle for orchestra came in the year 1874 with Brahms' *Variations on a Theme by Joseph Haydn*. Despite this auspicious beginning, the character variation for orchestra did not become popular; and, apart from Brahms' great set, the only other well-known example is Reger's *Variations on a Theme by Mozart*, written almost 40 years later. The true realm of the independent orchestral cycle was destined to be the free variation, in which connection we shall later see abundant example of it.

9 See also Beethoven's *Righini Variations*, the *Allegretto* from his *Quartet*, Op. 74, and Brahms' *Haydn Variations*.

10 Here the following groups can be discerned: 2–5; 6, 7; 11, 12; 16, 17; 26, 27; 29–31. See also Mendelssohn, *Variations sérieuses*. The use of groups signifies, of course, a temporary return to the spirit of the pre-nineteenth-century variation. Sometimes, in fact, the origin of certain groups can be traced back definitely to specific prototypes. The use of pairs, still occasionally present, recalls the baroque song variation; and the group of slow variations, numbers 29–31, in Beethoven's *Diabelli* cycle represents an expansion of the *adagio* member of the ornamental species.

11 The arrangement of this work, is tripartite: 1–7, 8–10, 11.

Karl Blessinger, in his *Grundzüge der musikalischen Formenlehre* (Stuttgart, n.d.), p. 293, sees in the nineteenth century the existence of a definite *group variation*, having in mind a cycle composed entirely of such opposing groups. One of the pieces he cites is Brahms' *Handel Variations*, which he says is grouped 1–12, 13–20, 20–25, 26. This analysis, however, is far-fetched; and in view of the scarcity of cycles which really conform to his definition, the usefulness of the term *group variation*, as Blessinger employs it, is limited.

12 See Schumann, *Impromptus on a Theme by Clara Wieck*, Op. 5; Brahms, *Variations and Fugue on a Theme by Handel*, Op. 24; Reger, *Variations and Fugue on a Theme by Mozart*, Op. 132.

13 In place of the 10 to 30 or more statements which comprise the typical independent character cycle, the incorporated pieces rarely show more than six.

14 Some character variations lack almost completely any marked change of expression. This apparent paradox is exemplified in the *Adagio* from Beethoven's *Quartet*, Op. 127, a movement which is distinguished from the ornamental variation only by its greater intricacy of style. See also the variation movements in this composer's Op. 111 and Op. 131, as well as in Brahms' Op. 36.

15 Occasionally, it is true, the character variation shows an abundance of new keys. The traditional illustration of extensive change is Beethoven's *Six Variations*, Op. 34, where each variation save the last is in a new key. This, however, is extreme. Schumann's *Etudes symphoniques* has but two key changes, Beethoven's *Diabelli* and Brahms' *Handel* cycles only one, and Brahms' *Haydn* set shows no change whatever. It would seem, therefore, that the extensive use of new tonalities is more an anticipation of the free variation than an essential attribute of the character variation.

16 See Beethoven, *Righini Variations*, var. 14; Op. 35, var. 15; Op. 120, vars. 10, 21; Op. 109, vars. 2, 3, 5, 6; Schumann, Op. 1, var. 2; Op. 5, var. 2; etc.

17 See Mendelssohn, *Variations sérieuses*, vars. 1, 2, 13; Brahms' *Handel Variations*, var. 1; etc.

18 Schwarz, p. 19.

19 Ad. Bernhard Marx, *Die Lehre von der musikalischen Komposition*, 4th ed., 4 vols. (Leipzig, 1868), III; 54 ff.

20 Approximately half of the subjects used in the character variation are original, a proportion greater than that of any previous form save possibly the basso ostinato variation.

21 In the nineteenth century the lyrical, expressive nature of the eighteenth-century themes continues, as well as the tendency toward occasional motival construction (see Beethoven, Op. 74, and Op. 131; and Schumann, Op. 41, No. 3). Binary structure prevails, the stock pattern being ‖: 8 :‖: 8 :‖. The stylistic proclivity of the 19th century for greater harmonic richness and thick-

ness of texture is also evident (*cf.* the themes of Mendelssohn's Op. 54 and Schumann's Op. 13 with those of Mozart's clavier variations). For comments regarding Brahms' themes see Luithlen, p. 294.

[22] Not all German musicians are satisfied with the term *thematische Arbeit*. Arnold Schönberg once told me that in his opinion a better term to designate the development of theme motives would be *motivische Arbeit*, for by using it the name *thematische Arbeit* could be reserved for the manipulation of complete themes, such as occurs in the overture to Wagner's *Die Meister-singer*. In this study the possibility of misinterpretation will be avoided, it is hoped, by the use of the English equivalent of *motivische Arbeit*, motival development.

[23] Leichtentritt, pp. 103–107.

[24] Klauwell, p. 77.

[25] Schwarz, pp. 62 f.

[26] Luithlen, p. 304 f.

[27] For a more complete analysis of the motives used in the *Etudes symphoniques* see Friedland, pp. 31–34 of the text, and pp. 1 f. of the musical examples. Friedland's analysis of études 7 and 8 is substantially the same as given in example 89, but he says that the melodic line of étude 2 has nothing to do with the theme.

[23] See Luithlen, p. 288.

[29] The basso ostinato variations examined include: Franz Liszt, *Grosse Variationen über ein Thema von Joh. Seb. Bach: Weinen, Klagen und Crucifixus* (Berlin, Schlesinger, n.d.); Johannes Brahms, *Finale* from *Variations on a Theme by Joseph Haydn*, Op. 56a (New York, Books and Music, 1939), and *Allegro energico* from *Symphony No. 4*, Op. 98 (New York, E. F. Kalmus Orchestra Scores, 1932); Max Reger, *Monologue: 12 Stücke für Orgel*, Op. 63 (Leipzig, F. E. C. Leuckert, 1902), *Chaconne für die Violine allein*, Op. 117, No. 4 (Berlin, Bote und Bock, 1910), *Introduktion, Passacaglia, und Fuge für zwei Pianoforte*, Op. 96 (Leipzig, Lauterbach und Kuhn, 1906), *Introduktion, Passacaglia, und Fuge für die Orgel*, Op. 127 (Berlin, Bote und Bock, 1913); Sigfrid Karg-Elert, *Chaconne and Fugue Trilogy with Choral*, Op. 73 (London, 1910).

[30] J. A. Fuller-Maitland, *Brahms*, 2d ed. (London, 1911), p. 153.

[31] Possibly the symphonic context may have influenced the structure of this movement, for it shows a resemblance to sonata form. The first 10 statements, predominantly assertive and bold, have the apparent function of a first theme; the slow, quiet variations, 13 to 16, that of a second theme. If one pursues the analogy further, 11 and 12 become the transition, 17 to 24 the development, 25 to 30 the recapitulation, and 31 to the end the coda.

CHAPTER VI

(Pages 112–120)

1 "Variations," *Grove's Dictionary of Music and Musicians*, 4th ed., 6 vols. (New York, 1940).

2 The following discontinuous variations were examined: Anton Dvořák, *Thema mit Variationen für Pianoforte*, Op. 36 (Berlin, n.d.), and *Symphonische Variationen über ein Original-Thema*, Op. 78 (Berlin, n.d.); P. I. Tchaikovsky, *Third Suite for Orchestra*, Op. 55 (Moscow, n.d.), 4th movement, *Variations sur un thème rococo*, Op. 33 (Moscow, n.d.), and *Trio für Klavier, Violine, und Violoncelle*, Op. 55 (Braunschweig, n.d.), last movement; Edward Elgar, *Variations on an Original Theme for Orchestra*, Op. 36 (London, 1899); A. Arensky, *Troisième suite pour deux pianos*, Op. 33 (Moscow, n.d.); A. Glazounov, *Thème et variations pour piano*, Op. 72 (Leipzig, 1901); S. Rachmaninov, *Variations pour le piano sur un thème de F. Chopin*, Op. 22 (Moscow, n.d.); Anatol Liadov and others, *Variations sur un thème russe* (Leipzig, 1903); Karol Szymanowski, *Variationen über ein polnisches Volksthema*, Op. 10 (Vienna, n.d.); Max Reger, *Variationen und Fuge über ein lustiges Thema von Joh. Ad. Hiller für Orchester*, Op. 100 (Leipzig, 1907); M. Enrico Bossi, *Thema und Variationen für grosses Orchester*, Op. 131 (Leipzig, 1908).

3 The following continuous variations were examined: César Franck, *Variations symphoniques pour piano et orchestre* (Paris, n.d.); Vincent d'Indy, *Istar*, Op. 42, miniature score (Paris, 1897); C. Hubert H. Parry, *Symphonic Variations for Full Orchestra* (London, n.d.); Richard Strauss, *Don Quixote*, Op. 35, miniature score (Vienna, n.d.); Frederick Delius, *Appalachia*, miniature score (Vienna, 1927); Ralph Vaughan Williams, *Fantasia on a Theme by Thomas Tallis for Double String Orchestra* (London, 1921). The Strauss work is discontinuous in part, but a majority of the variations are connected without pause.

It should be noted that continuity alone does not make a free variation. The basso ostinato variation, in spite of its continuity, adheres closely to the structure of the theme. The variations movement in Beethoven's *Eroica Symphony*, made continuous partly through the use of transitions, is likewise predominantly a structural variation. For the free variation to exist there must be an abandonment of the theme structure in a majority of the variations.

4 For a similar example see the sixth variation in Tchaikovsky's *Piano Trio*, Op. 50. Here, as above, the variation opens with a development of figures which are later united contrapuntally with the transformed melodic subject. The formation of these two examples recalls the cantus firmus chorale variation, in which imitative preludes lead up to the announcement of the chorale subject.

5 See Donald Francis Tovey, *Essays in Musical Analysis*, 6 vols. (London, 1935–1939), II (*Variations and Orchestral Polyphony*), 140 f.

6 D'Indy's *Istar* reverses the customary order by proceeding from *variations* to *theme*, the theme being heard in its simplest form at the close of the work rather than at the beginning. This novel plan is the result of the program, which tells how the Babylonian goddess Istar, descending to the lower world, is progressively disrobed at each of seven gates, until finally she stands in naked splendor.

7 See, in addition to the examples just mentioned, Tchaikovsky's *Suite*, Op. 55, vars. 1–4; Glazounov's *Pianoforte Variations*, Op. 72, vars. 1–6; and Rachmaninov's *Chopin Variations*, vars. 1–3, 5, 7, 9, 13, and 21.

8 Vienna, 1929.

9 New York, 1932.

10 Such as are found in *Das Marienleben* (Mainz, 1924) and the *Fourth Quartet* (Mainz, 1924).

CHAPTER VII
(Pages 121–127)

[1] George Santayana, *The Sense of Beauty* (New York, 1895), pp. 106 f.
[2] Quoted in Victor Luithlen, "Studie zu Johannes Brahms' Werken in Variationenform," Denkmäler der Tonkunst in Österreich, *Studien zur Musikwissenschaft*, XIV (1927), 286–320. The musical quotation is an allusion to Brahms's *Variations on a Hungarian Song*, Op. 21, No. 2.
[3] Vincent d'Indy, *Cours de composition musicale*, 2 vols. (Paris, 1909), II, 443 f.

Appendix
(Pages 131–154)

[1] *Hispaniae Schola Musica Sacra*, ed. P. Pedrell, 8 vols. (Leipzig, 1898), VIII, 3 ff.

[2] See J. B. Trend, "Cabezón," *Grove's Dictionary of Music and Musicians*, 4th ed., ed. H. C. Colles, 6 vols. (London, 1940).

[3] J. K. F. Fischer, *Sämtliche Klavierwerke*, ed. Ernst v. Werra (Leipzig, n.d.), pp. 30–32; also in *Antologia di musica antica e moderna*, ed. G. Tagliapietra, 18 vols. (Milan, 1931), X, 60 ff.

[4] The score shows this figuration as a temporary middle part (see measure 93, example 129). This is an idiosyncrasy of the notation, inasmuch as the figuration is definitely in the soprano from measure 94 on.

[5] J. S. Bach, *Orgelwerke*, ed. F. C. Griepenkerl and F. Roitzsch, 9 vols. (Leipzig, 1928), V, 76 ff.

[6] Harvey Grace, *The Organ Works of Bach* (London, n.d.), p. 205.

[7] Full score: Paris, n.d. Two-piano arrangement ed. E. Hughes (New York, 1921). The examples quoted are from the two-piano arrangement, and are occasionally reduced by omitting duplicated parts.

The variations have been analyzed briefly by Vincent d'Indy in *Cours de composition musicale*, 2 vols. (Paris, 1909), II, 482; by Walter R. Spalding in *Music: An Art and a Language* (Boston, 1920), pp. 274–280; and by Donald F. Tovey in *Essays in Musical Analysis*, 6 vols. (London, 1936), III, 166–169.

BIBLIOGRAPHY

Bibliography

APEL, WILLI. "Early German Keyboard Music," *The Musical Quarterly*, XXIII (1937), 210–237.
———. "Early Spanish Music for Lute and Keyboard Instruments," *The Musical Quarterly*, XX (1934), 289–301.
———. *Harvard Dictionary of Music*. Cambridge, Harvard University Press, 1944.
———(ed.). *Musik aus früher Zeit*, 2 vols. Mainz, B. Schott's Söhne, 1934.
———. "Neapolitan Links between Cabezón and Frescobaldi," *The Musical Quarterly*, XXIV (1938), 419–437.
Archives des maîtres de l'orgue, ed. Alexandre Guilmant and André Pirro, 10 vols. Paris, A. Durand et Fils, 1898 ff.
ARENSKY, A. *Troisième Suite pour deux pianos*, Op. 33. Moscow, P. Jurgensen, n.d.
BACH, J. S. *The Art of the Fugue*, transcribed for string quartet by Roy Harris and M. D. Herter-Norton. New York, G. Schirmer, n.d.
———. *Orgelwerke*, ed. F. C. Griepenkerl and F. Roitzsch, 9 vols. Leipzig, C. F. Peters, 1928.
———. *Sonaten und Partiten für Violine Solo*, revised ed. Carl Herrmann. Leipzig, C. F. Peters, n.d.
———. *Werke*, 47 vols. in 60. Leipzig, Breitkopf und Härtel, 1851–1926.
BEETHOVEN, L. VAN. *Klavier Trios*, ed. R. Fitzner and J. Brandts Buys. Vienna, Universal Edition, n.d.
———. *Sonatas for Pianoforte Solo*, ed. H. von Bülow and S. Lebert, 2 vols. New York, G. Schirmer, n.d.
———. *String Quartets*, miniature score, 2 vols. Vienna, Wiener Philharmonischer Verlag, A. G., n.d.
———. *Symphonies*, miniature score, 3 vols. New York, E. F. Kalmus Orchestra Scores, 1932.
———. *Variationen für Pianoforte*, ed. A. Door, 2 vols. Vienna, Universal Edition, n.d.
———. *Violin Sonatas*, ed. M. Jacobsen. Vienna, Universal Edition A. G., n.d.
———. *Werke*, 25 vols. in 35. Leipzig, Breitkopf und Härtel, 1862–1904.
BLESSINGER, KARL. *Grundzüge der musikalischen Formenlehre*. Stuttgart, J. Engelhorns Nach., n.d.
BLUME, FRIEDERICH. *Die evangelische Kirchenmusik*. Potsdam, Akademische Verlagsgesellschaft Athenaion, m.b.H., 1931.
BÖHM, GEORG. *Sämtliche Werke*, ed. J. Wolgast, 2 vols. Leipzig, Breitkopf und Härtel, 1927.
BORREN, CHARLES VAN DEN. *The Sources of Keyboard Music in England*. English trans. James E. Matthew. London, Novello and Co., Ltd., n.d.
BOSSI, M. ENRICO. *Thema und Variationen für grosses Orchester*, Op. 131. Leipzig, J. Rieter-Biedermann, 1908.
BRAHMS, JOHANNES. *Klavier-Werke*, ed. E. von Sauer, 2 vols. Leipzig, C. F. Peters, n.d.
———. *Sonata for Clarinet and Piano*, Op. 120, No. 2. Berlin, N. Simrock, 1895.
———. *String Quartet*, Op. 67. Vienna, Wiener Philharmonischer Verlag, A. G., n.d.
———. *String Sextets*, miniature score. Leipzig, Ernst Eulenburg, n.d.
———. *Symphonies*, miniature score. New York, E. F. Kalmus Orchestra Scores, 1932.
———. *Variations on a Theme by Joseph Haydn*, Op. 56a. New York, Books and Music, Inc., 1939.
———. *Variationen über ein Thema von Paganini*, Op. 35. Leipzig, J. Rieter-Biedermann, n.d.
———. *Werke*, 121 vols. in 136. Berlin, N. Simrock, G. m. b. H., 1869–1911.
BURK, JOHN N. (ed.). *Philip Hale's Boston Symphony Programme Notes*. New York, Doubleday, Doran and Co., Inc., 1935.
BUSZIN, WALTER E. "Dietrich Buxtehude (1637–1707): On the Tercentenary of His Birth," *The Musical Quarterly*, XXIII (1937), 465–490.
BUXTEHUDE, DIETRICH. *Orgelcompositionen*, ed. P. Spitta, 2 vols. Leipzig, Breitkopf und Härtel, n.d.
The Chamber Music of Beethoven, ed. Albert E. Wier. New York, Longmans, Green and Co., 1940.
The Chamber Music of Brahms, ed. Albert E. Wier. New York, Longmans, Green and Co., 1940.
The Chamber Music of Haydn and Schubert, ed. Albert E. Wier. New York, Longmans, Green and Co., 1940.

The Chamber Music of Mozart, ed. Albert E. Wier. New York, Longmans, Green and Co., 1940.

CHAPPELL, W. *Popular Music of the Olden Time*, 2 vols. London, Cramer, Beale, and Chappell, n.d.

CHOPIN, FREDERIC. *Complete Works for the Pianoforte*, ed. R. Joseffy. New York, G. Schirmer, n.d.

CLEMENTI, MUZIO. *Twelve Celebrated Sonatas for Pianoforte*, ed. G. Buonamici, 2 vols. New York, G. Schirmer, 1896.

COPLAND, AARON. *Piano Variations*. New York, Cos Cob Press, 1932.

CORELLI, ARCANGELO. *Œuvres*, ed. J. Joachim and F. Chrysander, 5 vols. London, Augener and Co., n.d.

COUPERIN, FRANÇOIS. *Pièces de claveçin*, ed. J. Brahms and F. Chrysander, 4 vols. London, Augener Ltd., n.d.

DAVISON, A. T., and W. APEL (eds.). *Historical Anthology of Music*. Cambridge, Mass., Harvard University Press, 1946.

DEJMEK, GASTON R. *Der Variationszyklus bei Max Reger*, dissertation, Rheinische Friederich-Wilhelms-Universität, Bonn. Essen, 1930.

DELIUS, FREDERICK. *Appalachia*, miniature score. Vienna, Wiener Philharmonischer Verlag A. G., 1927.

Denkmäler deutscher Tonkunst, 1st series, 65 vols. Leipzig, Breitkopf und Härtel, 1892–1931; 2d series, 36 vols., 1900–1931.

Denkmäler der Tonkunst in Österreich, 83 vols. Vienna, Universal Edition, A.G., 1894–1938.

DVOŘÁK, ANTON. *Symphonische Variationen über ein Original-Thema*, Op. 78. Berlin, N. Simrock, n.d.

——. *Thema mit Variationen für Pianoforte*, Op. 36. Berlin, Bote und Bock, n.d.

EITNER, ROBERT. *Biographische-Bibliographisches Quellen-Lexikon*, 10 vols. Leipzig, Breitkopf und Härtel, 1900–1904.

ELGAR, EDWARD. *Variations on an Original Theme for Orchestra*, Op. 36. London, Novello and Co., 1899.

Encyclopédie de la musique et dictionnaire du conservatoire, ed. Albert Lavignac, 11 vols. Paris, Librairie Delagrave, 1926.

ERPF, HERMANN. "Der Begriff der musikalischen Form," *Zeitschrift für Ästhetik und Allgemeine Kunstwissenschaft*, IX (1914), 355–386.

EVANS, EDWIN. *Beethoven's Nine Symphonies*, 2 vols. New York, Charles Scribner's Sons, 1923.

——. *Handbook to the Chamber and Orchestral Music of Johannes Brahms*, 2 vols. London, William Reeves, 1933–1935.

FAURÉ, GABRIEL. *Thème et Variations*, Op. 73. Paris, J. Hamelle, n.d.

FISCHER, JOHANN KASPAR FERDINAND. *Sämtliche Werke für Klavier und Orgel*, ed. Ernst v. Werra. Leipzig, Breitkopf und Härtel, n.d.

FISCHER, WILHELM. "Instrumentalmusik von 1600–1750," *Handbuch der Musikgeschichte*, 2d ed., ed. G. Adler, 2 vols. (Berlin, 1930), I, 540–573.

——. "Zur Entwicklungsgeschichte des Wiener klassischen Stils," *Studien zur Musikwissenschaft*, III (1915), 24–84.

The Fitzwilliam Virginal Book, ed. J. A. Fuller-Maitland and W. Barclay Squire, 2 vols. Leipzig, Breitkopf und Härtel, 1899.

FRANCK, CÉSAR. *6 Pièces d'orgue*, Op. 18. Paris, Durand et Cie., n.d.

——. *Variations symphoniques pour piano et orchestra*. Paris, Enoch et Cie., n.d.

——. *Symphonic Variations for piano and orchestra*, two-piano arr. ed. E. Hughes. New York, G. Schirmer, Inc., 1921.

FRIEDLAND, MARTIN. *Zeitstil und Persönlichkeitsstil in den Variationenwerken der musikalischen Romantik*. Leipzig, Breitkopf und Härtel, 1930.

FULLER-MAITLAND, J. A. *Brahms*, 2d. ed. London, Methuen and Co., Ltd., 1911.

GEDALGE, ANDRÉ. *Traité de la fugue*, 1ʳᵉ partie: de la Fugue d'Ecole. Paris, Enoch et Cie., n.d.

GLAZOUNOV, A. *Thème et variations pour piano*, Op. 72. Leipzig, M. P. Belaiev, 1901.

GOETSCHIUS, PERCY. *The Larger Forms of Musical Composition*, 2d ed. New York, G. Schirmer, Inc., 1915.

GRACE, HARVEY. *The Organ Works of Bach*. London, Novello and Co., Ltd., n.d.

GRESS, RICHARD. *Die Entwicklung der Klaviervariation von Andrea Gabrieli bis zu Johann Sebastian Bach*, dissertation, Tübingen. Stuttgart, Ges. Nachf. L. Zechnall, 1929.

GRIEG, EDVARD. *Ballade für Pianoforte*, Op. 24. Leipzig, C. F. Peters, n.d.

GROVE, GEORGE. *Beethoven and His Nine Symphonies*. London, Novello and Co., Ltd., n.d.

Grove's Dictionary of Music and Musicians, 4th ed., ed. H. C. Colles, 6 vols. London, Macmillan and Co., Ltd., 1940.

HAAS, ROBERT. *Aufführungspraxis der Musik*. Wildpark-Potsdam, Akademische Verlagsgesellschaft Athenaion, G.m.b.H., c1931.

Handbuch der Musikgeschichte, 2d ed., ed. Guido Adler, 2 vols. Berlin, Heinrich Keller, 1930.

HANDEL, G. F. *Werke*, ed. F. Chrysander, 96 vols. in 98. Leipzig, Breitkopf und Härtel, 1859–1901.

HAYDN, JOSEPH. *Klaviersonaten*, ed. H. Zilcher, 4 vols. Leipzig, Breitkopf und Härtel, n.d.

———. *24 Symphonien*, miniature score, 4 vols. Leipzig, Ernst Eulenburg, n.d.

———. *Symphonien*, 4-hand piano arr. H. Ulrich, 4 vols. Leipzig, C. F. Peters, n.d.

———. *Sonaten für Pianoforte und Violine*, ed. Ferd. David. Leipzig, C. F. Peters, n.d.

———. *Sämtliche 83 Streichquartette*, miniature score, 3 vols. Leipzig, Ernst Eulenburg, n.d.

———. *Twenty Piano Compositions*, ed. Xavier Scharwenka. Boston, Oliver Ditson Co., 1907.

HILL, EDWARD BURLINGAME. *Modern French Music*. Boston, Houghton Mifflin Co., 1924.

HINDEMITH, PAUL. *Das Marienleben*, Op. 27. Mainz, L. Schott's Söhne, 1924.

———. *Fourth String Quartet*. Mainz, B. Schott's Söhne, 1924.

I Classici della musica italiana, ed. G. d'Annunzio, 36 vols. Milan, Societa Anonima Notari, n.d.

D'INDY, VINCENT. *César Franck*, English trans. Rosa Newmarch. London, John Lane, 1909.

———. *Cours de composition musicale*, 2 vols. Paris, A. Durand et Fils, 1909.

———. *Istar*, Op. 42, miniature score. Paris, A. Durand et Fils, 1897.

JAHN, OTTO. *W. A. Mozart*, 6th ed., ed. H. Abert, 2 vols. Leipzig, Breitkopf und Härtel, 1923–1924.

KARG-ELERT, SIGFRID. *Chaconne and Fugue Trilogy with Choral*, Op. 73. London, Novello and Co., 1910.

KINKELDEY, OTTO. *Orgel und Klavier in der Musik des 16. Jahrhunderts*. Leipzig, Breitkopf und Härtel, 1910.

KLAUWELL, OTTO. "Ludwig van Beethoven und die Variationenform," *Studien und Erinnerungen*. Langensalza, Hermann Beyer und Söhne (Beyer und Mann), 1906, pp. 56–80.

KÖCHEL, L. R. VON. *Chronologisch-thematisches Verzeichnis sämtlicher Tonwerke Wolfgang Amade Mozarts*, 3. Auflage bearbeitet von Alfred Einstein. Leipzig, Breitkopf und Härtel, 1937.

KREHL, STEPHAN. *Musikalische Formenlehre*. I Teil: Die reine Formenlehre. Leipzig, G. I. Goschen'sche Verlagshandlung, 1902.

KURTH, ERNST. *Grundlagen des linearen Kontrapunkts*. Bern, M. Drechsel, 1917.

LANG, PAUL H. *Music in Western Civilization*. New York, W. W. Norton and Co., 1941.

LEICHTENTRITT, HUGO. *Musikalische Formenlehre*, III Auflage. Leipzig, Breitkopf und Härtel, 1927.

LIADOV, ANATOL, AND OTHERS. *Variations sur un thème russe*. Leipzig, M. P. Belaiev, 1903.

LISZT, FRANZ. *Grosse Variationen über ein Thema von Joh. Seb. Bach: Weinen, Klagen und Crucifixus*. Berlin, Schlesinger, n.d.

———. *Spanish Rhapsody*, 2-piano arr. F. Busoni. New York, G. Schirmer, Inc., 1894.

LITTERSCHEID, RICHARD. *Zur Geschichte des Basso ostinato*, dissertation, Marburg. Dortmund, Karl Strauch (Inh. Ernst Meinhard), 1928.

LUITHLEN, VICTOR. "Studie zu Johannes Brahms' Werken in Variationenform," Denkmäler der Tonkunst in Österreich, *Studien zur Musikwissenschaft*, XIV (1927), 286–320.

Les Maîtres francaises de l'orgue, ed. F. Raugel, 2 vols. Paris, Editions de la Schola Cantorum, n.d.

MARLIAVE, JOSEPH DE. *Beethoven's Quartets*, Eng. trans. H. Andrews. London, Oxford University Press, 1928.

MARX, ADOLF BERNHARD. *Die Lehre von der musikalischen Komposition*, 4th ed., 4 vols. Leipzig, Breitkopf und Härtel, 1868.

MASON, DANIEL GREGORY. *The Chamber Music of Brahms*. New York, The Macmillan Co., 1933.

MENDELSSOHN-BARTHOLDY, FELIX. *Compositions for the Organ*, ed. E. H. Lemare. New York, G. Schirmer, n.d.

———. *Original-Compositionen für Pianoforte zu 4 Händen*. Leipzig, C. F. Peters, n.d.

MENDELSSOHN-BARTHOLDY, FELIX. *30 Piano Compositions*, ed. Percy Goetschius. Boston, Oliver Ditson Co., 1906.

——. *Werke*, 19 vols. in 40. Leipzig, Breitkopf und Härtel, 1874–1877.

MIES, PAUL. "Die Chaconne (Passacaille) bei Händel," *Händel-Jahrbuch*, II (1929), 13–24.

——. "W. A. Mozarts Variationenwerke und ihre Formungen," *Archiv für Musikforschung*, II (1937), 466–495.

MORPHY, G. (ed.). *Les Luthistes espagnols du 16e siècle*, 2 vols. Leipzig, Breitkopf und Härtel, 1902.

MOSER, ANDREAS. "Zur Genesis der Folies d'Espagne," *Archiv für Musikwissenschaft*, I (1918), 358–371.

MOSER, HANS JOACHIM. *Musiklexicon*. Berlin, M. Hesse, 1935.

MOZART, W. A. *Elf Konzerte für Pianoforte mit Orchester*, miniature score. Leipzig, Ernst Eulenburg, n.d.

——. *Klavier Variationen*. Leipzig, C. F. Peters, n.d.

——. *Sonaten für Pianoforte solo*, ed. Louis Koehler and Richard Schmidt. Leipzig, C. F. Peters, n.d.

——. *Sonaten für Violine und Klavier*, ed. Carl Flesch and Arthur Schnabel. Leipzig, C. F. Peters, n.d.

——. *Streich-Quartette*, miniature score. Vienna, Wiener Philharmonischer Verlag A. G., n.d.

——. *Werke*, 24 vols. in 75. Leipzig, Breitkopf und Härtel, 1877–1905.

MÜLLER-BLATTAU, J.M. "Beethoven und die Variation," *Internationaler Musikhistorischer Kongress, Beethoven Zentenarfeier*. Vienna, Universal Edition, 1927, pp. 55–57.

NETTL, PAUL. "Zwei spanische Ostinatothemen," *Zeitschrift für Musikwissenschaft*, I (1918–1919), 694–698.

——. "Die Bergamaska," *Zeitschrift für Musikwissenschaft*, V (1922–1923), 291–295.

NEUDENBERGER, LUCIA. *Die Variationstechnik der Virginalisten im Fitzwilliam Virginal Book*, dissertation, Berlin, 1937. Berlin, Triltsch und Huther, n.d.

Old English Composers for the Virginal and Harpsichord, ed. E. Pauer, 6 vols. London, Augener Ltd., n.d.

OREL, ALFRED. "Skizzen zu Joh. Brahms' Haydn-Variationen," *Zeitschrift für Musikwissenschaft*, V (1922–1923), 296–315.

ORTIZ, DIEGO. *Tratado de glosas*, German trans. M. Schneider. Berlin, Leo Liepmannsohn, 1913.

PARRY, C. HUBERT H. *Symphonic Variations for Full Orchestra*. London, Novello and Co., n.d.

PARRY, C. HUBERT H., and H. C. COLLES. "Variations," *Grove's Dictionary of Music and Musicians*, 4th ed., 6 vols., ed. H. C. Colles. London, Macmillan and Co., Ltd., 1940.

PEDRELL, P. (ed.). *Hispaniae Schola Musica Sacra*, 8 vols. Leipzig, Breitkopf und Härtel, 1898.

PIRRO, ANDRE. "L'Art des organistes," *Encyclopédie de la musique et dictionnaire du conservatoire*, ed. Albert Lavignac, 11 vols. (Paris, Librairie Delagrave, 1926), 2d part, II, 1181–1374.

POHL, C. F., and H. BOTSTIBER. *Joseph Haydn*, 3 vols. Leipzig, Breitkopf und Härtel, 1878–1927.

PROPPER, LILI. *Der Basso ostinato als technisches und formbildendes Prinzip*, dissertation, Friederich-Wilhelms-Universität, Berlin. Hildburghausen, F. W. Gadow und Sohn, n.d.

PROUT, EBENEZER. *Applied Forms*, 3d ed. London, Augener and Co., 1895.

PURCELL, HENRY. *Original Works for Harpsichord*, ed. W. Barclay Squire, 4 vols. London, J. and W. Chester, 1918.

——. *Works*, 26 vols. London, Novello and Co., Ltd., 1878–1928.

RACHMANINOV, S. *Variations pour le piano sur un thème de F. Chopin*, Op. 22. Moscow, A. Gutheil, n.d.

REESE, GUSTAVE. *Music in the Middle Ages*. New York, W. W. Norton and Co., 1940.

REGER, MAX. *Monologue: 12 Stücke für Orgel*, Op. 63. Leipzig, F. E. C. Leuckert, 1902.

——. *Chaconne für die Violine allein*. Op. 117, No. 4. Berlin, Bote und Bock, 1910.

——. *Introduktion, Passacaglia, und Fuge für die Orgel*, Op. 127. Berlin, Bote und Bock, 1913.

——. *Introduktion, Passacaglia, und Fuge für zwei Pianoforte*, Op. 96. Leipzig, Lauterbach und Kuhn, 1906.

——. *Variationen und Fuge über ein Thema von G. Ph. Telemann für Klavier zu zwei Händen*, Op. 134. Leipzig, C. F. Peters, n.d.

————. *Variationen und Fuge für Orchester über ein Thema von Mozart*, Op. 132, miniature score. Berlin, N. Simrock, G.m.b.H., n.d.

————. *Variationen und Fuge über ein lustiges Thema von Joh. Ad. Hiller für Orchester*, Op. 100. Leipzig, Lauterbach und Kuhn, 1907.

REICHERT, ERNST. "Die Variationenarbeit bei Haydn," unpublished dissertation, Vienna, 1926.

RIEMANN, HUGO. "Basso ostinato und Basso quasi ostinato," *Liliencron Festschrift*. Leipzig, Breitkopf und Härtel, 1910, pp. 193–202.

————. *Musik Lexicon*, 11th ed., ed. A. Einstein, 2 vols. Berlin, Max Hesses Verlag, 1929.

RONGA, LUIGI. *Gerolamo Frescobaldi*. Turin, Fratelli Bocca, 1930.

SAINT-SAËNS, CAMILLE. *Variations pour deux pianos sur un thème de Beethoven*, Op. 35. Paris, Durand et Schoenewerk, n.d.

SANTAYANA, GEORGE. *The Sense of Beauty*. New York, Charles Scribner's Sons, 1895.

SCHERING, ARNOLD (ed.). *Geschichte der Musik in Beispielen*. Leipzig, Breitkopf und Härtel, 1931.

SCHÖNBERG, ARNOLD. *Variationen für Orchester*, Op. 31. Vienna, Universal Edition, 1929.

SCHUBERT, FRANZ. *Klavierwerke*, ed. Eduard Beninger, 5 vols. Vienna, Universal Ed. A. G., n.d.

————. *Original-Kompositionen für Klavier zu vier Händen*, ed. J. V. Wöss, 4 vols. Vienna, Universal Edition A. G., 1928.

————. *Symphony No. 2*, miniature score. Leipzig, Ernst Eulenburg, n.d.

————. *Werke*, 21 vols. in 42. Leipzig, Breitkopf und Härtel, 1884–1897.

SCHUMANN, ROBERT. *Andante und Variationen für 2 Pianoforte*, Op. 46, ed. C. Kühner. Braunschweig, Henry Litolff's Verlag, n.d.

————. *Klavier Werke*, ed. E. von Sauer, 5 vols. Leipzig, C. F. Peters, n.d.

————. *Sonaten für Pianoforte und Violine*, ed. Friedr. Hermann. Leipzig, C. F. Peters, n.d.

————. *String Quartets*, miniature score. Vienna, Wiener Philharmonischer Verlag A. G., n.d.

————. *Werke*, 14 vols. in 31. Leipzig, Breitkopf und Härtel, 1879–1893.

SCHWARZ, WERNER. *Robert Schumann und die Variation, mit besonderer Berücksichtigung der Klavierwerke*, XVI Band der Königsberger *Studien zur Musikwissenschaft*. Kassel, Bärenreiter-Verlag, 1932.

SCHWEITZER, ALBERT. *J. S. Bach*, English trans. Ernest Newman, 2 vols. London, A. and C. Black, Ltd., 1935.

SHAW, H. W. "Blow's Use of the Ground Bass," *The Musical Quarterly*, XXIV (1938), 31–38.

SIMPSON, CHRISTOPHER. *The Division-Violist: Or an Introduction to the Playing upon a Ground*. London, William Godbid, 1659.

SPALDING, WALTER RAYMOND. *Music: An Art and a Language*. Boston, The Arthur P. Schmidt Co., 1920.

SPITTA, PHILIPP. *Johann Sebastian Bach*, English trans. Clara Bell and J. A. Fuller Maitland, 3 vols. London, Novello and Co., Ltd., 1899.

STANFORD, CHARLES VILLIERS. *Musical Composition*. London, Macmillan and Co., Ltd., and Stainer and Bell, Ltd., 1911.

STÖHR, RICHARD. *Musikalische Formenlehre*, 4th ed. Leipzig, Kistner und Siegel, 1921.

STRAUBE, K. (ed.). *Alte Meister [des Orgelspiels]*. Leipzig, C. F. Peters, 1904.

———— (ed.). *Alte Meister des Orgelspiels*, neue Folge, II Teile. Leipzig, C. F. Peters, 1929.

———— (ed.). *Choralvorspiele alter Meister*. Leipzig, C. F. Peters, 1907.

STRAUSS, RICHARD. *Don Quixote, fantastische Variationen über ein Thema ritterlichen Characters für grosses Orchester*, Op. 35, miniature score. Munich, Jos. Aibl Verlag, n.d.

STRAVINSKY, IGOR. *Concerto per due Pianoforti Soli*. Mainz, B. Schott's Söhne, 1936.

SWEELINCK, J. P. *Klavierwerke*, ed. M. Seiffert. Leipzig, Breitkopf und Härtel, 1894.

SWOBODA, HENRY, "Die nachbeethoven'sche Variationenform," unpublished dissertation. Prague, 1922.

SZYMANOWSKI, KAROL. *Variationen über ein polnisches Volkstema*, Op. 10, Vienna, Universal Edition, n.d.

TAGLIAPIETRA, G. (ed.). *Antologia di musica antica e moderna*, 18 vols. Milan, G. Ricordi e C., 1931.

TCHAIKOVSKY, P. I. *Suite no. 3 pour orchestre*, Op. 55. Moscow, P. Jurgensen, n.d.

————. *Trio für Klavier, Violine, und Violoncell*, Op. 50. Henry Litolff's Verlag, n.d.

————. *Variations sur un thème rococo*, Op. 33. Moscow, P. Jurgensen, n.d.

THAYER, A. W. *The Life of Ludwig van Beethoven*, English trans. H. E. Krehbiel, 3 vols. New York, G. Schirmer, Inc., 1921.

TOMAĚ-WUKADINOVIC. *Die Veränderungs* [sic] *bei den Hauptmeistern der Klavier-Musik vor Bach*, unpublished dissertation. Prague, 1928.

TORCHI, L. (ed.). *L'Arte musicale in Italia*, 7 vols. Milan, G. Ricordi e C., n.d.

TOVEY, DONALD FRANCIS. *Essays in Musical Analysis*, 6 vols. London, Oxford University Press, 1935–1939.

———. *The Goldberg Variations: An Essay in Musical Analysis*. London, Joseph Williams, n.d.

———. *Essays in Musical Analysis: Chamber Music*. London, Oxford University Press, 1944.

VAUGHAN WILLIAMS, RALPH. *Fantasia on a Theme by Thomas Tallis for Double String Orchestra*. London, J. Curwen and Sons, Ltd., 1921.

VIECENZ, HERBERT. "Über die allgemeinen Grundlagen der Variationskunst, mit besonderer Berücksichtigung Mozarts," *Mozart Jahrbuch*, II (1924), 185–232.

WEBER, C. M. VON. *Klavierwerke*, ed. L. Köhler and A. Ruthardt, 3 vols. Leipzig, C. F. Peters, n.d.

WOLF, JOHANNES (ed.). *Sing- und Spielmusik aus älterer Zeit*. Leipzig, Quelle und Meyer, n.d.

WYZEWA, THEODORE DE, AND G. DE SAINT-FOIX. *Wolfgang Amédée Mozart*, 3 vols. Paris, Desclée de Brower et Cie., 1936.

INDEX

INDEX

DATE DUE

APR 17 '74			

DEMCO 38-297